my kitchen in rome

my kitchen in rome

recipes and notes on italian cooking

rachel roddy

Photography by Rachel Roddy
with Nicholas Seaton

GRAND CENTRAL
Life & Style
NEW YORK · BOSTON

Five reasons for five quarters

There is an alternate title for this book, *Five Quarters*, and there are five reasons for this.

The quarter of Rome that I call home, Testaccio, is shaped like a quarter, or a large wedge of cheese. Although in the heart of the city, it feels like a village.

Quinto quarto (the fifth quarter) is the name of the distinctive style of cooking created by the workers of the Testaccio slaughterhouse during the 1890s. Partly paid in kind with offal—which makes up a quarter of the animal's weight, hence "fifth quarter"—the workers (or their wives) found clever ways of transforming their wages into nourishing and tasty meals.

If we develop the idea that the fifth quarter is made up of the things that are usually discarded, the Romans are masters at using them, like the starchy pasta-cooking water, a ladle of which is the key to bringing the pasta and sauce together; the bean-cooking water, which is often the foundation and flavor in classic Roman soups; old bread, which is dampened back to life and tossed with chopped tomatoes, salt, and olive oil or used as a base for soup; and ricotta, the soft, curd-like cheese that is so important to Roman cooking and is a by-product of *pecorino* making.

A classic Roman meal, too, is made up of five parts: the antipasti, or starter; a pasta *primo*; a meat or fish *secondo*; a vegetable *contorno*; and a sweet *dolce*.

There are, of course, only four quarters. In cooking, I think of the fifth quarter as the other thing (or things), in addition to ingredients, that are needed when you prepare food: common sense, good taste, imagination, and experience. It's what you bring to a recipe by making it again and again until it is your own.

How it began

Of course I thought Rome was glorious, but I didn't want to stay. A month, three at most, then I'd take the train back to Sicily to finish the clockwise journey I'd interrupted before moving farther southward somewhere. I had no plan, only a vague notion that I would know the place I could settle in when I found it. It was about halfway through that first reluctant month—April 2005, to be exact—that my oldest friend, Joanna, came to stay for a few days, bringing with her a suitcase the size of a few weeks and the

itinerary of an architect. We spent her first three days negotiating maps, disconcerting curves in the river, and other tourists in search of fluted columns and flights of steps. Then, on her fourth day, we visited one of the most Roman of all Roman quarters: Testaccio.

Approaching Testaccio for the first time, as we did by bus that day, I was caught off guard. Linear and grid-like, the blocks of undistinguished-looking nineteenth-century buildings seemed hard, passionless even, after the warren of medieval alleys and the exhilarating sprawl of imperial ruins we'd been lost in. We walked, or wandered really (the best way, and invariably a happy adventure in Rome), down tree-lined *vie,* past tenement blocks and clusters

of chattering *signore,* and pressed our noses up against the frosted-glass windows of local trattorias. In the courtyard of one block, while Joanna made notes about the internal stairwell and talked about public housing schemes, I watched a wicker basket being lowered from a window, filled with shopping, reeled back up, and swallowed by a clotted lace curtain. In another courtyard, which had washing hung like smiles under almost every window, we dodged a trio of boys playing, their ball ricocheting from the internal walls, until a voice called out *'tacci tua!* and the boys scattered like marbles, us too. Years later, now that I fully understand the connotations of *'tacci tua,* I cringe at our thick tourist skins, walking around a private courtyard admiring the washing, only to be shooed away by an old lady and this very best of Roman insults.

We must have walked along via Branca because I remember thinking that trattoria Agustarello looked plainly appealing. We certainly walked along via Beniamino Franklin, because at the end of it we stood looking up at the statue of a winged god punching out an innocent bull sitting above the entrance to Rome's sprawling ex-slaughterhouse. We stood for quite some time getting our bearings before walking all the way through the vast complex, the meat hooks on long rails still hanging where they had been left 30 years ago. The slaughterhouse led us to the base of what appeared to be a hill, but was actually an ancient pile of broken terra-cotta amphorae. Curving round the hill of broken pots, we came upon a section of the Aurelian wall, which led us to a cypress-shaded cemetery where Keats is buried, juxtaposed with a Futurist post office and a sharply pointed ancient pyramid. Joanna read dates and details from the guidebook: 1872, 1st century AD, 1821, 1933, AD 271. It looked and felt a little like a scene from a pop-up book illustrating buildings from more than 2,500 years of history, except they were all coexisting in the present, both preposterous and wonderful. From the pyramid we walked, me in the heavy boots I'd bought in Naples and Joanna in yellow heels, around the perimeter of Testaccio with its two cut sides and deep curve along the river. We barely caught sight of another tourist.

Eventually we found ourselves at the center of the coarse and chaotic old market, with its iron uprights and grimy glass roof, the air damp and bosky. We wandered, staring at whole waxed wheels of pecorino cheese, hind legs of prosciutto and a tom-tom-drum-sized can of salted anchovies, over which a woman sat poised, spoon in hand, ready to scoop and wrap her silver-streaked, salt-encrusted fish in waxed paper. We marveled at the unruly heaps of wild *cicoria* (chicory), crates of globe artichokes with violet-stained petals and

silvery leaves, piles of peas, *fave* (fava beans), lemons, and the first of the tomatoes, deeply fluted and smelling of the tangled vine on which they grew. In return for our stares we received stares back, mostly aimed at Joanna it must be said, who, although happy to accept a free pear and an impertinent *che bella!,* was actually more interested in the 1970s roof elevations.

It was at least midday by the time we sat at one of the small tables outside Zia Elena for ill-timed cappuccinos and sweet yeasted buns called *maritozzi.* Then, as we have done since the ages of three and four respectively, we thought, and then raced to say, the same thing at the same moment: that Testaccio was extraordinary and I should find a flat here. That night we had supper at the trattoria that had caught my eye, Agustarello, where I ate my first *cacio e pepe* (pasta with cheese and pepper), a dish infinitely more delicious than it sounds if the maker has the know-how and flick of the wrist to turn the cheese and the pasta-cooking water into a seductive, soft sauce. There were also lamb chops and braised Roman artichokes, I think, although I can't be sure, as we also drank far too much of a pleasant Frascati. We finished the meal with the herbal digestif Amaro, which made us shudder, before walking back through the piazza to catch our bus.

Two weeks later, with Joanna gone, I signed a year-long contract for a small flat at a gentrified rent next to the market. Did I know at this point that Testaccio was the somewhere I'd been looking for? Looking back, that was possibly so; certainly, I celebrated with a bottle of Sicilian red, which left me unfit for anything, let alone unpacking or mattress shifting, and fell asleep on the sofa. The next day I fell into life in Testaccio. That is, the coffee bar for breakfast, then the bakery (*il forno*) for bread, before walking round the quarter, and occasionally beyond it, always ending up where I'm happiest: wandering round the market, figuring out what to have for lunch and dinner. Within weeks I had met more neighbors and shopkeepers than I'd met during seven years in east London. My days continued just so, contrasting sharply but softly with my old London life. They felt simple and straightforward, punctuated with waves of relief that I had finally got away, and idealistic, possibly clichéd delight at finding myself living this particular life in this particular corner of Rome.

The idealism faded, of course, into something worn and occasionally jaded, but more appropriate. The delight remained bright and constant, though, as did the routine, which was fortified when work and reality seeped its way back into my life—bar, bakery, market, fishmonger, butcher, my kitchen, bar again— fixed points around which everything else rotated. I had never

enjoyed living anywhere as much as my wedge-shaped quarter
with its fierce sense of community and rich but commonplace
history. I should note that Testaccio, and its shops, bars, and most
certainly the market itself, is a far cry from any rustic, whimsical,
or Mediterranean idyll you might imagine, for although charming
and charismatic, it is straightforward, traditional, ordinary. It is
also an area tangibly struggling with change and the age-old story
of gentrification, of which I was the surest sign: rising rents pushing
out the traditional parts of the community and replacing them with
a new crop of people with deeper pockets. My guilt wasn't going
to change anything, but my loyalty to the local shops might. So I

was loyal, and embraced *la vita del quartiere* (the life of the quarter) wholeheartedly.

In December 2005, in much the same way that I'd fallen into life in Rome (that is, reluctantly and unexpectedly), I fell in love with Vincenzo, a Sicilian who'd been living in Rome for 25 years. I began writing my blog in September 2008, when I'd been in Testaccio for three and a half years, and Vincenzo and I were still living next to the market, directly above a bakery called Passi and across the courtyard from the boisterous trattoria Il Bucatino. I was teaching full-time by now, mostly English to children through theater and

music. The rest of the time I spent cooking, eating, and writing. I'd always enjoyed them, but these three things really came together—collided, if you like—in this small kitchen in this distinct part of Rome. I was plainly happier than I'd been in a long time.

In Rome, my writing took on a new importance as I tried to understand a completely different way of buying, preparing, eating, drinking, and thinking about food: the sheepy nature of pecorino cheese, the consistency of a carbonara, the way Romans mix garlic, rosemary, and white wine; the way they braise veal slowly, roast lamb with rosemary and the knack of *ripassare* (re-passing) cooked vegetables in fearless quantities of garlic-scented olive oil, which makes everything taste so sensual and good.

I began to observe similarities as well as differences. Roman food, I noticed, had much in common with traditional English food, particularly that of my northern relatives: the simplicity and straightforwardness of it (my grandfather would have said "no fuss"); the resourcefulness; the use of offal; the long, slow braises using less popular cuts of meat; the battered cod; the love of peas and potatoes, asparagus and mint; the jam tarts, stewed fruit, and spiced fruit cakes. These connections were reassuring to me and made cooking even more of a newfound pleasure. I took pleasure, too, in taking the photographs that became central to the story, always taken in my flat, always in real time—which means meal times.

Difficulties, I suppose, were inevitable. At first it seemed like a summer storm, the sort that appears to come from nowhere and rains off the lunch. Of course, storms—actual or otherwise—have their antecedents, they come from specific conditions and have usually been rumbling away somewhere in the background. In creating a new life, I'd run away from an old one, but of course I hadn't really, I'd simply brought myself and my difficulties with me, and there they were, sitting on the sofa like unwanted visitors in an Alan Ayckbourn play. The details aren't important here; I mention this simply as a counterbalance to the idealistic delight I've been going on about. I imagined I might leave, although for where I'm not sure. It was an unedifying time.

I spent a couple of months across the river in a part of Rome called Trastevere as a guest in a friend's studio in a grand frescoed palazzo overlooking Palazzo Farnesina. It was, I thought each morning as I set my feet on the cobbles of via della Lungara, the quintessential Roman setting. It was also, for me at least, ill-fitting, and where I realized the importance of Testaccio, the people, place, and the life I had created within it. Storms can wreak havoc, but they do pass. That's not to say that suddenly everything was

fine—far from it—but like after the rain, when the air is clean, color returns, and the light sharpens detail, things became clearer.
I moved back to Testaccio. I was also having a baby.

The routine I had fallen into so happily when I first arrived took on a new, reassuring significance during my pregnancy. I walked increasingly slowly during that long, hot summer, from the bar (the coffee kind), to the bakery, to the market, collecting shopping and extraordinary amounts of prenatal advice at each pit stop. Luca, a bonny boy, was born in September and was with me at the market three days later. Three years later, he runs along beside me, shouting in English or Italian and shooting imaginary spiderwebs at old ladies.

We outgrew the small two-roomed flat on via Mastro Giorgio, the one above the bakery and across the courtyard from the noisy trattoria. It's still ours, though, acting as a studio in which I have written most of this book, with the smell of bread, the clatter of plates, and an occasional kitchen outburst providing a familiar and reassuring backdrop. We now rent a flat on via Galvani, one of Testaccio's busier streets, which is probably the best positioned in that it lies between my trusted shops and just minutes from the new market. The market has moved, and the old structure with its iron uprights and grimy glass roof has been replaced with a bright, white structure just opposite the old slaughterhouse. The stallholders remain the same, though, notably my fruit and vegetable stand, my butcher, and my cunning fishmonger, Mauro.

It is Mauro's fish, a sea bass shining like a newly minted coin fresh from Anzio this morning, that is sitting on the drain board as I write. The stainless-steel drain board made my heart sink when I first saw it, but now suits me fine. It's large, functional, and flooded with light, and the place I am happiest to stand (I never feel tied to it) and appreciate the good things I have bought from the market that morning. Talking of which, I'd think I'd better go and make lunch.

Working on the principle we all know—that good ingredients are the basis for good food—why do we often skimp on the most important one, the fragrant, flavorful foundation of so many dishes: olive oil? It really is the essence of your cooking, so seek out a basic, good-quality, extra-virgin olive oil, ideally with specific provenance (Italy is too general—look for a region, for example Lazio, Umbria, or Abruzzo) and a guarantee of origin such as DOP or IGP. It won't be cheap, but neither should it be very expensive. Extra-virgin olive oil is, of course, as complex as wine, and different oils from different regions possess different qualities. However, rather than having a shelf full of different bottles, I would focus on finding one good-quality oil that suits you, and use that for everything.

The same goes for the rest of the ingredients. Seek out the best you can afford: onions, garlic, seasonal fruit and vegetables, good-quality dried pasta, canned plum tomatoes, ideally San Marzano, canned chickpeas, dried lentils, a jar of anchovies, olives, eggs, bread, and a piece of Parmesan or pecorino. These are my basics, reassuring me that I can make myself and however many people happen to be around something good to eat. If there are also butter, cured pork (either pancetta or *guanciale*), frozen peas, and a bar of chocolate, better still.

As a rule, I use free-range eggs, granulated sugar, unwaxed organic lemons, unsalted butter, Italian 00 flour (a finely ground soft wheat flour), and decent red wine vinegar. I have three types of salt: coarse sea salt for pasta-cooking water, fine salt for seasoning when cooking, and English flaky sea salt for seasoning at the table.

As for herbs, I had great hopes for my small balcony and how it would become home to a small potted kitchen garden. As I write, the rosemary plant and small bay tree are hanging on for dear life, but the sage is a goner. The basil plant on the drain board, however, is thriving, and the stalks of flat-leaf parsley in a glass covered with a shower cap are holding out well. Keeping herbs fresh is an ongoing battle for me, but one I continue to fight because they are so important to the food I like to cook, particularly rosemary, sage, bay leaves, basil, and parsley. With the occasional exception of oregano and marjoram, I don't use dried herbs.

Kitchen equipment

Some of the best meals I've eaten in Italy have been cooked in small, ordinary kitchens on straightforward stoves using simple, basic equipment. I have also eaten some wonderful meals cooked in large kitchens equipped with every conceivable tool and appliance, and armies of pans. It's not that one is better than the other—good food can be prepared in either way, in either kitchen. However, it is the ordinary and simple that appeals to me, since it's more inclusive and uncomplicated, rather like the food itself.

I arrived in Italy with nothing, which meant I had the opportunity to start again in terms of kitchen equipment. I took my lead from what I saw in the kitchens of cooks I liked and whose food I wanted to eat. I was determined to keep things simple (which is not necessarily in my nature) and to remember the logistics of my own small kitchen. Over the last ten years I have accumulated a set of kitchen equipment that serves me well and is all I need to prepare the food I like to make and eat. Much of it was bought locally (several bits secondhand), other things were brought back from England, and several of the nicest pieces were gifts. I have one electric appliance. Because we decided it was best that I cooked and photographed all the food for the book in my kitchen over the course of a year in real time, you will see all my equipment pictured in the following pages.

A big pan
The workhorse of the kitchen is the 6-quart pan that I use to cook 2–6 portions of pasta. It is medium-weight aluminum, which means it's manageable even when full of boiling water. I also boil potatoes and large quantities of vegetables, and wilt spinach in this pan.

Small pans
A 1-quart heavy-bottomed stainless-steel pan for cooking one portion of pasta, a few vegetables, frying in small quantities, and watering the plants nearest the door. I also have a small pan for milk, cream, and custard, which is just the right shape for balancing a bowl on for a makeshift bain-marie.

A colander
The partner to the big pan is a three-legged colander I found in a secondhand shop. It hangs above the sink, ready to be plonked in it to drain or rinse vegetables.

A deep frying/sauté pan

I have a large, deep sauté pan with a long handle, the kind you see in trattoria kitchens, which I mostly use to make sauce or prepare vegetables for pasta. You will see it again and again in the book. It has a heavy enough base to cook evenly, but is light enough to lift and flip when you add the pasta to the sauce. It also has a lid.

A heavy casserole dish

My oval orange Le Creuset was a birthday present from Vincenzo. I call it my peperonata pan because of the sheer quantity of stewed peppers I insist on making in it. I actually use it for countless things, though: braising meat, making thick soups, poaching fruit, and occasionally baking bread. From time to time I convince myself I need a bigger version of this. I really don't.

A food mill (*mouli*)

This is a favorite kitchen tool, which warrants a whole paragraph in part 2 (page 126).

A special sauté pan

Worth almost as much as everything else in the kitchen put together, my copper sauté pan was a gift from my sister and her husband and my brother and his wife for my fortieth birthday. Although by no means ordinary or essential—the sauté pan and casserole have it covered—it is a joy to cook in because of the way it conducts heat and cooks evenly and slowly. I fry, braise, stew, poach, coddle, and simmer in this beautiful pan. It too has a lid.

A grill pan

The heavy sort made from cast iron with ridges, which sits on the stovetop and leaves pleasing black lines and a smoky tang on steak, fish, and vegetables, and sends smoke rushing through your hair. I leave it to cool on the balcony and then forget about it, so it gets rained on and by the next day rust is taking hold, which I then have to scrub away. I am extremely fond of my grill pan.

Roasting pans

With the exception of cookies and cakes, almost everything else that goes in the oven is in one of two enamel roasting pans I bought from Emanuela's stall on Testaccio market.

An immersion blender

This is my only electric appliance. I use it for soups, sauces, making cakes (or, rather, cake, since I only really make one), and occasionally whipping cream.

A manual pasta roller

This was a gift that sat in the cupboard for a year before I first used it. These days it gets clamped to the table at some point most weeks.

A mortar and pestle

Which I no longer have, because I broke it the week I began work on the book. I have been using the end of a rolling pin in a thick glass jar to grind spices and the immersion blender to make pesto, which means it isn't the same. I would like another one.

Knives

I have three very good knives, which are slowly being worn away by the knife sharpener who drives into Testaccio once a week in his white Fiat Panda with a sharpening wheel in the trunk. There is a small, sharp vegetable knife, a large 8-inch cook's knife, and a cleaver that I wish I could use more skillfully. I also have an inexpensive bread knife that I use all the time.

Moka stovetop coffee pots
I have 2-cup, 3-cup, and 6-cup sizes.

Mixing bowls
I'm not sure which of the family of five extremely light, extremely inexpensive stainless-steel bowls that sit in a nest I use the most.

Utensils
I use my box grater most days, usually for cheese. I often use scissors instead of a knife for trimming beans, cutting herbs, and chopping tomatoes directly in the can. Of the various utensils, my wooden spoons, wooden fork, tongs, whisk, and spatula are the ones I use most.

Miscellany
My beloved ring-shaped cake pan, the Bonne Maman jam jar I use for green sauce, a tart pan I found in the road outside a trattoria being refurbished, a curved knife for scoring chestnuts that is endlessly useful, a stumpy cheese knife, Vincenzo's grandmother's cutting board, a disconcertingly heavy bowl for making mayonnaise, a flat iron I bought at Porta Portese that I use when I need a heavy weight (which is more often than you might imagine), the strand of spaghetti that is always in with the wooden spoons for testing whether the cake is cooked, an enamel bowl for soaking beans, the chipped 4-ounce Duralex glass I use for measuring, a curved nutmeg grater not much larger than a coin that I keep in the nutmeg jar, and a shallow Tupperware box that long ago lost its lid, which I always use to make granita.

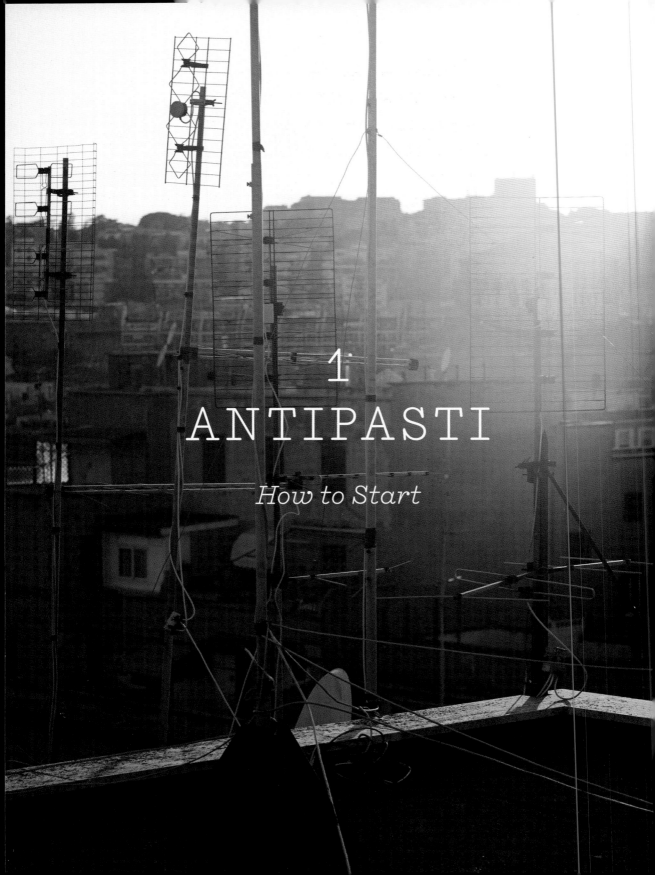

1
ANTIPASTI

How to Start

Fava beans and pecorino

Salami and marinated olives

Roman-style sweet-and-sour onions

Marinated zucchini with mint

Batter

Deep-fried sage leaves

Deep-fried apple or pear with pecorino

Deep-fried squash blossoms

Deep-fried artichokes

Potato and Parmesan croquettes

Ricotta and spinach fritters

Rice croquettes filled with mozzarella

Bruschetta with garlic and olive oil

Bruschetta with tomatoes and basil

Bruschetta with white beans and rosemary oil

Bruschetta with ricotta and fava beans

Bread and tomato salad

Mozzarella with oven-roasted tomatoes

Prosciutto, melon, and figs

Pizza with olive oil and salt

Frittata with potato

Frittata with ricotta and mint

Roast bone marrow, parsley salad, and toast

Bread or toast, butter, anchovies, and radishes

Octopus and potato salad

Marinated fresh anchovies

May 2005. I'd been in Rome for two months and had just moved into a neat studio flat next to the old Testaccio market. I'd already had several lunches at Agustarello, a single-roomed trattoria with frosted windows and a reputation for good Roman food, but it wasn't until the fourth or fifth one that I witnessed a Roman ritual for the first time. A table of men, deep in conversation and seemingly able to order purely by gesture and nod, were brought a plate of *fave* (fresh fava beans in their pods) and an entire wheel of young *pecorino romano* cheese. While the conversation continued unabated, the men opened the *fave* by pinching the tip, tugging on the thread like a zipper and easing the beans from their pod. Having liberated their beans, they then ate them with pieces of pecorino chiseled from the wheel.

I remember staring, thinking it both odd and wonderful. I wondered if I too might be brought a plate of *fave* and the wheel of cheese, if I too could tug the threads and dig my knife into the quarry of cheese. I wasn't, of course; I'd just finished my pasta, and *fave* didn't even seem to be on the menu I'd studied in the careful way a solitary diner studying Italian might. I stared at the men as they continued podding, talking, and hewing chunks of cheese from the wheel, their arms crisscrossing the table as easily as the conversation. The plate of empty pods and the wheel were whisked away into the kitchen as my bill arrived. I paid, pushed my chair back under the table, and left the trattoria before seeing what they had to follow.

Later I would learn that the peeling and eating of fava beans with young pecorino (by nature a fleeting pleasure) is a distinctly Roman ritual, one traditionally enjoyed during a symbolic trip to the countryside after winter. It is not often noted on menus but you will always be given it if you have the know-with-all to ask. It's a habit that unites Romans and transcends class, eaten in starched-linen restaurants, paper-mat trattorias, kitchen tables, parks and picnic fields on the first of May.

Fave e pecorino is a good way to start this first part of the book, because it is a quintessential *antipasto* (which literally means "before the meal"): something tasty and with great flavor—Italians say *saporito*—intended to pique the appetite but not to overwhelm what will come next. The contrast of sharp, salty cheese with tender, waxy beans does this job admirably. *Fave e pecorino* also illustrates the shared ritual of antipasti, the physical coming together, like the group of men around a bowl of beans and a wheel of cheese.

I start here too because, far from being restricted to Rome and Lazio, this is a way to begin a meal that translates well anywhere you

can find fresh fava beans and sharp cheese; Dorset, for example, and my parents' house, where the first English fava beans, every bit as tender and good as their Roman counterparts, find their partner in a sharp, creamy Godminster Cheddar.

Fave e pecorino
Fava beans and pecorino

It took me a while to come around to *pecorino romano*, the sheep's-milk cheese so beloved of the Romans. It's a distinctive, strong, and surly cheese, with a semisharp, almost muttony taste about it. If *Parmigiano reggiano* is a smooth, sophisticated type with a history of art degree and a flat in Kensington, then *pecorino romano* is a bit of a rogue with an accent as thick as molasses, a great record collection, and plenty of charm.

Most *pecorino romano* is aged for eight months to a year and is considered a grating cheese. Once grated, it's launched liberally, lending its distinctive nature and a salty wink to some of Rome's most famous pasta dishes: *amatriciana, carbonara, cacio e pepe,* as well as the aromatic *trippa alla romana.* Some *pecorino romano,* however, is eaten younger, at three to five months, which means it's less pungent, softer, and milder mannered, and makes a good table cheese, especially with the first fava beans of spring. You want young ones, those tender enough to eat in their opaque coats. If you do meet a larger bean whose coat is thick and starchy, simply nick it with a nail and then ease it away to reveal the bright green disc of a bean, which sounds like a faff and is, but no more than, say, opening a pistachio nut.

lots of fresh young fava beans in their pods
a piece of pecorino cheese, or sharp Cheddar

Put the beans and the cheese on the table or kitchen counter along with a knife, ideally a stubby one, for the cheese and a bowl to collect empty pods. Serve with a white wine from Lazio, or better still a Prosecco Colfòndo, which is a prosecco whose fermentation is interrupted and then resumed, making it softly sparkling, and perfect with beans and cheese.

<u>Negroni</u>

Clink, clink, clink go the three cubes, an icy base for equal measures of gin, sweet vermouth, and Campari and a slim half-moon of orange. Remember to stir purposefully before raising your glass to something, then drink.

I don't often drink cocktails, an admission which once won me a snooty look from a friend of a friend as she sipped her Martini and I lifted my pint of bitter. I do, however, like the not-so-occasional Negroni as an *aperitivo*, a word which comes from the Latin *aperitivus* (to open or dilate)—in this case your appetite, in anticipation of the meal to come. I first had a Negroni nearly ten years ago in a bar in Trastevere. "*Ne - gro - knee*" said the supercilious Sicilian barman as he finished the ruddy orange drink with a slice. Ten years later, that same barman still makes me a

Negroni in our kitchen, and still stresses the *gro - knee*. He might also tell me that it was invented in Florence for Count Negroni, and that bitter Campari used to be colored with carmine dye derived from crushed cochineal insects, all of which I am happy to hear again and again, as long as I have a drink in my hand.

The key to Negroni, I've learned, is fastidiously using equal parts gin (we use whatever we have, which at the moment is Sipsmith from London), sweet vermouth (Martini Rosso or the more opinionated Punt e Mes), and Campari over ice with a half-moon of orange or, better still, a strip of zest pared from an unwaxed orange with a peeler, twisted over the glass, and dropped in. I think the glass should be short and stout, and certainly stemless.

The strongest element makes its presence felt first—at least the juniper scent of it does. The first taste, though, is bitter-sweetness from the Campari, which burrows into your tongue and throat warmly before the gin comes through, only to be tempered by the sweet vermouth. The balance of smooth, bitter, aromatic, and sweet is spot on, punch-pleasant and stimulating, making it—for me—the perfect *aperitivo*. Clink.

Salame e olive marinate
Salami and marinated olives

Antipasti are all about anticipating the meal to come. A glass of Lambrusco, perhaps—not the sickly sweet stuff of jokes, but a bone-dry one that tastes of wild berries and whose soft bubbles excite the appetite. A wine to match an opinionated antipasti of salami and olives. Maybe you're sitting at the table, but most likely you're standing around the kitchen, possibly with an overtired and overactive toddler running around, the supper simmering, looking forward to the good things to come.

As far as I'm concerned, salami and olives is one of the best ways to start a meal, a ritual repeated often because it's so easy and good. When it comes to choosing salami, try to find a good and accommodating Italian deli that will let you taste until you find something you like. Look out for *finocchiona*, a cured meat with fennel seeds, or Corallina di Norcia, a very long salami that is smoked with juniper berries. Ideally, you want to cut the salami just before you eat it, so try to buy a section rather than pre-cut slices. For olives, try to find a place that sells different varieties marinated in different ways, sold by weight. When it comes to jars, look out for olives from Gaeta, *taggiasca* olives from Liguria, and the huge, fleshy, straw-green ones from Abruzzo. Alternatively, you could buy good-quality olives in brine and try marinating them yourself.

This recipe comes from Sabina, about 20 miles north of Rome, a land of undulating hills and olive groves. The combination of the dark, meaty olives with the gently acerbic citrus, the aromatic, almost piney marjoram, and warm chile is a delicious one. The olives need to sit for at least three hours, or better still overnight, to really assume the other flavors. They will keep happily for weeks in a screw-top jar in the fridge.

serves 6–8 as part of a mixed antipasti
1 small organic orange
1 small organic lemon
about ⅔ cup extra-virgin olive oil
1 tablespoon fresh marjoram, chopped,
  or 1 teaspoon dried marjoram
1 small fresh or dried red chile
2 bay leaves
salt
10 ½ ounces small black or brown olives in brine, drained

Pare the orange and lemon zest very carefully so as not to include any white pith, then slice it into very thin strips. In a large bowl, mix together the zest with the olive oil and 2 tablespoons lemon juice. Finely chop or crumble in the marjoram and chile and add the bay leaves and a good pinch of salt. Add the olives, stir well, and leave to sit for at least 3 hours, stirring every now and then.

Cipolline in agrodolce alla romana
Roman-style sweet-and-sour onions

Another small round companion for *salame* is *cipolline in agrodolce alla romana,* or Roman-style sweet-and-sour onions, a perennial favorite on Roman tables in cooler months. It's an ancient recipe, which reminds us that Romans have had a taste for *agrodolce* (sweet and sour) since ancient times, when honey or grapes would have been used in lieu of sugar.

I searched for a recipe for years, having eaten them as part of an otherwise pretty terrible antipasto, washed down by crummy white wine in a loud trattoria some years back. While the rest of the food eaten that evening was quickly forgotten, the memory of the savory-sweet onions sitting in a thick, dark syrup stuck. Then, while researching the olive recipe, I came across a recipe for onions, a satisfyingly simple one too.

Peeling the weepingly large quantity of small onions is a fiddly chore. Putting a teaspoon in your mouth does help (with the weeping, that is, not the fiddlyness); I have no idea why. It's probably for the same reason that drinking backward from a glass cures hiccups. Alternatively, you could try covering the onions with boiling water briefly, which I'm told loosens the skins. Whether you have wept over them or not, once peeled, you soak them in water for at least 4 hours, after which you cook them very slowly in half vinegar, half water with a tablespoon of sugar and a pinch of salt until tender. Serve with salami and olives as an antipasto. They're also good as a side dish with simply cooked meat, acting rather like a pickle or chutney. Talking of which, two onions sliced crosswise and tucked into a Cheddar cheese sandwich are a good antidote for nostalgia cravings and provide a Roman alternative to Branston Pickle chutney.

serves 6–8 as part of an antipasto or as a condiment
about 1½ pounds very small onions or shallots
1 garlic clove
3 tablespoons olive oil
salt
1 heaped tablespoon sugar
red wine vinegar

Peel the onions and soak them in cold water for 4 hours, then drain them. Chop two of them very finely along with the garlic and cook them gently in the olive oil in a heavy-bottomed frying pan.

Once the chopped onion and garlic are soft, golden, and translucent, add the rest of the whole onions, stirring so that they are all well coated with oil. Sprinkle with salt and sugar, then almost cover them with a mixture of half water and half vinegar—the amount will depend on the size of your pan.

Bring to a boil, then reduce the heat to a simmer. Half cover the pan and leave it to bubble gently for about 2 hours, turning the onions every now and then. They're ready when all the liquid has evaporated and the onions are very soft, sitting in dark, shiny, sticky sauce.

Zucchine alla scapece
Marinated zucchini with mint

Zucchine alla scapece are thin rounds of zucchini fried until golden in olive oil, then dressed with vinegar, salt, garlic, and mint, a recipe that gives the sweet but often timid zucchini some serious appeal, with a sharp suit and a musky scent.

I first ate this dish at my friend Josephine's house. The zucchini rounds had been sitting on a clean tea towel all night and most of the morning, and were consequently dry, wrinkled, and unprepossessing. However, having given up much of their water, they fried in a most possessing way and mingled obediently with the garlic, mint, and vinegar. They looked curious, like crêped discs, but they were delicate and delicious, soft with crisp edges, the vinegar cutting through the oil and the mint lending sweet mustiness. Eaten straight away, they are mild mannered, but left for a few hours, they get tarter and bolder. They can also be kept covered with olive oil in a jar in the fridge, and in this form they're a classic Roman conserve.

This recipe is best with the pale-green, ridged _zucchine romanesche,_ but any small, bright, firm zucchini will work well. I particularly like them as part of an antipasti lunch alongside a frittata. Good red wine vinegar is really important in this recipe.

about 1½ pounds zucchini
about ⅔ cup extra-virgin olive oil (depending on size of pan)
2 garlic cloves
salt
1 scant tablespoon red wine vinegar
1 small handful mint leaves

Wash and dry the zucchini and slice them into ¼-inch slices. Place the slices on a clean tea towel, pressing each one gently into the cloth, and leave to dry out—on a hot day you could leave them in the sun for a few hours, otherwise in the sunniest spot in the kitchen or a very cool oven—for a few hours.

Warm a generous ¾ inch cm olive oil in a frying pan over a medium heat. Put a single layer of zucchini slices in the oil and fry, turning the slices once, for about 5 minutes, or until golden and crisp. Lift out with a slotted spoon, shaking it slightly over the pan to allow some of the oil to drip away, then park them first on paper towels to blot, then into a shallow bowl. Continue frying the zucchini in batches and transferring them, via paper towels, to the bowl.

Peel and slice the garlic into thin batons, add it to the zucchini, and sprinkle them with salt and vinegar. Some people like to pour over a little more olive oil at this point. Tear the mint leaves into small pieces and add these too. Using a spoon, or better still your hands, mix everything together. Eat immediately or wait a few hours for the flavors to sharpen and the dish to become tarter and, I think, even better.

Frying tonight

"I wouldn't bother with recipes that involve deep-frying," said a well-meaning acquaintance. "Nobody deep-fries anymore because nobody wants their kitchen and hair to smell like a fish-and-chip shop, and of course it isn't healthy." At which I nodded and mentally added another fried recipe to the list.

She was right, of course, about the flat smelling like a fish-and-chip shop, but then you turn up your exhaust fan or fling open the windows. We know we shouldn't eat fried things too often, but every now and then, something dipped in a well-made batter and fried until golden and tantalizingly crisp is absolutely delicious, and no more unhealthy than depriving yourself of something you love.

My frying roots were laid in the north of England. Both my granny and grandma knew how to fry a chip until crisp on the outside but forgiving within, and a piece of fish into a golden cocoon. They also knew the best places for a fried tea, so we would drive to the Magpie in Whitby, then sit on the wall looking out over the bay, eating what seemed like huge arcs of battered cod and vinegar-sodden chips, with Grandpa Roddy telling us not to kick our heels against the bricks. However, it wasn't until I came to Rome that I really learned how to fry: to heat the oil until the tester bread cube dances around the pan in its coat of tiny bubbles; to work out how long to cook a sage leaf or a cylinder of potato coated with bread crumbs; to keep the door of the flat open so that the smell drifts through my hair and into the courtyard.

Romans are, for the most part, fantastically fond of deep-fried food. Golden squash blossoms, trimmed whole artichokes, florets of broccoli, slices of apple, wild flowers and herbs, fillets of salt cod, rings of squid, tiny silver fish, balls of mozzarella cheese and rice are all dipped in flour or batter and fried until golden. It's a tradition that has its roots in Roman Jewish cooking, but is now diffused throughout the city, particularly in pizzerias, which fry and serve up hot, freshly fried *fritti* before the pizza. That's by no means to say that all *fritti* in Rome are good, far from it: there are some shockingly bad ones to be found, but I am not going to take you there.

Three of my favorite places to eat—trattoria Cesare, pizzeria La Gatta Mangiona, and my local trattoria La Torricella—all do great *fritti*, but that doesn't stop me frying at home now and again, with the kitchen door wide open on to the balcony, a bottle of prosecco open, fried things blotted on paper towels and then eaten as soon as you can touch them. As much as I'd like you to imagine me effortlessly whipping up *fritti* for 12 with dinner to follow, I have to admit that I don't enjoy frying for a lot of people. Four, six at most; enough to warrant another bottle, but not too many to cramp the stove. My kitchen, as I have already mentioned, is not that much larger than an *Encyclopedia Britannica*. When I fry, I fry several things and make it a *fritti* dinner, preparing little else—a salad, probably—and then sending someone up the hill to get gelato from Il Gelato for dessert.

Everybody thinks their batter is the best, and mine is no exception. It did take me a very long time to find it and even though I knew it was the one, I still strayed and experimented using seltzer, fresh yeast, and whole eggs. But then I came back to the recipe that works best for me and the three favorite fried things I have chosen for the book: battered sage leaves, apple or pear slices, and squash blossoms. The batter is light and delicate and I leave it in the fridge until it is the spoon-clinging consistency of thick cream. I then fold in a couple of egg whites, beaten so vigorously that they stand to attention in peaks. I used to fry in sunflower or peanut oil, but I've now returned to olive oil, which is expensive and more impertinent in terms of flavor, but deliciously so. This also means that I fry in a small pan with just a few inches of oil, which I then use two or three more times. I do own a thermometer and I occasionally use it to check my standard frying temperature of 375°F. However, most of the time I have absolutely no idea where I have put the damn thing, and I judge it by eye. I do this by checking to see if the heat has made the oil less syrupy—it should err on the liquid side—by gently swirling the pan; if circular ripples form, the oil is ready for frying. I then double check by tossing a cube of bread in the oil, which should dance around and take about 40 seconds to turn golden. My amateur approach is also why I prefer a small pan, a few inches of oil, and frying in small batches, which feels more manageable.

1¼ cups all-purpose flour
2 tablespoons extra-virgin olive oil
a pinch of salt
2 egg whites

Make the batter by beating the flour, olive oil, and salt into a smooth, thick cream with 1 cup cold water, using an electric mixer or hand whisk. Allow it to rest in the fridge for at least 1 hour. Just before frying, place the egg whites in a large, clean bowl and whisk until they form stiff peaks, then fold them into the batter.

A note: I have suggested the amount of one thing to be fried for one quantity of batter, knowing there is a very good chance you will fry a mixture of things. The other day, one quantity of batter was enough for 25 or so sage leaves, a large apple, and about 8 squash blossoms, which we shared between three with a bottle and a half

of prosecco. This batter also works well for salt cod, rings of squid, small fish, and most vegetables.

Salvia fritta in pastella
Deep-fried sage leaves

Silvery green and moleskin-like to the touch, with a musty smell reminiscent of a room that has been closed up for a bit too long, sage is a very particular herb. A surprisingly delicious one too, especially when its leaves are dipped in batter and fried until golden. You need prosecco as well, its bubble and acidity contrasting beautifully with the crisp batter, then cleansing the mouth in anticipation of more. This is one of the best ways of whetting your appetite (or *stuzzicare,* as Vincenzo says), to poke and tease in readiness of the things to come, which I hope is a second batch of *fritti.* If you can, try to buy a small plant rather than a packet of ready-cut sage. That way, you can pull off the most suitable leaves—not too big and not too small—with a long enough stem to provide a handle for swooping through the batter.

serves 4–8 as part of an antipasti
olive, sunflower, or peanut oil, for frying
50 fresh sage leaves, washed and dried
1 quantity batter (page 49)
salt

Heat the oil in a deep frying pan or saucepan to 375°F. Use the stalk as a handle to drag a sage leaf through the batter, then lower it into the hot oil. Repeat with 6 or 7 leaves, depending on the size of your pan.

Nudge and turn the leaves with a wooden fork or spoon so that they fry evenly. Once crisp and golden, scoop the leaves out of the oil onto a plate lined with brown paper or paper towels using a slotted spoon. When they have drained a little, slide them onto a clean plate, sprinkle with salt, and serve immediately.

Mela o pera fritta in pastella con pecorino
Deep-fried apple or pear with pecorino

I first had battered and deep-fried wedges of apple and pear
dusted with pecorino cheese at an osteria called Iotto in a town
called Campagnano di Roma. They came as part of *fritto romano*
(fried things Roman style), which included artichokes, onion,
zucchini, and balls of mozzarella. It was all excellent, but it was the
fruit, sweet and soft within, crisp on the outside, and dusty with
sharp cheese, that got the whole table talking excitedly with their
mouths full. Another plate, with extra apple and pear, was ordered
immediately. When we have a standing Friday *fritti* supper, I always
make these, one of us frying and lifting, the other blotting, grating
over the cheese, and seeing how asbestos-like our mouths are. This
is another reason—as if you needed one—for classic prosecco.

serves 4–8 as part of an antipasti
**3 apples or pears (I like Golden Delicious apples and
  Bosc pears)**
olive, sunflower, or peanut oil, for frying
1 quantity batter (page 49)
freshly grated pecorino, to serve

Peel, core, and quarter the apples or pears, then slice them into ¼-inch thick slices, or use an apple corer, then cut them crosswise into rings. Heat the oil in a deep frying pan or saucepan to 375°F.

Dip an apple piece into the batter and lower it into the hot oil. Repeat with 6 or 7 more pieces, depending on the size of your pan.

Nudge and turn the apples with a wooden fork or spoon so that they fry evenly. Once crisp and golden, scoop them from the oil onto a plate lined with brown paper or paper towels, using a slotted spoon. When they have drained a little, slide them onto a clean plate, dust with grated pecorino, and serve immediately.

Fiori di zucca in pastella fritti Deep-fried squash blossoms

The golden, orange-tipped flowers attached to the end of each squash are female. The slightly smaller flowers with long, firm stems that grow directly, shooting really, from the main stem of the plant, like the ones in the picture on page 50, are male. Both are called *fiori di zucca* and both can be eaten. The male flower is perfect for deep-frying because the stem provides a tail you can hold on to while dipping the flower into the batter, then lowering it gently into the pan.

In August, when the market stalls in Testaccio are heavy with crates of pale green, blossom-tipped *zucchine romanesche* and bunches of their delicate flowers, we often have squash blossoms in salad, ripped into green leaves or, even better, into zucchini shavings dressed with olive oil and salt. I like a couple of bright yellow flowers tucked into a sandwich with mozzarella, or added, along with a handful of basil, to zucchini carbonara. But perhaps the nicest and most delicious way to eat squash blossoms is to buy a bunch of male flowers and fry them in very hot oil until they are crisp and golden.

In Rome, the flowers are stuffed with mozzarella and anchovy before frying. If they are freshly made, as opposed to the ready-prepared and frozen ones you'll spot a mile off, they are quite delicious things, usually served on a small white plate on a square of brown paper. They should be freshly fried, oddly shaped, and eaten straight from the hot oil, tongue-scaldingly hot. You wait a few seconds, then grab the crisp, golden cocoon with a paper napkin. You bite into the crisp batter, which gives way to the soft, forgiving flower petals—a nice contrast—and finally a soft pool of anchovy-infused mozzarella. For those among you who are dubious about fish and cheese together, I suggest you try these.

Much as I adore the Roman *fiori di zucca*, though, the best fried squash blossoms I've ever eaten were in Puglia, where they were dipped in the lightest batter and fried with no stuffing. Crisp and golden on the outside, the batter puffed with pride, giving way to a soft flower. The secret, the cook willingly told us, was beaten egg whites folded into the flour, water, and olive oil batter. Make sure you coat each flower thoroughly with batter. Again, sparkling wine is a delight here. Ask a trusted wine merchant for a nice, decently priced Franciacorta and see what he gives you.

serves 4
16 fresh male squash blossoms, with stems
olive, sunflower, or peanut oil, for frying
1 quantity batter (page 49)
salt

Soak the flowers in cool water for 1 minute. Remove and blot them gently, then leave them to dry completely on a clean tea towel.

Heat the oil in a deep frying pan or saucepan to 375°F. Using the stem as a handle, drag a flower through the batter until it is well coated, then drop it into the hot oil. Depending on the size of your

pan, fry the flowers in batches of 2–5, but ideally no more. Nudge and turn the flowers with a wooden fork or spoon so that they fry evenly. Once crisp and golden, scoop the flowers from the oil onto a plate lined with brown paper or paper towels using a slotted spoon. When they have drained a little, slide the flowers onto a clean plate, sprinkle with salt, and serve immediately.

Variation: To make the classic Roman *fiori di zucca*, stuff each flower with a small piece of mozzarella and half an anchovy. Pinch and twist the flowers so that they close. Fry as described above.

Carciofi alla giudea
Deep-fried artichokes

You often hear *fritti* called *sfizi*, which comes from *sfizio*, meaning "whim" or "fancy," in other words something you really don't need, but then again do: that golden squash blossom dipped in batter and fried, or a whole artichoke fried twice so that it looks like a bronze flower whose petals break away like crisps, and whose heart is velvety and soft. If you have been to Rome and eaten *carciofi alla giudea* you will understand what I am talking about.

I thought quite hard about including this recipe, as it really does depend on finding suitable artichokes, like the ones in Rome: huge, purple globes without inedible chokes that can be trimmed neatly and fried whole. "Come to Rome at the right time of year," I would tell you, "and among other things, eat artichokes." However, since good artichokes are becoming more readily available, and more of us are overcoming our fear of trimming, they are extremely possible at home. Here is the recipe. The key is the trimming, which I describe below, then frying twice, the first time slowly at a lower temperature, the second time quickly at a higher temperature for the definitive crisp. Unlike the other recipes, a thermometer is vital here.

serves 4
4 whole globe artichokes
2 lemons
olive oil, for frying
salt and freshly ground black pepper

Prepare the artichokes by removing the dark, tough outer leaves, pulling them downward and snapping them off just before the base.

Using a sharp knife, pare away the tough green flesh from the base of the artichokes and the stem. Cut the top third of the artichoke off completely. As you work, rub the cut edges with a lemon half, or place them in a bowl of water with lemon juice.

Heat about 3 inches olive oil in a saucepan over low to medium heat to about 300°F. Add the artichokes and fry them gently for about 10 minutes, poking them with a fork every now and then and letting them roll around so that they cook evenly.

Remove the artichokes with a slotted spoon and transfer to paper towels to drain the excess oil. Once cool enough to handle, gently open out the leaves with your fingers, remove the hairy choke if there is one, and press the artichoke head down on paper towels to flatten it slightly. Heat the oil again, this time over medium-high heat, to 375°F, and deep-fry the artichokes, head down, for 2–3 minutes, or until they are crisp and a deep golden brown. Tongs are helpful here. Remove and drain on paper towels, sprinkle with salt and pepper, and serve immediately.

Crocchette di patate e parmigiano
Potato and Parmesan croquettes

I'd never really considered the croquette before coming to Italy. I'd eaten them, mostly in St George's School dining room between 1984 and 1989, straight from a catering-size pack and fried two hours before consumption. They were floppy and soggy with a suspiciously orange coat that concealed a gluey, unctuous filling, which inevitably resulted in mild heartburn. Similar digestive challenges were presented by the potato cylinders I insisted on buying from dodgy fish-and-chip shops in London after long nights at the pub. There were some good ones in France, during a traumatic exchange holiday when I was 14, but like everything else to do with that trip, I try not to think about them.

I discovered the true potential of the potato croquette in a pizzeria in Naples when one was deposited in front of me at such speed that the plate spun round twice. I knew straight away it wasn't your average croquette, but even so I wasn't particularly excited by the prospect of a cylinder of deep-fried mashed potato, however golden it looked. Then I tasted it, and the shell gave way to an extremely soft, well-seasoned, cheese-spiked cushion of mash. This high was followed by various lows, during which I encountered much croquette disappointment. It seems that many of the pizzerias in Rome, even some of the best, aren't much more discerning than St George's School dining room. Just as I was about to give up all hope, I went to La Gatta Mangiona in Monteverde and there it was, the second: a modest little roll, reassuringly wonky, with a golden-brown texture like the sun, a hot, crisp, crunch on the outside, then a soft pillow of mash inside, with a sliver of mozzarella hiding in the center. There are variations using salt cod, others with herbs and other cheeses, reminding you that the possibilities are many.

Simple they may be, but it took me a while to settle on a recipe at home. I experimented with butter, with dipping in beaten egg, and with various methods such as mashing, ricing, and grating, until I settled on this: grated potatoes enriched with lots of Parmesan and an egg, seasoned with plenty of black pepper, dipped in polenta or bread crumbs, fried until golden, and eaten immediately. I repeat, immediately: gather guests around the stove and eat, ideally with other *fritti* and cold beers. Please note that my croquettes are wonky because, as everybody knows, very neat croquettes—like very neat people and houses—are suspicious.

makes 12
3 large russet potatoes
1 cup grated Parmesan
2 eggs, lightly beaten
salt and freshly ground black pepper
flour, for dusting
1 cup fine dried bread crumbs or instant polenta
2 cups olive or vegetable oil
lemon wedges, to serve

Scrub the potatoes, then cook them whole in a pan of well-salted boiling water until tender. Drain well. Once they are cool enough to handle, peel off the skin and then either grate them, press them through a potato ricer, or pass them through the largest holes of a food mill. Mix the potatoes with the Parmesan and one of the eggs and season with salt and pepper. Mold the potato mixture into 12 croquette shapes or cylinders, roll them in flour, then the other egg, roll them in the bread crumbs or polenta, and sit them on a plate lined with wax paper.

Heat the oil to 375°F in a small shallow pan, or until a cube of bread takes about 40 seconds to turn golden. Fry the croquettes 3 or 4 at a time for about 2 minutes, or until they are golden all over. Use a slotted spoon to lift them out onto paper towels to drain the excess oil. Serve immediately with lemon wedges.

My norcineria

In 2013 we moved from one side of Testaccio to the other. It was only a matter of 400 yards, give or take a corner, but everything felt different. The bar where I have my coffee each morning and the stall where I buy my fruit and vegetables felt entirely different approached from another direction. Streets rarely walked became suddenly familiar. Courtyards peered into from one side appeared entirely different from the other. A drinking fountain I'd only drunk from a handful of times became my local. A bakery, a launderette, a minuscule sewing shop, a pet shop whose window we spend at least 10 minutes a day peering through while Luca barks, and a *norcineria* I'd never noticed became part of my daily stroll—or grind, depending on the day.

It's not surprising that I'd never noticed the *norcineria,* as we both moved to via Galvani at more or less the same time. The shop used to be about a mile away before Bruno and Sergio, the two brothers who own it, decided to come back to Testaccio. A *norcineria* is a shop that specializes in cured pork products, which may also sell cheese, *salame,* and other dried goods. The name derives from the town of Norcia in Umbria, whose inhabitants (or some of them, at least) are historically renowned and much sought after for their meat-curing skills. *Norcinerie* are places of pink flesh and seasoned fat, of pancetta, *guanciale, lonzino,* coppa, *ciauscolo,* shoulder steaks, loins, fillets, and air-dried delights.

Norcineria Martelli is a neat, pleasing place, with a meat counter to the left, dried goods to the right, and the altar to *porchetta*—a large boneless pork roast seasoned with salt, black pepper, garlic, rosemary, and fennel seeds typical to Lazio—straight ahead as you come through the door. Which I do most days, with Luca in tow shouting loudly enough to arouse concern. Bruno and Sergio are amicable and honest, as are their pork and products. On Fridays they have ready-soaked chickpeas and salt cod, and on Tuesdays and Saturdays they also have a nice, naturally leavened bread and a dome or two of the best sheep's-milk ricotta.

I am disproportionately fond of ricotta: brilliant white, compact but wobbly enough to remind you not to be so serious, and embossed with the ridges of the cone it was molded in. We eat it several times a week, its creamy, sweet-but-sharp, and sheepish nature indispensable in both sweet and savory dishes. I shape it into lumps, stir it into pasta, smear it on bread (which I then finish with lots of salt, black pepper, and olive oil), slice it over beans, spoon it next to fruit, nuts, and honey, whip it into desserts, and bake it into tarts and cakes.

I also mix it with wilted spinach (I never fail to be impressed by
the way that disobedient spinach, once disciplined in a pan, wilts
so obediently), lots of freshly grated Parmesan, an egg, a nip of
nutmeg, salt, and plenty of black pepper, to make *polpette di ricotta
e spinaci.*

Polpette di ricotta e spinaci
Ricotta and spinach fritters

This recipe is inspired by the *polpette* we eat as often as possible
at what is probably my favorite *tavola calda* (a kind of self-service
café) in Rome these days: C'è Pasta e Pasta! on the other side of the
river on via Ettore Rolli. The key is to make a relatively firm mixture
of ricotta and spinach—and the key to that is to make sure you drain
the spinach meticulously. Drain, then squeeze and press until you
have an almost dry green ball. The ricotta, too, should be drained
of any excess liquid. If the mixture is firm you shouldn't have any
problems shaping it into *polpette*, which you then flatten slightly
with the palm of your hand. Why this is so satisfying I'm not sure,
but it is. Then, the triple roll: first in flour, next in a bath of beaten
egg, then in fine bread crumbs.

Once rolled, you fry them in hot oil; these days I prefer olive oil,
but vegetable oil works well too. They take just minutes to shimmy

in a disco coat of bubbles until they're deep gold and crisp. *Polpette di ricotta e spinaci* or *bon bon di ricotta e spinaci* are best eaten while they are still finger-scaldingly hot, while their coating is sharp, decisive, and shatters between your teeth before giving way to a soft, warm filling of cheese and spinach.

> makes about 15
> **about 1 pound spinach**
> **1½ cups ricotta (ideally sheep's milk, but cow's milk works well too)**
> **3 large eggs**
> **½ cup grated Parmesan or pecorino**
> **freshly grated nutmeg**
> **salt and freshly ground black pepper**
> **flour, for dusting**
> **1 cup fine dried bread crumbs or instant polenta**
> **olive or vegetable oil, for frying**

Soak the spinach in several changes of water. Discard any wilted or bruised leaves and trim away any very thick, woody stalks. Put it in a large pan with nothing but the water that clings to the leaves, cover, and cook over medium heat until it has collapsed and is tender. This should take 3–5 minutes, depending on the freshness and age of the spinach.

Drain the spinach, and once it is cool enough to handle, squeeze and press it gently with your hands to eliminate as much water as possible. Chop it roughly, then transfer it to a large bowl. Add the ricotta and stir gently but firmly with a wooden spoon. Add 1 egg, the grated Parmesan, and a grating of nutmeg and season with salt and pepper. Stir the ingredients until they are evenly combined, then taste and adjust the seasoning if necessary. Let the mixture rest in the fridge for an hour.

Prepare 3 plates, one with the remaining eggs, beaten, one with seasoned flour, and one with the bread crumbs or polenta. Using a teaspoon, scoop out a golf-ball-size lump of the spinach-and-ricotta mixture. Shape it into a ball and flatten it into a patty. Dip it in flour, then egg, and finally roll it in the bread crumbs or polenta until evenly coated. Put the polpette on a plate lined with parchment paper while you prepare the rest.

In a deep frying pan or saucepan, heat the oil to 375°F (I judge this by eye, using a cube of bread—see page 49) and carefully lower in 3 or 4 polpette at a time. Cook for about 2 minutes, or until crisp and deep gold. Use a slotted spoon to lift them onto a plate lined with paper towels. Once drained, slide them onto the serving plate, sprinkle with salt, and eat immediately.

Supplì al telefono
Rice croquettes filled with mozzarella

When you break a golden *supplì* in two, the mozzarella hidden inside the cylinder of rice doesn't tear but stretches like an old-fashioned telephone cord, hence the name. Luca, who is nearly three and whose favorite food, after *pizza rossa,* is *supplì,* will never fully understand this concept. *Supplì* are another example of resourceful fifth-quarter cooking—traditionally, they would have been a way of using up leftovers, whether leftover rice, cheese, bread crumbs, chicken livers, or ground meat from ragù. Although that would be delicious, I usually make these vegetarian, which is why I would favor stock over water and be generous with the seasoning.

Supplì are what I would call a kitchen project. Not that they are particularly complicated, it's simply that they require time (ideally a night) and organization for molding, dipping, and frying. However, when I do get my act together and make them, ensuring there are plenty of cold beers in the fridge, I make not just Luca but everybody else extremely happy. It is always the case that you don't fry the first couple of *supplì* for long enough, and the mozzarella is warm but not fully melted. But then you fry the third and someone tears it in half and there it is, the cord stretching before your eyes.

makes about 15
1 onion
3 tablespoons extra-virgin olive oil
14.5 ounces canned plum tomatoes
salt and freshly ground black pepper
4 cups light stock or water
2½ cups Arborio rice
4 tablespoons butter
½ cup grated Parmesan
4 eggs
7 ounces mozzarella
flour, for coating
fine bread crumbs or instant polenta, for coating
olive or vegetable oil, for frying

Dice the onion. Heat the extra-virgin olive oil in a deep sauté pan over low heat and cook the onion gently until soft and translucent. Pass the tomatoes through a food mill or sieve or blast them with an immersion blender, and add them to the pan with the onion. Season with salt and plenty of pepper, then stir and leave to bubble away for a few minutes.

Warm the stock or water in a small pan. Add the rice to the pan with the tomatoes and stir. Now, cook the rice as if you were making a risotto; in other words, add the liquid gradually and let it bubble away gently while you stir. As the liquid is absorbed, add another ladleful of stock or water and stir again. Keep stirring and slowly adding stock until the rice is swollen and tender. This should take about 17 minutes.

Remove the pan from the heat and, using a wooden spoon, beat in the butter, grated Parmesan, and 2 of the eggs, lightly beaten. Leave the rice mixture to sit in the fridge for at least 5 hours or overnight. Cut the mozzarella into ¾-inch-long, ¼-inch-wide batons. Using a tablespoon, scoop out a ball of rice mixture. Using your finger, make a hole in the center and tuck a mozzarella baton inside. Use your hands to mold the rice over the hole and shape the ball into a stout croquette. Arrange the flour, bread crumbs, and remaining eggs, beaten, on separate plates. Dip the *supplì* in flour, then egg, then roll in the bread crumbs.

In a deep frying pan or saucepan, heat the oil to 375°F. Fry the *supplì* in batches until golden brown and crisp, then remove with a slotted spoon and drain on paper towels. Serve immediately.

The bakery

Although we outgrew the flat above the bakery, it's still ours, providing a home for Vincenzo's vinyl and CD collection and most of my cookbooks. This means it's the place Vincenzo goes when he wants to listen to Miles Davis and The Meters, and where I go to write. As I write now, on a warm May afternoon, I can hear the faint clatter of baking trays and pans, and if I sniff I can catch the scent of afternoon baking, tarts I think (possibly cherry and ricotta), that has curled through the back window of the bakery into the courtyard, up two floors, and into my open front door.

In the morning, if you stand near the front door, as I did every morning for five years to make coffee, it is the smell of bread, thick, yeasty waves of it, that creeps under the front door. According to Vincenzo, there is also the smell of *piazza bianca*, one so seductive that he would often run down the two flights of stairs, out of the front gate, ten paces along the street, and make the purchase, to be back with two hot slices of pizza before the coffee had bubbled out of the coffee pot.

The bakery is called Passi, which means "steps"—fitting if you live just steps away. It is a family-run business, which was

established in 1976 and these days is managed by the children—a handsome shop on the corner of via Mastro Giorgio, with a classic Roman typeface on its sign. The assistants all wear white jackets and hats and the bakers wear white T-shirts, flour-dredged aprons, and caps. The glass counter is high and domed, displaying cookies, tarts, and buns at one end, and cooked dishes at the other. On the wooden work surface behind the counter there is pizza, and then, in sections on the back wall, the bread. The shelves above the bread are stacked with dry goods: Gentilini biscuits, crackers, pasta, coffee, and bright yellow packets of tea. If you stand at the end of the counter farthest from the door you can see into the back room where the bakers paddle *pizza bianca* out of the stacks of ovens. Passi is perennially busy and its charm comes not only from the place, but also from the boisterous sense of family it exudes and the pervading sense of neighborhood generated by the loyal local customers, who wait patiently for their daily bread: hot *pizza bianca* or *rossa, patate with rosmarino, rosette* (a shaped bread roll often filled with mortadella), *scrocchiarella* (a very thin, very crispy, cracker-type pizza), or freshly fried, sugar-encrusted *ciambelle*.

I am still trying to get to the bottom of Passi's bread, which changes from day to day. But one thing is certain: there is always *pane casareccio* (home-style bread), usually in two forms, one round, *la pagnotta,* and one long, *il filone*. It is an open, chewy bread with a light, cracking crust. There are also *rosette:* hollow, domed bread rolls cut to resemble rosettes, the type I never won when growing up. On any given day Passi will also have bread brought in from other bakeries, some near and some farther away, such as *pane di Genzano*, a semi-whole-grain bread cooked in wood-fired ovens from Genzano, a town north of Rome, or the pale, saltless bread from Terni in Umbria. Occasionally there will be the majestic *pane di Altamura* from Puglia, a yellow-crumbed bread shaped like a broad-rimmed hat that wouldn't look out of place at Ascot, made from twice-ground local durum wheat. My favorite is *pane di Lariano;* naturally leavened, it has a chewy crumb that's slightly sour, a good crust, and a bottom hard enough to tap a tune on (thanks to the wood oven), and can be bought by weight.

Whichever bread Romans choose to buy, or indeed make, it is central to the way they eat, so much so that it's taken for granted and is noticed only by its absence. Which is likely to cause a furor, at least among the Romans I know. More often than not, bread is the first thing to arrive on the table, usually in a basket lined with a napkin, and the last thing to be removed. It is nourishment that predates pasta in Rome by centuries; an accompaniment; a utensil (when the dish permits, many Romans eat with a fork and a crust of bread); and the agent of the final swipe, or *scarpetta*, of most plates. Quite simply, a meal is unthinkable without bread.

Bruschetta four ways

I am no stranger to the resourceful use of old bread. Both Grandma Roddy and Granny Jones were good at putting faded bread to good use, and my mum was too, in bread sauce, bread-and-butter pudding, to coat whatever needed to be crumbed (and then fried), or for toast and more toast. In Rome, where tradition still rules, people are (mostly) equally resourceful with old bread, similarly reducing it to bread crumbs, which are then used in cakes, as toppings and coatings, soaked in milk to pad out meatballs, mixed with tomatoes for panzanella, and toasted for bruschetta.

Bruschetta comes from the word *bruscare* or *abbrustolire,* which means "toast lightly," in this case so that the bread is golden and

hard enough to withstand a deft swipe with a cut garlic clove. Traditionally, bruschetta was toasted over a wood fire and iron grill, but nowadays is mostly made on a grill pan over the heat if you want that slightly smoky flavor and deep grill lines, or in the toaster, or under the broiler, or in the oven. It's entirely up to you.

If the bread is good, the olive oil is decent extra-virgin, the garlic is fresh, and the salt is the sort that could cut the pads of your fingers, then plain bruschetta is hard to beat. In trattoria Agustarello, Sandro brings plain bruschetta, branded with dark lines from the grill and streaked with olive oil, with *fave* and pecorino cheese, and it is simply delicious. Beyond plain, the possibilities are endless, but I particularly like tomato and basil, white bean with rosemary, and my lunch at least once a week while they're in season: peeled fava beans with ricotta.

Bruschetta con aglio e olio
Bruschetta with garlic and olive oil

I give you the method from *La Cucina Romana* by Rosa D'Ancona because I think it captures the spirit of bruschetta so well.

serves 4
day-old country or sourdough bread
2 garlic cloves
extra-virgin olive oil
salt and freshly ground black pepper

Cut 4 slices from a loaf with a compact crumb. They mustn't be too thin. Position the slices on the grill over the coals. When the slices are golden and toasted on both sides, rub both sides with a cut clove of garlic. Pour plenty of olive oil over the slice and give flavor with salt and a grind of black pepper. Serve very hot so the oil doesn't have time to impregnate the bread.

Bruschetta con pomodoro e basilico
Bruschetta with tomatoes and basil

serves 4
⅔ **pound good tomatoes**
salt
a few leaves of basil
extra-virgin olive oil
4 slices day-old country bread with a compact crumb
2 garlic cloves

Rinse and cut away the tough central core of the tomatoes, then dice them into a bowl, taking care to catch the juices. Add a pinch of salt, some ripped basil leaves, and a good dousing of olive oil. Let the tomatoes sit for an hour or so. Toast the bread in whichever way you choose, until golden. Rub with the cut side of a garlic clove and top with a mound of chopped tomatoes and a little of the oily juices. Eat immediately.

Bruschetta con cannellini e olio con rosmarino
Bruschetta with white beans and rosemary oil

serves 4
7 tablespoons extra-virgin olive oil
a sprig of rosemary
2 cups cooked cannellini beans
salt and freshly ground black pepper
4 slices day-old country bread with a compact crumb
1 garlic clove

Make a rosemary oil by gently warming the olive oil in a small pan with the rosemary over a low heat. Leave the rosemary oil to infuse for 20 minutes or so.

Put the beans in a bowl and season them with salt and pepper. Either mash them gently with a fork or blend them to a smooth paste with an immersion blender, depending on how you like them. Toast the bread in whichever way you choose, until golden. Rub with the cut side of a garlic clove and spread with some of the beans. Spoon over some rosemary olive oil and eat immediately.

Bruschetta con ricotta e fave fresche
Bruschetta with ricotta and fava beans

serves 4
2¼ pounds fava beans in their pods
salt
extra-virgin olive oil
4 slices day-old country bread with a compact crumb
1 garlic clove
1 cup ricotta
freshly ground black pepper

Remove the fava beans from their pods, put them in a bowl, and cover them with boiling water. Wait for 1 minute, then drain and cover them with cold water. Now the opaque coats should slip away easily, leaving you with a small bowlful of bright green beans.

Sprinkle over a little coarse salt, pour over some olive oil, and stir. Toast the bread in whichever way you choose, until golden. Rub with the cut side of a garlic clove and spread with some ricotta. Spoon a quarter of the fava beans over each bread slice, grind over a little black pepper, and eat immediately.

Panzanella
Bread and tomato salad

Testaccio in August: hot, sleepy, and slightly squalid, which I put down to the dust and arbitrary rubbish collection. There is just enough life to reassure—including my preferred bar, market stall, and *forno* (bakery)—but no more. The whole quarter behaves like a cat; that is, lying low in the shade all day, rousing only when absolutely necessary (meaning meals), then prowling at night. I like Testaccio in August. I say rouse for meals, but in our case for ridiculously simple food: granita, melon and figs, mozzarella and tomatoes, potatoes I cooked the night before with anchovies, or a dish that tastes like late summer: panzanella.

Traditionally, like bruschetta, panzanella was a way of using up old bread and the glut of juicy tomatoes, a good example of resourcefulness tasting as good as it feels. Decent bread is important, and Tuscan unsalted bread or sourdough work best. Ideally, the bread should be at least a day or two old so it has a decent chew. Very old bread that you could knock someone out with can be dampened back to life with a little water, squeezed, and then ripped. The inclusion of mint is not traditional alongside the basil, but I think it works really well.

We eat panzanella with grilled fish, meat, or halloumi if I'm lucky enough to find it, with hard-boiled eggs crisscrossed with a pair of anchovies and, thanks to my friend Hande, now with a big spoonful of warm ricotta on the top. Panzanella pairs beautifully with chilled rosé wine, particularly one called Cerasuolo di Montepulciano.

serves 4
2¼ pounds mixed tomatoes, the best you can find
a handful of basil leaves
a few mint leaves
extra-virgin olive oil
salt
7 ounces day-old bread, preferably sourdough

Chop the tomatoes roughly and put them in a large bowl. Tear in the basil and mint leaves, and add oil and a pinch of salt. Stir and leave to sit for about 10 minutes. Meanwhile, tear the bread into manageable pieces and, using your hands, toss it with the tomatoes and their juices. Leave to sit for another 10 minutes or so, before tossing again and serving.

Mozzarella con pomodori al forno
Mozzarella with oven-roasted tomatoes

I make two sorts of oven-roasted small tomatoes. The first I think of as neat (or neatish), which take a couple of hours in a low oven and emerge semidried, as wrinkled as a prune and with an intense, almost sunburned, flavor. You can use them just so, or keep them in oil in a jar in the fridge. Either way, they are good in sandwiches, salads, added to pasta dishes, or next to a slice of frittata.

The others I think of as messy. This involves tomatoes still on the vine, if possible, lots of salt and olive oil, and about an hour in a hot oven, at which point you have rich and roasted tomato chaos, which (once you've picked out the vine) can be stirred into pasta, squashed on toast, or served alongside roast chicken. Alternatively, both neat and messy go beautifully with milky-white mozzarella.

serves 4–6
2¼ pounds small plum or cherry tomatoes, ideally on the vine
2 (8-ounce) balls mozzarella di bufala

Neat and almost dried
Preheat the oven to 300°F. Wash and cut the tomatoes in half. Line a baking sheet with parchment paper and arrange the tomatoes, cut-side up, on the paper. Roast for 2–3 hours, or until the tomatoes have shriveled, wrinkled, and half dried.

Messy and squashy
Preheat the oven to 360°F. Rinse the tomatoes on the vine and pat them dry. Put them on a baking sheet, sprinkle with salt, pour over some olive oil, and roast for an hour or so, until the tomatoes are soft, and starting to turn golden, and the edges are splitting.

Serve either with mozzarella alongside.

Prosciutto, melone e fichi
Prosciutto, melon, and figs

For years it was a choice between figs or melon. I'd flip the two back and forth in my mind, weighing fragrant over sweet and vinous, moons over torn flesh. Then, in a domestic eureka moment at my market stall, I realized I can have both: I can have my melon and eat my figs with prosciutto too.

serves 4
1 ripe melon, ideally cantaloupe or honeydew
8 ripe figs
8 slices of prosciutto, ideally San Daniele

Cut the melon in half, scoop out the seeds, slice it into 1-inch-thick wedges, and pare away the rind. Cut the figs in half. Arrange the melon, figs, and prosciutto on a large platter and serve.

White pizza

When I first arrived in Rome, I walked and walked. In retrospect, this was the best thing to do. In order to understand Rome you must be physical, pound hard, touch, inhale, and taste, and allow the city with its stone and dust to work itself into you. The senses are much more honest than studious intelligence. In truth, though, it wasn't a conscious decision. I didn't know what else to do, so I walked as a way of continuing to flee, to keep running, counting steps, counting churches, counting coffees.

Caffè was of paramount importance and fueled my walking. The Roman habit of paying up front at the cashier, then drinking your short, dark espresso standing up against the bar suited me as I shifted from foot to foot, never really stopping, exchanged two words, and then moved on. For sustenance there was *pizza bianca*, Rome's adored street food, which is bought by the slice and eaten while you rove or dawdle around the city.

My local baker, Passi, makes a good everyday *pizza bianca*, but for some of the best you need to walk up the river to Il Forno di Campo dè Fiori or Roscioli. Better still, you can cross Rome to Pizzarium, a small but almost perfectly formed *pizza al taglio* (pizza by the slice) just up from Cipro metro station. It's a Tardis-like place,

where Gabriele Bonci and his crew of broad-handed, flour-dusted *pizzaioli* make some of the best *pizza bianca* you could hope to taste: firm-bottomed and crisp at first, then giving way to a proper, mouth-arresting chew, with oil and salt clinging to your lips.

It never crossed my mind to make *pizza bianca* at home until I started working on this book. I felt it was one of those things that's better left to the experts, most of whom spend their days in tiny Roman *forni*, paddling hot pizza daily from the gaping mouths of ovens, brushing them with olive oil, strewing them with salt, and slicing them just for me. Then I kept finding myself writing "good with *pizza bianca*," "serve with *pizza bianca*." Figs and prosciutto, mozzarella and tomatoes all cried out for *pizza bianca*. I realized I would have to learn.

Pizza bianca
Pizza with olive oil and salt

This is the recipe from the man who knows: Gabriele Bonci. It's an intimidating one at first glance, or it was for me at least. You need to seek out the right flour, deal with a particularly sticky, putty-like dough, have patience for the long, slow, 24-hour rise, then handle it with a puttering touch. But when you try it you realize that it's actually not that much bother at all. Yes, there are the three rounds of folding, but it's actually pretty straightforward. It requires that you wait, but don't all good things? The puttering touch is easily mastered and the final pizza is worth every moment, especially if you are someone who has been dreaming of *pizza bianca* ever since you left Rome (it is, among my friends at least, one of the things people miss most).

The key to this recipe, I've learned, is the *piegature di rinforzo,* or "folding to reinforce." By stretching and folding the dough gently, developing the gluten and incorporating air into it, you render it altogether more manageable. Important, too, is the long, slow rise in the fridge, where the cool inhibits a fast inflate and forces the dough to work, stretch, and develop. It is this slow rise that produces an extremely digestible pizza. As for the baking, there are no two ways about it: domestic ovens are not going to come close to the temperatures or conditions of a professional oven. However, don't let this stop you from giving it a try at home—just turn your oven up as high as it will go. There's a reason why Romans hang around in bakeries and *pizza al taglio* places waiting for the pizza to come out of the oven. Eat it as soon as you can.

makes 5 pizzas (can be halved)
2¼ pounds Italian farina 0 or bread flour
3½ teaspoons fast-action dried yeast, or 2 tablespoons plus
   ½ teaspoon fresh yeast
2½ teaspoons salt
3 tablespoons extra-virgin olive oil

You'll need a standard square or rectangular, thin-based, rimmed baking sheet or pizza stone. I use a run-of-the-mill 12 x 12-inch rimmed baking sheet.

In a large bowl, mix together the flour and yeast with a wooden spoon. Then add a scant 3 cups water gradually, and once it is incorporated, add the salt and the oil. Mix until you have a pale, sticky, putty-like mixture. Cover with a clean tea towel or plastic wrap and leave to rest for 1 hour at room temperature in a draft-free part of the kitchen.

Scrape the mixture onto a lightly floured board; it will still be sticky. Now for the *piegature di rinforzo*. With lightly floured hands, gently stretch and pull the edges of the dough and fold them back over themselves. Try as best as you can to turn the dough 90 degrees (it will stick) by using a dough scraper or spatula and repeat the pull-and-fold motion. With this repeated pulling and folding,

the incorporation of air and a little flour from your hands means the dough will get more soft and manageable. Bonci suggests you repeat this pulling-and-folding motion 3 times, wait for 20 minutes, repeat, wait for 20 minutes, then repeat.

Put the soft dough in an oiled bowl, cover it with a tea towel or plastic wrap, and leave it for 18–24 hours in the bottom half of the fridge.

Remove the bowl from the fridge and leave it for 10 minutes. Carefully lift the dough out of the bowl and cut it into 5 pieces of more or less 12 ounces each—you can use a scale to check. Working piece by piece, shape the dough into a ball, fold it over once as you did for the *piegature di rinforzo,* and leave it to sit for another 30 minutes at room temperature, away from any drafts. Preheat the oven to 500°F and oil your baking sheet or pizza stone.

The final stage needs to be done with a delicate touch; you don't want to squash out the air you have so patiently incorporated. On a lightly floured board, use your fingertips to push and massage the dough into a square or rectangle the same size as your baking sheet, starting from the borders and working into the center. Once it is more or less the right size, drape it over your arm and lift it onto your prepared baking sheet. Zig-zag the dough with a thin stream of olive oil.

Bake it directly on the floor of the oven for 15 minutes, then check the pizza by lifting up the corner and looking underneath—it should be firm and golden. If it seems nearly done, move it to the middle rack for 10 more minutes. Take it out, brush it with more olive oil if you think it needs it, and sprinkle with salt. Slice and eat.

Figs and pizza bianca

In July and August, when figs are ripe but *sodi* (vinous and sweet), Romans tear and tuck them, along with a slice or two of prosciutto, between the two ripped halves of *pizza bianca*. The salty prosciutto contrasts deliciously with the sweet, floral fig, the seeds grate gratifyingly against the smooth meat and get caught in your teeth, and the pizza acts as a slightly crisp, oiled, and salted pillow to envelop everything.

Frittata di patate
Frittata with potato

When I don't know what to cook and I'm too tired and hungry
to think, the answer is usually frittata. Far from being a tired
compromise (which it is), it's almost always the most reassuringly
tasty and comforting thing.

A frittata is a fat, open, Italian omelet that can be enriched with
whatever you like—vegetables, herbs, cheese, meat, leftover pasta—
and eaten hot, warm, or cold. I adore frittata with ricotta and peas,
with masses of fresh herbs and bacon, with wild asparagus, but best
of all I like frittata with potatoes, because it is good and because it
has, and will, continue to save our supper and what feels like my
sanity for years to come. You can, of course, make it with leftover
cold boiled potatoes, but the best way is to gently fry slices of potato,
possibly with a little sliced onion, until they are very soft, then add
them to some beaten, well-seasoned eggs before tipping the whole
lot back into the newly buttered pan. You then let it cook gently until
it is nearly cooked through. The next stage is where (without making

this precious—after all, we are tired) opinions differ. You can finish it under the broiler, but this tends to make it tough; you can turn off the heat, cover the pan with a lid for a couple of minutes, then serve so you have an incredibly tender, slightly wobbly, almost custard-like frittata (Vincenzo's favorite), or you can invert it onto a plate and slide it back into the pan for just a minute. I prefer the third option.

Frittata can be sliced and served as an antipasti—or, as my grandma might have said, nibbles—or as a meal with a green salad and a glass of wine, perhaps something crisp and white from Friuli such as Sauvignon Blanc.

serves 4 as a meal, 8 as part of an antipasti
about 1¼ pounds potatoes
3 tablespoons extra-virgin olive oil
salt
1 mild onion
6 large eggs
freshly ground black pepper
butter, for cooking

Slice the potatoes into ⅛-inch-thick rounds. Warm the olive oil over medium heat in a nonstick or cast-iron frying pan, add the potatoes and a pinch of salt, then stir until each round is well coated with oil. Cover the pan and cook over low heat for 10 minutes.

Thinly slice the onion. Uncover the pan, by which time the potatoes should be softening, and add the onion. Stir, re-cover the pan, and cook for another 10 minutes. Uncover the pan, stir, and keep cooking until the onions and potatoes are very soft and collapsing. Remove the pan from the heat.

In a large bowl, beat the eggs lightly and season well with salt and pepper. Add the potatoes and onion to the eggs and stir well. Return the pan to medium heat, add a dot of butter, and allow it to coat the pan. Pour in the egg, potato, and onion mixture and even it out with a fork. Cook for about 20 minutes over gentle heat, using a wooden spatula to ease the frittata away from the sides as it starts to set. Once it is almost set and still just a little wet on top, invert it upside down onto a plate and slide it back in the pan for another minute. Invert it back onto a serving plate. Wait at least 10 minutes (and up to a few hours) before eating.

Frittata di ricotta e menta
Frittata with ricotta and mint

This is an excellent frittata for lunch or supper, or sliced into wedges as an *aperitivo*.

> serves 4 as a meal, 8 as part of an antipasti
> **1 small white onion**
> **3 tablespoons extra-virgin olive oil**
> **6 eggs**
> **1⅓ cups ricotta**
> **a handful of mint**
> **salt and freshly ground black pepper**
> **butter, for cooking**

Thinly slice the onion. Warm the olive oil in a nonstick or cast-iron pan and add the onion. Cook gently until soft and translucent, then remove the pan from the heat. In a large bowl, whisk the eggs with a fork. Add the ricotta and mash it so it breaks up into the egg. Using your fingers, rip the mint into tiny pieces and add it to the egg and ricotta. Add the onion and season generously with salt and pepper.

Return the pan to medium heat, add a dot of butter, and allow it to coat the pan, then pour the egg mixture into the pan. Use a fork to even it out. As the mixture starts to set, use a wooden spatula to ease it away from the sides of the pan. After 20 minutes or so, when you can see the frittata is almost set through and only a little wet on top, invert it upside down onto a plate and slide it back into the pan for another 30 seconds. Slide it onto a serving plate. Allow the frittata to sit for 10 minutes or up to several hours before serving in small slices as part of antipasti, or in much larger wedges for lunch or supper.

Midollo con insalata di prezzemolo e bruschetta
Roast bone marrow, parsley salad, and toast

I have hazy memories of sucking or poking bone marrow from the bones of a Sunday roast, but a clear one of the first time I ate bone marrow at a restaurant called St John in London. I was taken by my friend Jo, an architect, to a cavernous, whitewashed place on St John Street that seemed to be full of other architects. The restaurant, I was told, served a kind of British cooking and lots of offal, which was disconcerting then. We drank in the bar and then ordered from a bar menu chalked up on the blackboard. I would order from that menu countless times over following years, so my memories are a muddle of many visits repaid with brilliantly simple and delicious things to eat: Welsh rarebit; boiled eggs and celery salt; radishes, butter, and salt; skate, chicory, and anchovy; rabbit terrine; smoked eel with watercress and horseradish; crispy pigs' tails; sorrel salad; soft roes on toast; cured beef with celeriac. A muddle, except for the first dish on the first visit: roast bone marrow with parsley salad.

Bone marrow isn't, as I used to think, all fat (not that this presented me with a problem): it is also protein, and a veritable collection of vitamins and good things. It is delicious, quivering, and rich, and melts into the warm toast luxuriously. Like butter and olive oil, bone marrow on toast cries out for salt, ideally tiny shards of it that catch the sides of your mouth. The pinch of parsley, caper, and shallot salad, grassy, salty, and sharp, is a welcome addition for its contrast with the marrow and bread. It's simple, purposeful, and delicious food that is also extremely at home in Rome, where bone marrow is called *midollo* and is traditionally squashed on bread for kids. What's more, my butcher is more than happy to give me veal bones for free.

serves 4
12 pieces veal marrow bones
a bunch of flat-leaf parsley
2 spring onions
1 tablespoon capers, preferably small ones
⅓ cup extra-virgin olive oil
juice of 1 small lemon
salt and freshly ground black pepper
8 slices sourdough bread
coarse sea salt, to serve

Preheat the oven to 400°F. Put the bones in an ovenproof frying pan and then into the oven for about 20 minutes, or until the marrow is soft and like jelly but not melting away. I start checking and prodding with the tip of a knife after about 15 minutes.

While the marrow is softening, make the salad by pulling the parsley leaves off the stems and chopping them roughly. Finely chop the spring onions and roughly chop the capers and mix them with the parsley (hands are best for this). Add the olive oil and lemon juice and season with salt and pepper.

When the marrow bones are nearly ready, make some toast and serve each person 3 bones, 2 pieces of toast, and a little pile of parsley salad. The best way to go about eating this, in the absence of a long, thin bone-marrow spoon, is to use the end of a teaspoon to dig out the marrow, squash it onto the toast, crunch over a little salt, pile on some parsley salad, and eat it immediately.

Bread and butter

Granny Alice, my mum's mum and my second namesake, loved
bread and butter. She was particular about how to unwrap and then
rewrap the foil or wax paper—after all, butter wrappers are not just
for keeping butter safe; later they can be used for smearing the last
bit of butter onto a pan or pie dish. Alice would have tutted at the
mess captured in the picture here. Actually, I want to tut at the mess
I made of the butter pack. I considered changing the picture until I
realized it was a good place to start because it is precisely this sort
of banal detail of a badly opened butter pack that can stir a thought
or memory, which then tumbles like a domino into more memories,
and suddenly bread and butter is so much more than just bread
and butter.

   After the picture was taken, I called my dad to ask him something
for the book and the conversation turned to bread and butter, of
which he is very fond too. I told him the wrapper had made me think
of Alice, and he told me that when he was a boy there was a plate
of buttered bread on the table at every meal. He also reminded me

that on Mum's side of the family, Alice's sister May used to butter the end of the loaf before cutting off a slice. As he spoke, a memory emerged of Auntie May, short and strong, in the kitchen in my granny's pub, the Gardeners' Arms, buttering the end of a white loaf. This memory then rolled into one of Uncle Colin in about 1980, when he was 23, more or less the age he remains in our minds as he died not long afterward. In this memory, Colin, still in his dressing gown with his bangs hiding his eyes, strolls as if to music into the kitchen in search of strong tea and a bacon sandwich.

There is Alice in the kitchen too, frying back bacon to be sandwiched between slices of bread, every now and then casting exasperated but adoring glances at her youngest son. While the bacon fries, Colin lights a cigarette and May chases him out of the kitchen with a pair of kitchen tongs, which we, his young nieces and nephew, think hilarious. Now the memories are spreading like soft butter on bread, of Colin and the unbearably sad things to come, so I think about the bacon butties eaten in the pub kitchen and the taste of the bread that was put in the empty pan to soak up the bacon fat. I think about Colin putting another coin in the jukebox. *Just take those old records off the shelf / I sit and listen to 'em by m'self.* Fat memories.

Now, in Rome, I'm playing a game of associations: bread and butter, bread and Flora margarine, bread and bacon fat, bread and dripping. "Bread and olive oil," Vincenzo says, with the knowing glint in his eye that drives me mad. "Yes, yes, of course bread and olive oil is delicious, but I'm thinking about England. Now, where was I? Bread and butter, bread, butter and Gentleman's Relish anchovy paste…" "Bread, butter, and anchovies," says Vincenzo. "When in Rome." He's right. Bread, butter, and anchovies is something you often come across in Rome, which suits me down to the ground, since good bread spread with good butter into which I squash a fat, pink, oily, salty little fish is one of my favorite things to eat.

When you order *pane, burro e alici* you are usually brought a plate striped with several anchovy fillets and curls of butter, and alongside it a basket of bread. I like to spread my butter thickly—as if plastering a particularly potholed wall—across the whole slice and then cross it lattice-like with whole fillets. Vincenzo prefers to butter a small section, top it with a bit of anchovy, bite, and then repeat. We have been known to argue about which method is best. However, at a favorite wine bar, *burro e alici* comes on bruschetta, which means the bread is toasted and arrives spread with butter spiked with lemon zest and crossed with three anchovies, which are rapidly melting into the warm base. I have adopted both ways at home.

Pane, burro e alici con ravanelli
Bread or toast, butter, anchovies, and radishes

Despite all this talk about a leisurely way to start a meal, this is just as likely to be the hurriedly prepared snack or supper that I gobble before rushing out, partly because it's a favorite, but also because the anchovies and butter are in the fridge door and the bread on top, so they are three of the first things I see when I stand in front of the fridge in hunger. Whether I toast the bread or not depends on the extent of the rush. I don't usually have radishes sitting around, but one day I did, and discovered how good alternating bites of anchovy and butter-drenched toast are with crisp, peppery radish, especially when leaning against the sink listening to *Desert Island Discs*.

Gobbled snacks aside, this does make a good, companionable start to a meal. I put a pile of toast or bread, a pat of butter, a jar of anchovies, and a couple of bunches of washed and dried radishes, ideally with leaves, in the middle of the table and tell everyone to get on with it. It is the inimitable Fergus Henderson of St John restaurant who reminds us to seek out radishes with happy leaves: pert, lively greens that reassure us of recent picking, thoughtful bundling, and minimal travel. He also reminds us to wash them in plenty of cold water and pat them dry gently. Finally, a favorite wine for a favorite antipasto: this is the moment for the Italian sparkling wine Franciacorta, which can stand up to and complement the strongly flavored anchovies.

Beans

I find that the hardest thing about cooking legumes is remembering to soak them. Positioning a package near the bottle opener during the afternoon serves as an effective reminder, the idea being that when you open the evening's bottle of wine you also open the package, tip the beans or peas into a bowl, and cover them with water. If you position the soaking bowl near the coffee maker or teapot, the next morning, as you grasp for your morning cup, you are met by a swelling panful, which you can bring to a boil while you have breakfast, then let them simmer away for an hour or so while you try to dress a two-and-a-half-year-old boy.

I did eat legumes growing up, mostly beans, from a green can. I am still fond of Heinz baked beans, especially on toast. We also sometimes had "foreign" beans: small, pale-green flageolet with roast lamb or burgundy kidney beans cooked in a vaguely *con carne* style. The family down the road ate them all the time, but they were vegan (so was their cat) and wore sandals. Heinz, foreign, or healthy: beans were "other."

That all changed when I came to Rome. Legumes, particularly borlotti, chickpeas, white cannellini beans, and lentils, have been one of the pillars of Roman food for thousands of years, and they are as beloved, but as ordinary and everyday, as bread, pasta, cheese, or tomatoes. Of course you can buy them in cans; in fact, good-quality, unsweetened, sparingly salted beans are, along with tomatoes, one of the few things that are not unduly affected by the canning process. They are also the busy cook's friend. That said, they aren't a patch on a pan of freshly cooked, dried and soaked beans, still warm, nutty, and creamy, sitting in a pool of broth. It's this broth that keeps me cooking beans; the cloudy, dubious-looking liquid that could be thin wallpaper paste is in fact a well-flavored, obliging broth that preserves the beans in the pan as you use them scoop by scoop for an antipasti, a bean salad, a side dish, or a bed for sausages. Then it offers itself as an exemplary broth for soup or a thick bean-and-pasta *minestra*.

I am, I admit, a disorganized cook, but the technique above, and the fact that a large pan of legumes in the fridge will happily last for several days and provide us with several meals, means that beans are one of the few things I almost always have on the go.

How not to cook an octopus

Some years ago, while touring around Sicily in a Ford Transit with eight musicians, I ate a simple but particularly good antipasti of octopus at a trattoria in Avola. The secret, said the son of the owner, is to plunge the creature into a pan of boiling water four times before leaving it submerged for 20 minutes, after which you pull the pan off the heat and let the octopus cool in its cooking water. If you wanted to make extra sure, you could add a cork to the pan. At another trattoria this method was reiterated, but with the additional note that the water should be seawater. The following year, while traveling in Puglia in the same rapidly aging van, we ate another dish of octopus, again perfectly tender, the tentacles sliced into thick pieces and dressed with olive oil and lemon. The secret, the cook told me, is to pummel and thwack the octopus into tenderness with a wooden mallet. Quite how was not elaborated, although I imagined it involved some force.

Back in Rome, I tried both plunging and pummelling, made sure the water was as salty as the sea, and added a cork (three actually), but every time, the *polpo*, although edible, was disappointing and rubbery. I decided I should step aside before I did another disservice to another octopus.

Years later I recounted my failure in another van, this time while surging down the *autostrada* with a friend called Chris who happens to be a chef. No water and no boiling, he said as we hurtled past dark fields of buffaloes on our way to a town called Grano. It might work for the freshly caught octopus you find in Sicily or Puglia, but not otherwise. No corks either, unless you want to add 75 of them. You need to freeze and then defrost the octopus before cooking, which tenderizes it. Then you could try cooking it slowly in its own juices with olive oil, black peppercorns, a couple of curls of lemon peel, and bay leaves for company, then let it cool. So I did.

Vincenzo said he could smell the octopus in the lobby of our building, the warm, salty smell of the sea getting more and more impertinent as the lift rose up three floors in its caged shaft. It had taken 1 hour and 15 minutes, by which time the liquid was a burnt pinky red and the octopus was deliciously tender. Once it was cool enough to handle, we sliced it and dressed it with a little olive oil and a spritz of lemon juice. Then, two days later, having frozen and then defrosted another beast, we ate it mixed with new potatoes and a handful of parsley. No pummelling, no plunging, no seawater, no corks. This is one way to cook an octopus.

Insalata di polpo e patate
Octopus and potato salad

serves 4

1 octopus, approximately 3¼ pounds
5 tablespoons extra-virgin olive oil, plus extra to serve
3 bay leaves
3 strips unwaxed lemon zest
a few black peppercorns
salt
6–8 small new potatoes
a handful of flat-leaf parsley
freshly ground black pepper
lemon wedges, to serve

Freeze the octopus overnight and defrost it the next morning, before cooking it during the early afternoon in time for supper. You need a large, heavy-bottomed pan or deep sauté pan with a tight-fitting lid.

Put the olive oil in the pan and add the bay leaves, lemon zest, peppercorns, and octopus, whole. Sprinkle over just a little salt, then cover the pan and place it over medium-low heat. After a few minutes, check the pan: the octopus should be starting to relinquish inky-colored liquid and the pan should be steamy. Reduce the heat, cover the pan, and let the octopus cook very slowly in its own juices. After about 30 minutes, turn the octopus and prod the main body to see if it is getting tender. It's cooked when it's tender enough to pull a tentacle away relatively easily, which should take 1–1½ hours. Once cooked, pull the pan off the heat and let the octopus cool in its own juices for an hour or so.

Meanwhile, scrub and boil the new potatoes in well-salted water until tender, then drain them. Chop the parsley finely. Once the octopus is cool enough to handle, pull the tentacles off the main body. Use a knife to pare away any particularly intrusive bits of red skin. Chop the tentacles and head into large pieces. Arrange the octopus and potatoes on a serving dish, sprinkle with parsley, season with salt and pepper, pour over a little olive oil, and use your hands to gently toss the ingredients. Serve with wedges of lemon.

Alici marinate
Marinated fresh anchovies

Fresh anchovies have fragrant, delicately flavored flesh. They are related to sardines and mackerel and have the same firm, slightly oily flesh but a notably milder flavor. Their size (they are generally about 2–4 inches long) means they are extremely tender. I learned to prepare and cook anchovies with Vincenzo's mum, Carmela.

First, the cleaning. Anchovies are a great way to get to grips with gutting and preparing fish if, like me, you're a novice. Along with artichoke taming and mixing the perfect batter, preparing these little fish is one of the most satisfying kitchen skills I have acquired in the last couple of years. It may seem complicated, but it's actually

pretty straightforward once you get the hang of it. Take an anchovy in one hand and use the thumb of the other to slit open the body. Then, grasping the head firmly between finger and thumb, detach it together with the guts. Gently ease and prize open the body, pull away the spine, and flatten the little fish, fanning it out like a butterfly, ready for the next stage.

As with preserved anchovies, Italians love and do great things with fresh ones. They grill them just as they are, coat them with batter and plunge them into hot oil, or dip them in egg and then bread crumbs and shallow fry them until crisp and golden. A friend of ours stuffs them with a mixture of bread crumbs, herbs, and Parmesan, sprinkles them with olive oil, and bakes them in the oven. Carmela fans them out like the spokes of a wheel in a shallow pan, sprinkles them with olive oil and parsley, then cooks them very gently so that they fry and steam at the same time. Delicious stuff.

But perhaps one of the nicest ways to enjoy the delicate flesh of fresh anchovies is to marinate them in lemon juice and olive oil along with finely chopped garlic, parsley, chile, and lemon zest for a few hours. The acid in the lemon literally cooks the flesh, turning it opaque and rendering it firm, tender, and sweet, and in turn the anchovies lend a fishy wink to the most delicious marinade-turned-dressing. Marinated anchovies are usually served as an antipasti in Italy, but we have them for lunch with lots of bread, a green salad for afterward, and a glass of minerally white wine from southern Italy.

serves 4–6 as an antipasti
1 pound 10 ounces fresh anchovies
2 garlic cloves
a big handful of flat-leaf parsley leaves
juice of 2 unwaxed lemons, plus 2 strips of zest
salt and freshly ground black pepper
1 dried or fresh chile, crumbled or chopped
⅔ to ¾ cup extra-virgin olive oil

Fillet the anchovies as described above. Very finely chop the garlic, parsley, and lemon zest and mix together.

In a serving dish large enough to accommodate the anchovies in 2 layers, arrange a layer of anchovy fillets, season with salt and pepper, sprinkle over some chile and half the garlic, parsley, and lemon zest mixture, then pour over about half the lemon juice and half the oil. Make another layer of anchovies, season with salt and pepper, and sprinkle over the remaining ingredients. Leave to marinate for 2 hours before eating.

2
SOUP & PASTA

Settling Down

Pasta and potato soup

Pasta and lentil soup

Pasta and bean soup

Pasta and chickpea soup

Pasta and chickpea soup 2

Minestrone

Spaghetti with olive oil, garlic, and chile

Fettuccine with butter and anchovies

Tomato sauce

Spaghetti with cherry tomatoes

Bucatini with tomato and cured pork

Spaghetti with tomatoes, anchovies, capers, and olives

Spaghetti with ricotta and black pepper

Spaghetti alla carbonara

Linguine with zucchini, egg, and Parmesan

Pasta and broccoli

Spaghetti with clams

Fettuccine with rich meat sauce

Shepherd's pie (of sorts)

Fresh egg pasta

Ricotta and spinach ravioli

Potato dumplings

Potato gnocchi with pork rib ragù

I was so intent on going back to Sicily that even when it became clear I was going to stay in Rome for a couple of months, I continued to read about Sicilian food and plan the route I would take when I got back. Moving to Testaccio was the first shift, as it was here, away from the domes and grand monuments in a fairly modern part of the city with a lively market and ordinary air, that I first wondered if I could settle for a while. But even then I persisted in thinking about Sicily, especially its cooking, because for me, food has always been a lens to look at the world through.

Roman food, though, is hard to ignore, particularly in Testaccio. Distinctive, traditional, and inextricably tied with the history and daily life of the place, it seems to permeate everything. The scent of *pizza bianca* curling up through the courtyard into my flat, the smell of dozens of pans of chickpeas simmering on a Friday morning to make *pasta e ceci* (pasta and chickpea soup)—not that I knew what it was yet—the reek of boiled broccoli on Tuesdays, the stench of the water swept from under the fish stalls into the gutter on a warm afternoon. Just minutes from my new flat, caper berries climbed the ancient city wall and wild mint sprouted in the cracks in the pavement. Most days during that first spring I'd see crates of saw-edged *cicoria* (chicory) and violet-tipped artichokes being wheeled deftly on nippy trolleys from the market next to my building to one of the trattorias nearby. It wasn't unusual to have my path crossed by a man carrying a halved animal carcass, its red flesh marbled with fat, balanced on his wide shoulders on its way into one of the many butchers. Some mornings I'd wake up thinking the world was falling in, only to realize it was an avalanche of wood for the pizza ovens tumbling down a hatch into a cellar.

Whereas the food of Sicily had thrilled me, the food of Rome tripped me up and then pulled me to my feet, charming me with its simplicity, certainty, and bold flavors—notably the *primi,* or first courses. A deep bowl of *pasta e ceci* scented with rosemary; spaghetti coated with a seductive creamy sauce that's nothing more than eggs, cheese, and cured pork; more spaghetti, glistening with olive oil, flecked with parsley and clams, and tasting indignantly of the sea; a plate of stout potato gnocchi, no bigger than acorns, topped with bright red sauce and a blizzard of pecorino cheese. I quickly realized I didn't just want to eat these dishes, I wanted to understand them. I wanted to make them.

At that time I lived in a flat on via Mastro Giorgio above the bakery, Passi, in a building still largely inhabited by people who were born there, many of whom cooked each day in the most resolutely traditional way, with their front doors open on to the

walkways hanging over the communal courtyard, across which voices and cooking smells bounced like balls. Through suspicion and occasional mockery, I persisted and began to gather advice in much the same way as I gathered ingredients at the market, attracted to anything that caught my eye. Looking back, I'm not sure whether to smile or cringe at my enthusiasm. Others certainly cringed. Then, with my door open—not least because the kitchen had no window and the stove no exhaust fan—I began to cook.

I did know how to cook, in an ordinary and capable way. However, since I'd left everything behind in order to travel, I adopted a similar approach to cooking, allowing myself to learn things all over again, especially the most blindingly obvious things. Such as how to fry onion, carrot, and celery to make a *soffritto* (the essential blend of aromatics cooked in fat, which comes from the verb *soffriggere*, to cook lightly in fat without frying); how to make the simplest tomato sauce; how to cook chickpeas; how to boil pasta; all things that I ostensibly knew how to do, but then again didn't. Things that, once re-learned and better understood, have changed the way I cook. Then, with these newly acquired skills, the first dishes I made were *primi*, which in Rome are almost always pasta, either as part of *minestra* (soup) or *pasta asciutta* (with sauce). This section is about these dishes that, nine years later, have become central to the way I eat.

Five soups

Or, more correctly, five *minestre*, which is a term used for dishes of pasta or rice cooked in broth or water with vegetables and beans— and therefore eaten with a spoon—rather than soups. Let's call them five substantial soups with pasta, which also work well without pasta if you prefer. You will find different versions and variations of *minestra* all over Italy, but mine are distinctly Roman ones, made my own because these are dishes that insist you do so.

While writing this book I asked friends, colleagues, cooks, and whoever else would listen how they made certain dishes, and I noticed something. While dishes like carbonara (pasta with eggs and bacon), *amatriciana* (pasta with tomatoes and cured pork), and *coda alla vaccinara* (oxtail stew) provoked strong, bold opinions that could turn into vigorous debates, *minestre* aroused something different. Reactions were soft, and opinions, although every bit as defined as other dishes, were what I can only describe as warm and generous. Vincenzo, as is so often the case, was the person to suggest the reason for this: *minestre* are the embodiment of childhood nourishment and comfort for many Italians, ladled from the pan or tureen. *Pasta e patate, pasta e fagioli, pasta e ceci* are dishes that stir up something elemental. More than any other, these were the dishes that people chose as their *piatto preferito* (favorite dish). If I'm making this seem overly sentimental I should make clear that it isn't—*minestre* are too functional and no-nonsense for that.

Despite my initial suspicion and reluctance about what felt like unlikely pairings (pasta and beans, pasta and potatoes, pasta and chickpeas) and my long-held idea that soup, however good, wasn't really a meal, they have become the cornerstones of my diet. Tasty, nourishing, economical to make, generous, infinitely accommodating, *minestre* are dishes that we eat a couple of times a week. All five are based on more or less the same principle, which is that beans or legumes are cooked until tender, then added to a *soffritto* of aromatics cooked in fat along with enough water, or their cooking water, to cook the pasta. Beyond these basic principles, *minestre* can be simple or more complex, brothy and distinct, or blended until they are creamy. They can be rich red with tomato, or just blushing, or have no tomato at all; they can include herbs or cured pork. In short, having understood the basic principles, you make the recipe your own.

<u>Odori</u>

You don't need to return to the same Roman market stall more than a couple of times to be asked if you need *odori*, literally "aromas," in other words the aromatic herbs and vegetables that will accompany whatever else you have bought and plan to cook. My kind and funny *fruttivendolo,* Gianluca—who is learning English and uses my visits as impromptu lessons—calls them "smells," which makes us laugh every time. Depending on the season, your plans, and the mood of your *fruttivendolo,* the *odori* could be a carrot, a rib of celery, and a small onion for broth, a bunch of parsley for sauce, a stalk of floppy-leaved basil for tomatoes or to dab behind your ears, a tuft of rosemary for potatoes, a sprig of sage for melted butter, or a pair of bay leaves for the beans. *Odori* are stuffed matter-of-factly into the top of your shopping bag at no further cost except loyalty.

It is *odori*, notably onion, celery, and the fat stems and flat leaves of parsley, that make up the *soffritto,* the foundation of the following soup recipes. Rather like knowing how to boil pasta, make tomato sauce, cook beans, or gently cook garlic in olive oil, making a *soffritto* was something I needed to re-learn. I wasn't that far off the mark, but that was more down to good luck than good planning, since I'd never really afforded much attention to that important task. A good

soffritto starts at the market or shops, and finding vegetables that taste as bright and vigorous as they should; tasteless, dull vegetables will make a tasteless, dull *soffritto*. Having washed or peeled the vegetables, they need chopping evenly and finely with a sharp knife, along with a little cured pork if the recipe calls for it. In Rome, the mixture of aromatics was traditionally parsley and onion with lard and was called a *battuto*, which takes its name from the verb *battere*, "to strike," and refers to the striking action of the knife.

Once you have a pile of finely chopped aromatics—which always reminds me of vegetable confetti—you put them in a suitable pan with plenty of extra-virgin olive oil over low heat and cook them gently. Now, the relaxed, familiar way in which Italian cooks execute a *soffritto* can be misleading, since it suggests that it doesn't really need much attention or thought, which it does, especially when you're learning how it should look and smell. The vegetables should sizzle gently and comfortably in adequate olive oil; they need the odd nudge and budge around the pan (a wooden spatula is best), making sure they aren't too close to a hot edge or neglected up on the side of the pan. The *soffritto* is ready when the vegetables are soft, translucent, and fragrant and your kitchen smells good. This usually takes about 8 minutes. You will know.

Pasta e patate
Pasta and potato soup

This seems a good recipe to begin with because it's a good example of both a *soffritto* and a quintessential *minestra*. The disconcerting, even improbable, name suggests something rather too dense, or beige, or starchy. At least, I thought so when I stood beside my friend Ezio as he began chopping vegetables. The bowlful he served me 30 minutes later turned out to confirm none of my fears, but was instead a tasty and satisfying *minestra* that I now make once a week— not because I find myself with nothing more than an onion, a potato, a stick of celery, and a carrot with alarming regularity, nor because it's so straightforward (although both are true), but because I like it so much.

Pasta e patate is pure-tasting, elemental even, but elemental along with substance from starchy, collapsing potatoes and tender pasta. Adults and children alike adore its sweet, satisfying simplicity. With plenty of freshly ground pepper and some bold *pecorino romano*, this innocent soup grows up and answers back.

I'll finish by noting that the best version I've ever made was in England, in my parents' old kitchen, with a pair of handsome English spuds and two strips of English bacon. My two food worlds collided in a bowl of soup, eaten while watching *Newsnight*.

serves 4
1 onion
1 large carrot
1 celery stalk
about 2 ounces guanciale or pancetta (optional)
5 tablespoons olive oil
2 large potatoes, about 1¼ pounds
salt
7 ounces small pasta or broken spaghetti
freshly ground black pepper
grated Parmesan or pecorino, to serve

Finely dice the onion, carrot, and celery. If you are using it, finely chop the guanciale or pancetta along with the vegetables. Heat the olive oil in a deep frying pan or heavy-based soup pan, add the vegetables and guanciale, and cook gently until soft and fragrant. This should take about 8 minutes.

Meanwhile, dice the potatoes into 1-inch cubes and add them to the pan, stirring so that each piece glistens with oil. Add 6½ cups of water to cover the vegetables by at least 2 inches. Bring to a boil, then reduce the heat to a simmer. Cook gently for 15 minutes, or until the vegetables are soft. Taste and season with salt.

Add the pasta and increase the heat so that the soup boils for 8 minutes, adding more hot water if necessary—it should be dense but soupy—and stirring so the pasta doesn't stick. Taste and add more salt if necessary, and a few grinds of black pepper. Serve directly from the pan, passing around a bowl of grated Parmesan or pecorino for people to stir into their soup. Or, more correctly—at least, more traditionally—you should pour the soup into a tureen or soup bowl, stir in 6 tablespoons grated cheese, then serve at the table.

Pasta e lenticchie
Pasta and lentil soup

This is one of the most deeply satisfying bowls of food I know. It's good value, too, and good luck if you eat it on New Year's Eve, when the more money-shaped lentils you consume, the more fortune you will have the following year. Also, for someone like me, who lacks bean foresight and nearly always forgets to soak in advance, lentils, which don't require a long bath, are a great kitchen standby.

The recipe starts with patience, just a little, enough to fan the lentils out on a tray and scan them with your eyes, as there's almost always a tiny stone hiding, especially if you are using good lentils. It's a task that probably takes a minute at most but it's the kind of instruction that can make me disproportionately irritated, as in "I really don't have time to be fussing with that." This is a reaction I've learned to interpret as a sort of kitchen alarm, because more often than not this is precisely when I need a moment of patient slow-motion, and to remember that it's often the details that make the difference between food that's just cooked and food that's cooked well. Even on the most fraught days, having taken the cooking equivalent of a deep breath, I proceed differently. I also don't have stones in my *minestra*.

The base is a *soffritto of* onion, celery, and if possible a couple of fat parsley stalks. If you eat meat, you could also add some chopped pancetta or *guanciale* (cured pork cheek). The best lentils for this dish are from Castelluccio in Umbria because they have a unique fragrant, nutty taste and almost floury texture when cooked, which means they absorb the flavors of other ingredients well. This is why they are cooked alone first with bay leaves before being united with the other ingredients, resulting in two layers of flavor.

The key to this dish is the consistency, the critical point somewhere between a soup and a stew: soft enough to ripple when scooped up with a spoon, but thick enough to have real body. To get to this point the pasta and lentils should be relatively brothy in the pan, so that by the time you get to the table they're still swelling, and the dish will have thickened up nicely. Rest assured that however good you are at finding this elusive point, by the time it comes to seconds, the pasta and lentils remaining in the pan will have seized into a stew that your spoon will stand to attention in. In this case, just add a splash of boiling water and another grind of salt to loosen it all up again. Also rest assured that catching the point of perfect *minestre* consistency is an art many Italians spend a lifetime trying to master. Perfect consistency or not, pasta and lentils finished with a little extra-virgin olive oil and a tumbler of fat Umbrian white wine like Orvieto is a simple, satisfying lunch.

serves 4
1 cup small brown lentils, such as Castelluccio or Orsano
2 bay leaves
salt
1 small onion
1 garlic clove
1 celery stalk with a few feathery leaves
2 stalks flat-leaf parsley
¾ to 1 cup canned plum tomatoes or passata
5 tablespoons extra-virgin olive oil, plus extra to serve
1 small chile, chopped
7 ounces dried pasta, such as ditalini, or 9 ounces fresh egg
    quadrucci (see page 157)
freshly ground black pepper

Spread the lentils out on a tray and check for any tiny stones with your hands and eyes. In a large pan, cover the lentils with 6½ cups of water and add the bay leaves and a teaspoon of salt. Bring to a boil and then cook, covered, over low heat until the lentils are tender but not mushy. This can take 20–40 minutes, depending on the type and age of the lentils. I start tasting them after 15 minutes.

Finely dice the onion and garlic and finely chop the celery and parsley. If you are using canned tomatoes, pass them through a food mill or puree them with an immersion blender. Heat the oil in a large heavy-based soup pot, add the vegetables, and cook gently over low heat until they are soft and fragrant. This should take about 10 minutes. Add the tomato, chile, and a pinch of salt, stir, and cook over low heat for 10 minutes, until the sauce has reduced and the oil is starting to float free. Add the lentils and their cooking liquid, stir, and taste to check for salt.

Add the pasta and bring the soup back to a gentle boil for as long as the pasta needs to cook until tender. For small dried pasta, this will probably be about 8 minutes, for fresh pasta, about 5 minutes. Keep stirring so that the pasta doesn't stick, and add a little more water if necessary. Check the seasoning. Serve immediately with a little best-quality extra-virgin olive oil poured over the top and pepper, for those who want it.

Cranberry beans

There's no two ways about it: fresh cranberry beans are beautiful, their pink-streaked ivory pods opening up to reveal similarly colored beans. When they're in season and turning heads at the market, I buy kilo after kilo, then upturn the bag to tumble the pods onto the kitchen table for the communal podding, which is fitting, since another name by which they are known, borlotti, comes from the verb *borlare,* which means "tumble" and evokes the way the oldest plants grow.

When fresh cranberry beans are not available I buy dried beans, which, although subdued in color to beige and burnt red, still have a mottled beauty. The dried beans are skittled into bowls, as they need soaking in cold water overnight. I'm not sure I'll ever stop being disappointed by the way the beans, both fresh and dried, lose their distinctive speckles and turn plainly brown as they cook. Their cooked flavor doesn't disappoint, though, and the texture is almost meaty and smoothly creamy. This flavor and texture is the reason cranberry beans make such brilliant *minestre*, especially the ones you add pasta to. Cranberry beans, particularly fresh ones, are also delicious boiled and dressed while still warm with good extra-virgin olive oil and salt, which we often have for lunch with a salad and some cheese, or piled on toast rubbed with garlic. Warm cranberry beans with olive oil and salt, and possibly a handful of peppery arugula withering obediently in the residual heat, are also great with grilled fish and meat, particularly lamb.

Pasta e fagioli
Pasta and bean soup

The cooking water surrounding just-cooked beans or chickpeas is a cloudy, murky affair that looks, particularly in the case of cranberry beans, decidedly unappealing, like the water somebody with a purple rinse has washed their hair in. For years, if I ever got my act together and soaked and cooked dried beans, I watched the cloudy bean broth spin and disappear down the drain like other murky liquids. I was a kitchen fool. Bean-cooking water is good stuff, cloudy with the almost sweet, nutty goodness that has seeped out of the beans as they cooked, and it will provide your soup or stew with body and depth. It is in some ways a secret ingredient—that fifth quarter, if you like.

Pasta e fagioli is one of my favorite recipes in the book. Not just because it's one of my favorite things to eat, but also because it embodies so much of what I like about Roman food. It's simple, tasty, resourceful, generous. In summer it's made with fresh cranberry beans and for the rest of the year, dried beans are used. Both fresh and dried (and canned, in a pinch) cranberry beans taste somewhere between a chickpea, a cannellini bean, and a chestnut and are, in my opinion, the best bean for *pasta e fagioli*.

Soaked cranberry beans are cooked in water with a couple of bay leaves until tender, producing a sweet, nutty, slightly starchy broth. The beans are then added to a *soffritto* of onion, celery, and olive oil, to which you add just a little tomato and the bean broth in order to make soup, in which you cook the pasta. This is a substantial dish that calls for a substantial wine, a big but soft and rounded red with lots of flavor, such as a Sagrantino di Montefalco.

serves 4

1¼ cups dried cranberry beans or 2¼ pounds fresh cranberry beans, podded

2 bay leaves

1 small onion

1 celery stalk

5 tablespoons good extra-virgin olive oil, plus extra to serve

7 ounces canned plum tomatoes

salt

7 ounces pasta (ideally dried tubetti or ditalini, or fresh maltagliati)

If you are using dried beans, soak them in plenty of cold water for at least 12 hours, or overnight. Drain the soaked beans or pod the fresh ones and put them in a large pan. Cover them with about 6½ cups water, add the bay leaves, bring to a boil, and reduce the heat to a gentle simmer. Cook for about 30 minutes, or until the beans are getting tender but are still just a little firm. The exact time will depend on the age of the beans; I start tasting after 20 minutes.

Meanwhile, finely dice the onion and finely chop the celery. Heat the olive oil in a large, heavy-based pan, add the onion and celery, and cook gently over low heat until soft and fragrant. If you have one, pass the tomatoes through a food mill before adding them to the pan. If you don't have a food mill, add the tomatoes as they are, but crush them with the back of a wooden spoon. Stir and allow the tomatoes to bubble for about 5 minutes, before using a slotted spoon to lift the beans into the pan. Stir, then add 4½ cups of the bean-cooking liquid you have just lifted the beans from, making it up with hot water if necessary.

Let the soup bubble away gently for about 10 minutes, or until the beans are tender. Remove a cup of beans and broth from the pan,

process it until smooth with an immersion blender or pass it through the food mill, and return it to the pan. Season generously with salt.

Bring the soup to a boil and add the pasta. Stirring fairly attentively, simmer until the pasta is tender. For small dried pasta, this will probably be about 8 minutes, for fresh pasta, 3–5 minutes. Keep a small pan of water boiling next to the soup, adding some if the soup seems too thick. Taste to check the seasoning and serve with a little extra-virgin olive oil poured on top.

Pasta e ceci
Pasta and chickpea soup

I first ate *pasta e ceci* at Bucatino, the sprawling trattoria that occupies the ground-floor left-hand corner of my old building, the one in which the impatient exchanges between fraught waiters and the temperamental chef, along with the clink of cutlery against crockery, provided a soundtrack to our kitchen life. It was probably a Friday, a traditional day for *pasta e ceci,* and I was with Vincenzo. It wasn't my *primo,* but his. It arrived in a deep bowl, steaming so intensely that if I'd had a tea towel to hand I'd have been under it, inhaling the rosemary-and-garlic-scented broth in which were suspended chickpeas and pieces of broken tagliatelle. I traded half a portion of *spaghetti con le vongole* for *pasta e ceci,* and there began a habit.

Pasta e ceci is one of Rome's iconic dishes, and one with a history almost as long as the city itself, dating back two thousand years to a dish of chickpeas cooked with onion and a rib of celery, then united with broken whole wheat pasta. *Pasta e ceci* appears twice in the informal, unscientific weekly recipe calendar still followed in Rome: it is eaten on Tuesdays and Fridays. Walk past any Roman trattoria on those days and it may be chalked up on a blackboard. Walk around Testaccio on those days and you may well catch the smell of dozens of pans of *pasta e ceci* simmering.

Pasta e ceci is as changeable and temperamental as the cooks that make it. Like so much good Italian cooking, the principles are clear: cooked chickpeas are added to *soffritto*, water or bean broth is added, and the soup simmered. Pasta is then added to the soup and cooked until tender. But beyond that, the variations are endless. *Pasta e ceci* can be brothy or creamy and dense; it can be made with or without tomatoes; it can include anchovies, potato, and celery; it can be scented with garlic, rosemary, or sage; the chickpeas can be whole or blended into a cream (at least partially); the pasta can be tubes, badly cut squares, or broken tagliatelle. No two pans are the same, and even the most meticulously followed recipe will turn out differently each time. It is a dish that invites improvisation and adjustment to taste.

To start improvisation for this infinitely variable dish, however, you need a working model. Two, even. This first *pasta e ceci* is inspired by, and probably most closely related to, the one I have eaten and still eat at trattorias in Rome. Brothy and scented with garlic and rosemary, it also includes anchovies, which, far from being fishy and intrusive, are anything but, discreetly giving the broth a salty, savory note and then disappearing subserviently. The chickpeas can be cooked hours, even a day, in advance; just keep them under their cooking water. *Pasta e ceci* is a substantial dish that needs little more than a salad or straightforward vegetable dish afterward, and alongside it a glass of white wine, ideally something with good steely minerality like Fiano from southern Italy.

serves 4
1¼ cups dried chickpeas
2 garlic cloves
2 sprigs rosemary
¼ cup extra-virgin olive oil

2 fat anchovies packed in oil, drained (optional)
3 plum tomatoes, peeled, seeded, and coarsely chopped
salt
7 ounces short tubular pasta, such as tubetti or ditalini,
   broken tagliatelle, or maltagliati
freshly ground black pepper

Soak the chickpeas in plenty of cold water for 12 hours or overnight, changing the water twice if you can be bothered. Drain the soaked chickpeas, cover them with 8 cups fresh water, and add a clove of garlic and a sprig of rosemary. Bring to a boil over medium heat, then reduce the heat and simmer for 1½ hours, or until the chickpeas are tender. Start tasting after 1 hour.

In a large, heavy-bottomed pan or casserole dish, heat the oil and add the anchovies, the remaining garlic crushed gently with the back of a knife, and the remaining rosemary. Cook them gently so that the anchovies dissolve into the oil and the garlic and rosemary are fragrant. Remove the rosemary and garlic. Add the tomatoes and break them up with the back of a wooden spoon. Cook for another few minutes.

Use a slotted spoon to lift the chickpeas from their cooking liquid into the pan, then add 4½ cups of a bean-cooking liquid, making it up with hot water if there isn't enough, and a pinch of salt. Increase the heat to bring the soup to a boil. Add the pasta and cook until tender, stirring, tasting and adding more bean-cooking liquid or water so as to keep a slightly soupy consistency. Serve with a grinding of black pepper.

Pasta e ceci 2
Pasta and chickpea soup 2

This second *pasta e ceci* is my own version, which owes everything to Roman food and lessons I have learned, but also much to the thick bean and vegetable soups made with canned beans that I ate growing up in England. This version is one I make with canned chickpeas, which, unlike other canned beans, are generally very good, and very useful. This version begins with a *soffritto* of onion, celery, and carrot. It includes rosemary, just a little tomato paste, and a Parmesan rind. I will be forever grateful to the person who taught me to keep the Parmesan rinds with an inch of cheese still attached in a bag in the freezer. Added to soup and stew, the rind imparts its intense, sweet, umami flavor, then provides an excellent treat for the cook. The big difference between this and the first recipe is the consistency. I puree half the soup, which makes it denser and creamier. Mostly I add dried *ditalini* pasta, but I also like fresh *maltagliati*.

serves 4

1 mild onion
1 garlic clove
1 carrot
1 celery stalk
6 tablespoons extra-virgin olive oil, plus extra to serve
2 tablespoons tomato paste
a sprig of rosemary
2 (14-ounce) cans chickpeas, drained
salt
a Parmesan rind (optional)
8 ounces short tubular dried pasta such as tubetti or ditalini, or broken tagliatelle

Finely dice the onion with the garlic, carrot, and celery. In a large, heavy-bottomed pan, heat the oil; add the vegetables and cook gently until soft and fragrant. Add the tomato paste and rosemary,

stir, and cook for a few minutes, or until the rosemary is fragrant. Add the drained chickpeas, stir, add 4½ cups hot water, a pinch of salt, and the Parmesan rind, then stir again. Bring to a gentle boil, reduce the heat to a simmer, and leave the soup to simmer gently for about 20 minutes.

Remove half the soup and pass it through a food mill or blend it with an immersion blender until smooth and creamy, then return it to the pan. Taste and add more salt if necessary. Bring the soup back to a boil, add the pasta, and then, stirring fairly attentively, cook until the pasta is tender, adding more boiling water if necessary. Taste to check the seasoning and serve with a little extra-virgin olive oil poured on top.

Minestrone
The big soup

In Italian, to denote largeness you add *-one, -ona,* or *-oni* to the end of a word. *Libro* ("book"), for example, becomes *librone* ("big book"), *culo* ("bottom") becomes *culone* ("big bottom"), *casa* ("house") becomes *casona* ("big house"), and *minestra* ("soup") becomes *minestrone* ("big soup").

Minestrone, as you probably know, is a very substantial mixed vegetable soup that may or may not include beans, and probably does include some pasta or rice. It is cooked very slowly over low heat, emerging dense with a deep, mellow flavor that recalls no vegetable in particular, but all of them at once. There are, as is natural with a dish of this kind, many recipes, ideas, and thoughts about minestrone, the character of each panful being shaped by its circumstances, the place it is made in, the season, the produce available, and, of course, the cook.

The big, bold, relaxed "everything in the pan" aspect of minestrone is accurate, but misleading if you think it means "chuck it all in the pan." Good minestrone, I have learned, is made with care, and needs time. True, a large part of this time requires minimal attention—a stir every now and then, the later addition of the beans—while the pan simmers for about 2 hours over very low heat. The initial steps do, however, need about 30 minutes of your cooking concentration. This is because the ingredients enter the pot gradually in a set sequence. The steady march of ingredients into the pot allows the essential underlying flavors to develop, imparting each one to the next vegetable. While one vegetable is cooking you prepare the next. It's actually a nice process if you're not in a rush and have some good chopping music and a glass of red wine, perhaps a Cesanese from Lazio.

When you get to the simmering, the heat should be low and the simmer tremulous, the kind that has you checking that the flame hasn't gone out because the pan looks so still, then you lift the lid, look closely, see that the surface is quivering and suddenly—*plop!*—a burp of a bubble breaks the surface of the soup, and you are reassured that all is well. Minestrone is even better the next day, so it's worth making plenty, which is why the recipe below is for 8.

serves 8
2 red onions
3 carrots
2 celery stalks
3 tablespoons butter
½ cup extra-virgin olive oil
7 ounces potatoes
12¼ ounces zucchini
5¼ ounces green beans
7 ounces savoy cabbage
4¼ ounces canned or fresh plum tomatoes
a large Parmesan rind
2½ cups cooked cannellini beans

to serve:
5¼ ounces small dried pasta
2 tablespoons grated Parmesan
or
4 slices good bread, toasted
2 tablespoons grated Parmesan
salt

Finely dice the onions, carrots, and celery. Gently heat the butter and oil over low heat in a very large, heavy-bottomed pan, add the onion, carrot, and celery, and cook gently, uncovered, until they are soft and fragrant and starting to deepen in color—only just. This will take a good 10 minutes.

Meanwhile, dice the potatoes, zucchini, and green beans. Add the potatoes to the soup, stir, and cook gently for 5 minutes. Shred the cabbage, and peel (if fresh) and roughly chop the tomatoes. Add the green beans and zucchini, and after 5 more minutes, add the shredded cabbage. Add the tomatoes, stir, and increase the heat so the contents of the pan bubbles more vigorously for a few minutes. Add 6½ cups water and the Parmesan rind, bring to a boil, then reduce the heat to a tremulous simmer. Cover the pan and leave it just so for 2 hours, stirring occasionally.

After 1½ hours, add the cannellini beans, stir carefully and firmly, then cook for another 30 minutes. If you find the soup is looking too thick before it has finished cooking, add a little more water. When the minestrone has finished cooking, pick out the Parmesan rind and transfer about a fifth of the soup to a separate bowl. Process it until smooth with an immersion blender before returning it to the rest of the soup.

There are different options for serving it. I generally divide the minestrone in half once I've made it, warm up the first day's half, and add 5¼ ounces dried pasta that I've cooked in a separate pan until al dente. I then stir in a couple of tablespoons of grated Parmesan, wait 5 minutes, and serve. The next day, while the remaining soup is gently reheating, I toast 4 slices of bread, put them in the bottom of 4 bowls, sprinkle them with grated Parmesan and a little salt, and then ladle over the minestrone.

"Pasta, pasta, pasta!" Luca shouts in a peculiar north London-Roman accent as it nears midday. Pasta is a small word for a big family that comprises hundreds of shapes and forms with a long, evolved history that's part of the history of Italy itself. It can be long or short, made in a factory or by hand, stuffed or rolled, served in broth, dressed simply or to the nines with sauce. It can be made of hard durum wheat or soft wheat flour, with eggs and or/water, and comes in a dazzling variety of shapes. Some of these speak of great wealth and privilege; think of a hand-rolled sheet of rich egg pasta, or a hand-twisted parcel of seasoned meat. Others speak of great poverty, like *struncatura*, which literally means "sawdust pasta" and was made from the sweepings from the floor of the flour mills. For many Italians, pasta's presence at the table signifies that all is right with the world.

Most Italian pasta is made from one of two basic doughs: the hard durum wheat flour-and-water pasta that traditionally comes from the south, or soft wheat flour-and-egg pasta that is traditionally from the north. Both doughs can be fresh or dried, factory-made or homemade, but the hard wheat flour-and-water pasta (the type I was most familiar with) is most commonly factory made, and soft wheat flour-and-egg pasta is often made at home, or in small, independent *pasta all'uovo* shops to be bought by weight.

I used to think that fresh pasta is better than dried pasta, but it isn't, it's just different, and possesses different qualities. Generally speaking, dried hard-wheat pasta is chewier and more robust, whereas well-made fresh egg pasta is silkier and more buoyant. The difference between the two is heightened by the shape. Fresh and dried pastas lend themselves to different shapes and are therefore a very different experience in the mouth. Consider the difference between a thin, rounded strand of hard-wheat spaghetti and a wide, soft egg noodle, a tube of ribbed *maccheroni* and a hand-twisted spiral of fusilli. Quite aside from the sauce, form leads to flavor. This explains why different shapes are better suited to different sauces; why a tiny tube is good for a chickpea soup and a flat ribbon of fettuccine is more fitting for a sauce of butter and anchovies. I have tried to share what I have observed, learned, and come to like. These are only suggestions, though, and imperfect ones at that, and should never override the fact that this is *your* lunch or dinner.

Buying dried pasta

We eat pasta almost every lunchtime, and it's usually dried. Vincenzo, who is from Sicily, where dried flour-and-water pasta is ubiquitous, actually prefers it to fresh, saying it has more soul *and* more balls. I'm not sure I'm in a position to make such a bold claim, but I do know that good-quality dried pasta is a wondrous thing: full-bodied, nutty, and chewy enough to engage your whole mouth. I've learned that when buying dried pasta you should look for the best-quality durum-wheat pasta, which can be listed as *grano duro*, semolina, or simply *farina*. If there are any other ingredients on the list except water, avoid it. Also, look out for pasta extruded through bronze, which gives it texture. Even the smoothest-looking spaghetti, if made well, has a slightly rough surface like fine sandpaper to which the sauce can cling. Price is a good indicator of quality, and good dried pasta should cost accordingly. Flour and water it may be, but decent machinery, good drying techniques, and craftsmanship all have a cost—it can't possibly be very cheap. If it is, it will probably be crummy. Neither should it be very expensive, however. Look for Garofalo, Setaro, and my favorite, the one in the yellow packet, Martelli.

Cooking pasta

One of the most useful lessons I've learned is one I had no idea I needed: how to cook pasta. I was incredulous when, after a few weeks of meeting and cooking together, Vincenzo suggested that I might like to do things differently. "What?" I said, placing the pan gauntlet quietly on the table in the old flat. "What should I do differently?" To which he replied: "Do you really want to know?"

There was a lengthy pause, during which my pride, irritation, and curiosity had a serious tussle before my curiosity and the anesthetizing effects of a new relationship won out. "Tell me," I replied. There was another long pause while he lit a cigarette, inhaled, then exhaled toward the window. "Use a bigger pan and more water, add more salt, but not until the water boils, stir the salt into the water, start tasting two minutes before the end of the recommended cooking time, drain the pasta one minute before the time is up, always save the cooking water, and never overcook the pasta." In short, a list so long and comprehensive, so infuriating, and so obviously true that I was silenced and we didn't have pasta for lunch.

A few days later, I did the most familiar thing in an unfamiliar way. I took the largest, lightest pan, the one that holds 6 quarts, and for the first time ever I measured the water into it. The rule of thumb is 1 quart water for every 4 ounces pasta, so for 16 ounces spaghetti I needed 4 quarts. It was more water than I'd ever used. I brought it to a boil, which took less time than I thought, then weighed out 3 tablespoons coarse salt—more salt than I'd ever used—stirred it into the water, and tasted. It was, as promised, pleasantly salty, which is precisely what pasta, which doesn't contain any salt, needs. I checked the time and added the pasta, gently pressing it down with the back of a wooden spoon before re-covering the pan until it came back to a boil. I stirred and tasted in good time, drained the pasta quickly, and saved a cupful of water for loosening the sauce if necessary. It wasn't. I'd warmed the serving bowl; I tossed the pasta first with cheese, then with tomato sauce, and served it. I'm not sure what I expected. After well-behaved initial thanks, what I got was silence as Vincenzo and Carlo wound the spaghetti round their forks and ate.

This is a long story for a task that's usually too obvious to mention, but it's one that's executed badly so often, by me at least. In short, pasta needs lots of water and space to cook correctly. Too little water and it's sticky, overly starchy, claustrophobic, and quite simply the pasta won't cook properly. The water must be well salted or the pasta will be *sciapa* (without salt), a mistake nearly as grave as *scotta* (overcooked) pasta. This brings us to *al dente*, which means "to the tooth" and refers to the firmness of the cooked pasta that is so desirable. Now, generally speaking, the farther south you travel, the more al dente pasta is eaten. Vincenzo is from nearly as south as you can go in southern Sicily and would ideally have his pasta so al dente that it's as stiff as a Scottish guard and, to some, raw. I am an Englishwoman who, before moving to Italy, cooked my pasta in much the same way my grandma cooked vegetables: for too long. (I now cook my vegetables like my grandma did, but more about that later.) We have found a middle ground, and it's usually a minute and a half before the end of the recommended cooking time, when the pasta has just lost its white chalky core, has bite, and engages the mouth, but not excessively.

Spaghetti aglio, olio e peperoncino
Spaghetti with olive oil, garlic, and chile

This is what Vincenzo knocks up when he is alone, or very late back, or both: spaghetti with garlic and chile fried gently in plenty of olive oil, with a handful of chopped parsley. He calls it *aglio e olio* (garlic and oil) and thinks it is one of the best pasta dishes there is. I agree. It's also a dish we often have on a Friday night when we finally admit that a large bag of crisps and a bottle of prosecco is not really a balanced supper, and need something else but don't really want to cook. While Vincenzo makes this I might make a salad and open another bottle of wine. After all, it is Friday.

It seems counterintuitive to give quantities for a dish that is by nature unquantifiable and personal. That said, when I first started making *aglio e olio* I appreciated some guidance about how to make this mysteriously delicious dish. While the 4 ounces or so per person of spaghetti cooks in plenty of well-salted water, warm a couple of tablespoons of olive oil per person in a frying pan. Bear in mind that the oil should coat generously but not overwhelm the pasta. Add a garlic clove per person, chopped if you like garlic and want to keep it in, or peeled and crushed if you simply want to scent the oil, in which case cook it gently until the garlic is fragrant, then remove it. Add half a teaspoon of chopped fresh or dried chile per person, let it sizzle gently for a minute, then add the pasta and stir until each strand is gleaming. Remove from the heat, stir in some chopped parsley, and eat.

Fettuccine con burro e alici
Fettuccine with butter and anchovies

I make two versions of this dish: one with dried egg fettuccine, a standby can of anchovies, and a slice of whatever butter happens to be in the fridge door; the other with homemade fettuccine, Spanish anchovies that cost a small fortune, and butter I have bought especially. Obviously the first version is the one I make more, and the second is the one I enjoy more. Not that I don't enjoy the first— even with dried pasta, the contents of an average anchovy can, and everyday butter, this is a completely delicious plate of pasta, gutsy and, like me after a few drinks, just a little bit loud. Loud, but then softening into a rich, salty, and rounded affair, especially with a glass of white with enough flavor to match the anchovies and stand up to the butter, such as a good Gavi.

serves 4

salt
1 pound fresh (page 156) or dried egg fettuccine
10 tablespoons (1¼ sticks) butter
10 best anchovy fillets packed in oil, drained

Bring a large pan of water to a fast boil, add salt, stir, then add the pasta. If fresh, it will take just a few minutes to cook, so keep tasting.

Meanwhile, melt the butter in a large sauté pan over low heat and add the anchovies, prodding them gently with the back of a wooden spoon so they dissolve into the butter. The butter should foam very slightly, but no more than that.

Once the pasta is ready, drain it and add it to the pan, stirring so that each strand is coated with anchovy butter. Serve immediately.

The food mill

In an ideal world we would have given a complimentary food mill, *mouli*, or *passaverdura* away with every copy of this book, making it possibly the most inconveniently shaped purchase you would have made in a while. A brilliantly simple, old-fashioned device that consists of a bowl with a removable perforated plate and a crank with a curved metal paddle that forces the food through the holes, a food mill is a sort of souped-up sieve. I'm not sure I've ever been in an Italian kitchen that didn't have one or three at hand. It does a job no other kitchen tool can: it purees cooked vegetables, fruit, legumes,

fish, and other ingredients, separating out the skin, seeds, fibers, bones, and bits, the unwanted from the wanted. In fact, the action of the crank and the plate extracts flavor from the unwanted as well. This is particularly notable in the case of tomatoes, which we will come to shortly, the crank and paddle pressing the intense flavor from the skin, fibers, and seeds. What's more, a food mill doesn't entirely break and blast down the texture of the pulp as a blender or food processor would, but leaves it with the lively texture and distinct personality that's so desirable for Italian soups, sauces, and purees.

I will, of course, give alternatives to the food mill, but I will also keep suggesting you buy one. It is without a shadow of a doubt my favorite and most-used kitchen tool.

Sugo di pomodoro
Tomato sauce

This is our standard tomato sauce, based on the one made by Vincenzo's Sicilian grandmother, who would have called it *salsa di pomodoro*. It's simply tomatoes, oil, garlic, and salt, and in summer, the most irritatingly likeable of herbs: basil. It's a rich, smooth sauce, thick enough to coat the back of a spoon, but not so thick as to stunt the flow. It's the sauce we use most often on pasta, in baked pasta, around meatballs or beef roulade. It can be made with either fresh or canned tomatoes. It really requires a *mouli* or food mill, although you can use an immersion blender to reduce the tomatoes to a smooth consistency. You'll need 3¼ pounds tomatoes, fresh or canned in juice, which you'll need to prepare.

With fresh tomatoes
Cut the tomatoes in half lengthwise, put them in a saucepan, and cover with a lid. Cook over medium heat for 3 minutes, then lift the lid and squash the tomatoes with the back of a wooden spoon to release some of the juices. Replace the lid and cook for another few minutes, by which point the tomatoes should be soft, collapsing, and surrounded by juice. Set your food mill, fitted with the largest-holed disc, over a bowl and pass the cooked tomatoes and their juices through the mill in batches.

With canned peeled tomatoes
Set your food mill, fitted with the largest-holed disc, over a bowl and pass the canned tomatoes and their juices through the mill in batches.

To make the sauce

Peel and crush 2 garlic cloves with the back of a knife or the heel of your hand. Put the garlic and 5 tablespoons extra-virgin olive oil in a large frying pan over low heat and cook the garlic gently until it is fragrant and lightly golden. Be careful not to burn it, or the sauce will taste bitter. Remove the garlic. Add the tomatoes to the pan, along with a pinch of salt and a sprig of basil. Reduce the heat and let the sauce cook for 20–40 minutes, or until it is visibly thicker and reduced and the oil is just starting to come to the surface. To test it, if a silky spoonful placed on a flat plate no longer emits a large watery halo around the dollop, it's done.

Rough fresh tomato sauce

In contrast with the smooth sauce above, there is also the rough, which is possibly my favorite sauce of them all. I say rough, but actually "textured" would be a better description, in that you peel 2¼ pounds tomatoes, but rather than milling them you chop them roughly, seeds and all, then fry them in about 5 tablespoons extra-virgin olive oil scented with garlic until it is visibly thicker but the pieces of tomato are still distinct. I only make this in high summer when the tomatoes are at their best and most plentiful.

Roasted tomato sauce

This is the simplest of the lot. Put 2¼ pounds tasty small tomatoes (cherry, plum, the Piennolo Vesuvio variety, ideally on the vine) in a roasting pan, sprinkle with salt, pour over plenty of olive oil, and bake for about an hour. I might open the oven door and prod the tomatoes halfway through the cooking time, and they often squirt. They're done when they're a big oily mess, some squashed, some whole, all sitting in a pool of red-tinted oil. Vincenzo picks the vine out while I cook the pasta. It's then drained and tipped straight into the roasting pan, which also acts as a serving dish. If you like, you can pass the roasted tomatoes through a food mill, which gives you a smooth, intensely flavored sauce with a smoky, oven-baked aftertaste.

Rich tomato sauce with canned tomatoes

A rich, thick, and almost burgundy-colored sauce made with a *soffritto* of onion, carrot, and celery, canned plum tomatoes, and a glug of red wine. It can be served with just about any shape of pasta or with a gently poached egg and some bread. This sauce is decidedly Italian, but I learned to make it in un-Italian circumstances. That is, in the old kitchen in my parents' house in Harpenden. I imagine my mum drew her original inspiration

from a recipe by Elizabeth David or Jane Grigson, but the need for the printed page had long since passed. I watched keenly as she chopped the vegetables, then gently cooked the harlequin heap in lots of oil, added a big can of imported plum tomatoes and a slug of wine, then let the sauce bubble away on the stove for a good long while. I watched even more keenly as she poured a glass of red wine for herself, drank some, and turned the music up. A little later, while the sauce simmered, Dad might have spun her round in a tiny kitchen dance, which I found both reassuring and mortifying, so I focused back on the sauce.

I spurned this sauce when I first came to Italy, enchanted by the simpler, fresher versions and sheepish about my anglicized Italian cooking. It took a few years and much obsessive questioning about how Italians make their tomato sauce to discover that this sort of hearty sauce made with a *soffritto* is typical all over Italy during the darker months. One difference, though: Italians (at least the ones I know) nearly always pass this sort of sauce through a food mill so that the texture is smooth. I rather like it chunky—you could say that makes it more of a ragù than a sauce—but I'm also extremely happy to go smooth if that's the general consensus.

I imagine you know the routine as well as I do: peel and very finely dice onion, celery, and carrot and cook them gently in as much olive oil as you dare for a long, slow sizzle; slide in about a pound of canned chopped plum tomatoes; glug in some red wine to meet the tomatoes; then keep it at a slow, burping simmer for 30–40 minutes, stirring from time to time. Don't be afraid to add a little more wine or water if the sauce is looking dense but still needs cooking for a bit longer. Season as you see fit and add a little sugar if it seems acidic. If you prefer a smoother sauce, pass it through a food mill or a sieve. This will make enough sauce to dress 1–1¼ pounds pasta, which will feed 4 people.

Spaghetti con pomodorini
Spaghetti with cherry tomatoes

There are as many versions of *spaghetti al pomodoro* (spaghetti with tomatoes) as there are cooks. This is a summer version using the sweetest plum or cherry tomatoes you can find: ripe, tight orbs that burst in your mouth. It was taught to me by a demon cook, a Roman capable of great culinary feats who tells me he would happily eat this every day for the rest of his life, give or take the odd bowl of *pasta e fagioli*.

You smash 2 garlic cloves against your work surface with the palm of your hand, so that the skin comes away and the cloves split but remain whole and your hand could ward off vampires. You then fry them gently in far more extra-virgin olive oil than is decent. Once the garlic is just turning light gold and its fragrance is swirling up your nose, you add some halved cherry or tiny plum tomatoes (about 1 pound for 3 people) and a good pinch of salt and let them sizzle for a minute or so. Once they start softening and releasing liquid, you squash them with the back of a wooden spoon and watch their red juices tint the oil bronze. You add a few torn basil leaves and stir the pan, still over the heat, for a minute or so longer.

While you have been doing all this, your spaghetti (probably about 12 ounces) has been rolling around a large pan of well-salted, fast-boiling water. Your timing is good, obviously, and the spaghetti is al dente as you inhale and the tomatoes' bubbles say "ready." You scoop the spaghetti from the boiling water straight into the tomato pan. I use tongs for this, which means that some of the cooking water clings to the spaghetti. You stir with tongs and a spoon, and the cooking water—useful stuff that it is—mixes with the oily, tomatoey juices, emulsifying and creating a thickened sauce that coats each strand.

Bucatini all'amatriciana
Bucatini with tomato and cured pork

Opinions about how best to make this simple sauce of cured pork, tomatoes, and cheese are passionately held. I've been caught in the middle of more than one fierce debate, most memorably in a sweaty van with seven Roman musicians driving down the *autostrada del Parchi* not that far from the town of Amatrice in northern Lazio, where the dish originates. Once a dish of shepherds, it is now one of the most beloved Roman *primi*. Everybody seems to agree on the use of *guanciale* (cured pork cheek). Everything else, though, is open to debate: the inclusion of olive oil, onion, chile, white wine, which pecorino is best—*pecorino romano* or the slightly less aggressive local one from Amatrice—the preference for canned or fresh tomatoes, and the use of bucatini, spaghetti, or short pasta.

I am with Stefano, one of the musicians in the van, a 6-foot-4-inch Roman trumpet player and great cook, who taught me how to make this bold and delicious dish. He cuts the *guanciale* thickly and uses lots of it. He doesn't include olive oil, saying the *guanciale* has enough fat, which renders better with no oil. Nor does he add onion, which according to him is superfluous. He does add a little chile and white wine to cut through the fat in the *guanciale,* and happily uses fresh tomatoes if they are available, canned if they are not. His preference is for *pecorino romano.* As for the pasta, Stefano will defend bucatini with the same tenacity with which he holds a high C, meaning longer than everyone else. You will have opened a bottle to make the pasta, so ideally it should be one you can finish with the meal, such as an aromatic white from Lazio.

serves 4

about 1 pound ripe tomatoes or canned plum tomatoes with their juice
5¼ ounces guanciale
½ cup dry white wine
1 small dried or fresh chile, finely chopped
salt
1 pound bucatini
¾ cup grated pecorino romano

If you are using fresh tomatoes, peel and roughly chop them. If using canned, pass them through a food mill or roughly chop them. Cut the guanciale into short, thick batons. Put the batons in a large frying pan over medium heat and fry until it renders some fat, has turned golden, and is crisp at the edges. Using a slotted spoon, put half the crisp guanciale on a warm plate, leaving the rest and the fat in the pan. Pour over the wine, which will whoosh, sizzle, and evaporate. Add the tomatoes and chile, stir, taste, and season with salt accordingly. Cook the sauce over low heat, stirring every now and then, for 15 minutes, or until it is dense and the fat is coming to the surface.

Meanwhile, bring a large pot of water to a boil. Add salt, stir, and add the bucatini, fanning it out and then gently pressing it under the water with the back of a wooden spoon. Cook the pasta until it is al dente (check the cooking time on the package and start tasting at least 2 minutes earlier). Stefano mixes it directly in the frying pan, draining the pasta and tipping it on top of the sauce, sprinkling with grated pecorino, then tossing energetically with a wooden fork and spoon and serving it quickly from the pan, finishing each plate with some crisp guanciale. Alternatively, drain the pasta, tip it into a warm serving bowl, sprinkle over the cheese, toss, then pour over the sauce, toss again, and serve with the crisp guanciale on top.

Spaghetti alla puttanesca
Spaghetti with tomatoes, anchovies, capers, and olives

There are several stories and myths about the origins of this happy combination of ingredients commonly known as *spaghetti alla puttanesca*, or "whore's spaghetti." The story I've been told most often suggests that it was invented at the beginning of the twentieth century by the proprietor—let's call him Ciro and imagine he is very rotund and with an exuberant nature—of a brothel in the Spanish Quarter of Naples who would make this simple and tasty dish for clients and his working girls between appointments. A smart flourish to the story is the suggestion that the colors of the sauce (the red of the tomatoes, the vibrant green of the parsley, the gray-green of the capers, the deep violet of the olives, and the burgundy of the peperoncino) mirrored the eye-catching colors of the clothes and undergarments of the girls working at the brothel.

Others say that the sauce was created just after World War II on the island of Ischia, which lies about 30 miles off the coast of Naples, by an eccentric and notoriously hospitable painter called Eduardo Colucci. During one of his summer retreats to a tiny, simple cabin that nestled among the olive groves at Punta Molino, he's said to have made an improvised supper for his various and eclectic group of friends who lounged on the terrace. It was based on his speciality, the classic marinara sauce, but as it evolved he renamed it *puttanesca,* the exact reasons for which are not clear. But who wants clear?

The third story I'm often told is that the dish was invented in the 1950s by a certain Sandro Petti, co-owner of the famous restaurant and nightspot Rancio Fellone on the island of Ischia. One evening, just as the restaurant was about to close, Petti found a group of hungry friends sitting at one of his tables. He shrugged his shoulders; it was late, he was low on ingredients, and he didn't have enough to make them a meal. But they raised their hands in despair and cried, "*Mamma mia! Abbiamo fame, facci una puttanata qualsiasi!*" ("Mamma mia! We are hungry, make us any kind of garbage!") Used like this, *puttanata* is a noun meaning "rubbish" or something worthless, even though it derives from the Italian word for whore, *puttana.* Petti, the story continues, had nothing more than four tomatoes, two olives, and some capers, the basic ingredients for the *sugo,* so he used them to make the sauce for the spaghetti. From that day forth, Petti included the dish on his menu as *spaghetti alla puttanesca.*

Anyway, whatever the origins, it is a most fiercely delicious and opinionated combination of flavors. It's useful and practical, too, because we always have the ingredients in the cupboard, and because the sauce takes about the same time to make as it does to bring the water to a fast boil and cook the pasta. A pasta with such strong and particular flavors has to be a very personal thing, so this recipe is a loose guide and not a set of rules; you can experiment. If you like anchovies, you might like to add more; if you find capers overwhelming, add less or leave them out completely. How salty are your olives? How hot is your chile? You know better than me. Choose a wine that can stand up to such a formidable pasta, one with taste and body, such as a red from Campania like Aglianico.

serves 4

1 garlic clove
6 anchovy fillets packed in oil, drained
5 tablespoons extra-virgin olive oil
1 small fresh or dried chile
1 tablespoon salt-packed capers, rinsed
3½ ounces black olives, ideally Gaeta or Taggiasca
6 ripe tomatoes, or 14 ounces canned San Marzano tomatoes
  with their juice
salt
1 pound spaghetti
2 tablespoons finely chopped fresh flat-leaf parsley

Bring a large pot of water to a boil and warm a serving bowl if you're going to use one. Finely chop the garlic along with the anchovies. Warm the olive oil in a deep frying pan over low heat and add the chopped garlic and anchovies, mashing them gently with the back of a wooden spoon so they disintegrate into the oil. Chop the chile and add it to the pan. Cook for another couple of minutes. Roughly chop the capers, olives, and tomatoes and add them to the pan. Stir and cook over medium heat for 10 minutes.

Meanwhile, salt the boiling water, stir, and add the spaghetti, fanning it out and pressing it gently into the water (without breaking it) with the back of a wooden spoon. Cook, stirring occasionally, until it is al dente (check the cooking time on the package and start tasting at least 2 minutes earlier). Drain the pasta and, having pulled the sauce off the heat, toss it with the sauce, sprinkle with the parsley, and serve immediately. Alternatively—and more correctly—transfer the drained pasta to a warm serving bowl, tip over the sauce, toss with a spoon and a fork, sprinkle with the parsley, and serve.

Pasta-cooking water

Having left language school after four months, verb conjugations tripping off my tongue but still unable to have even the most basic conversation in Italian, I got a job as a waitress in a questionable trattoria that thought it was a restaurant. Looking back, it was all vaguely ridiculous. I was only ferrying bread baskets and bottles of water, placing plates in front of people and retrieving empty ones, but I was a waitress and people therefore asked me things, almost none of which I understood.

On every shift I scuttled like an irritating insect from one misunderstanding to the next, second-guessing, pointing, and on one occasion having a woman frog-march me over to the bar in order to get herself a packet of artificial sweetener. "*Dol-ci-fi-can-te*," she articulated through suspiciously plump lips, while waving the blue-and-white packet like a small bell in front of my nose. I became an expert at spending as much time as possible in the cellar, behind the bar polishing a low shelf, or in the corner of the kitchen. It was in this corner that I learned about pasta-cooking water.

The kitchen had a professional pasta cooker with metal baskets that were lifted in and out of boiling water, which over the course of the evening became more and more cloudy, and more and more dubious looking. I was already disconcerted to note that the pasta would often be dripping with water, like un-wrung clothes on a washing line, as it was united with its sauce in the pan waiting on the stove. It was even more disconcerting to see the chef, Gennaro, scooping a further ladleful into the frying pan and swirling it around. It seemed so bizarre. But slowly, through shift after shift spent hovering in the corner with my hands ready to receive a plate, I realized that rather than diluting it, the water was being absorbed into the dish and doing marvelous things in the process, loosening some sauces and apparently thickening others.

When I asked friends about this I received knowing looks, as if to say, "What, you didn't know about the cooking water?" One friend and good cook explained that the water, cloudy with thickening starch from the pasta and well salted, is, if not a secret ingredient, at least a key one. It loosens sauces that are too thick, creates an emulsion for others, and for the group of pastas that are inseparable from their condiment, acts as a catalyst and brings the elements together into a "sauce" that is created there and then on the hot pasta. A good example of this is carbonara, in which the beaten egg, cheese, *guanciale*, and pasta-cooking water unite to form a creamy sauce that clings to each strand or tube.

Domestic pasta-cooking water is, of course, not as potent as the type that rolls around in a professional pasta cooker, water so thick with the starch seeped from portion after portion of pasta that it actually gloops. The water in your pot, however, is starchy and salty enough to be fundamental in countless dishes, which is why Italians often remind you to reserve some of it when you drain the pasta. I took a friend's advice and started keeping a jug near the sink to remind me not to slosh the whole pot down the drain, and began experimenting, adding a ladleful here and there, often too much, sometimes too little, my timing off and then on, until I gradually learned how to use this cloudy substance. Meanwhile, back at the trattoria, I also learned never to put mozzarella in the fridge, how to make a *sgroppino* (lemon sorbet, prosecco, vodka, blend), and how to zig-zag fake chocolate sauce across a slice of crummy ricotta cheesecake, before we all acknowledged that until I had a slightly better grasp of Italian, waitressing in Rome probably wasn't an ideal job for me, and we parted ways.

Spaghetti con ricotta e pepe nero
Spaghetti with ricotta and black pepper

A simple, quick, and trusted favorite, which never fails to please and quiet everyone in this house. Three things are important. First, remember to remove a ladleful of pasta-cooking water and mix it with the ricotta and Parmesan until it looks like thick cream. Second, be extremely generous (although not foolish) with the freshly ground black pepper, as its throat-tickling heat is vital. Third, reserve some of the cooking water when you drain it, since once you have tossed the spaghetti in the ricotta, you may find you need a little more water to ensure that the spaghetti is slippery and curls around the fork willingly, as opposed to clumping.

serves 4
salt
1 pound spaghetti
¾ cup ricotta
½ cup grated Parmesan
freshly ground black pepper

Bring a large pot of water to a rolling boil. Add salt, stir, then add the spaghetti, fanning it out and using a wooden spoon to gently press and submerge the strands. Cover the pot until the water comes back to a boil, then remove the lid and continue cooking until it is al dente (check the cooking time on the package and start tasting at least 2 minutes earlier).

Meanwhile, in a large warmed bowl (I wash mine under hot water, then dry it), mash the ricotta with the grated Parmesan and grind lots of black pepper over the top. Scoop out a ladleful of cooking water from the pasta pot, add it to the ricotta mixture, and stir until you have a soft, creamy sauce.

Drain the pasta, reserving a little more cooking water, tip it into the bowl, and, using a spoon and a fork, toss the pasta in the sauce rapidly, lifting it up from the bottom of the bowl, turning and swirling to make sure each strand is coated with creamy sauce. The pasta should be soft and slithery; if it seems dry or too sticky, add a little more of the cooking water and toss again. Serve.

Spaghetti alla carbonara
Spaghetti with cured pork, eggs, and cheese

Carbonara is the best example of a pasta dish in which the sauce is inseparable from the pasta. It's one in which the elements—*guanciale* and its fat, beaten eggs, grated cheese, and a slosh of starchy pasta-cooking water—come together to form a soft yellow cream on strands of spaghetti or fat tubes of rigatoni. It is, like most good things, simple, but requires *la pratica* (practice), which I don't say in order to be off-putting, just honest. Having said this, you will now of course go off and make a perfect carbonara on your first attempt and wonder what on earth I was going on about.

For me, the key to carbonara is understanding what happens and when: that if you put the drained pasta into the pan with hot *guanciale* fat at the right moment, add the beaten eggs and grated cheese and enough pasta-cooking water, then pull the pan from the heat and stir purposefully, you should get a creamy sauce that clings to each strand or tube. Having understood this, you'll also understand the need for practice: it can't possibly be any other way. You'll notice how the cured pork renders its fat and how much fat there is, which will of course be different for everyone's *guanciale*, pancetta, or bacon cooked on their idiosyncratic stove. You'll find the best arrangement of frying pan, pasta pot, colander, tongs, slotted spoon, and vessel for the reserved cooking water, so as to make the sequence as easy as possible. But most of all, you'll become familiar with the series of movements: tipping the drained pasta into the

hot fat; adding the egg mixture and cooking water; the purposeful stir. You'll start to know if you need to add more cooking water, and notice when the sauce thickens to a batter-like consistency, coating each piece of pasta but still allowing it to slide seductively. You'll be able to spot the moment when the eggs scramble and seize and the pasta clumps together unhappily, which is still tasty, but not enough to risk doing that again. Or, in an attempt not to scramble, the moment when you flood the pan and everyone eats a tasty but rather soupy lunch.

Most of all, you need practice so that you can enjoy the eureka moment when it comes out just right, which must be brief because you need to rush the plates to the table—there is no time to waste. Someone just about manages to say *buon appetito* before forks start turning and pasta starts coiling, interrupted only by sips of cold Frascati. You too are engrossed in your lunch, but also in trying to remember precisely how much cooking water you added and when, making a mental note that the wooden fork does indeed work better than a spoon, and that you can always add more *guanciale*. Next time.

In Rome, *guanciale* is traditionally used for carbonara (purists claim it is indispensable). That said, quite a few Romans I know prefer pancetta. I like both and use both. If you can't find either, bacon works too.

serves 4
5¼ ounces guanciale, pancetta, or bacon
a little olive oil
salt
1 pound spaghetti
2 whole eggs and 2 extra yolks
¾ cup grated pecorino or Parmesan, or a mixture of both
freshly ground black pepper

Bring a large pot of water to a rolling boil. Cut the guanciale into short, thick strips. In a large frying pan over medium heat, cook the guanciale in a little olive oil until the fat has rendered and the pieces are golden and crisp. Remove from the heat.

Add salt to the boiling water, stir, then add the spaghetti, fanning it out and using a wooden spoon to gently press and submerge the strands. Cover the pot until the water comes back to a boil, then remove the lid and continue cooking until it is al dente (check the cooking time on the package and start tasting at least 2 minutes earlier).

While the pasta is cooking, in a largish bowl whisk together the eggs, egg yolks, grated cheese, a pinch of salt, and plenty of black pepper. Heat up the meat pan again, and once hot, use a slotted spoon to transfer three-quarters of the guanciale pieces to a small plate, leaving the last quarter and the fat in the pan.

Drain the pasta, reserving a cup of the cooking water. Add the pasta to the frying pan, stirring so that each strand is coated with fat. Turn off the heat, then add the egg and cheese mixture and a little cooking water. Using a wooden spoon or fork, mix everything together vigorously so each strand is coated with a creamy sauce. Add just a little more cooking water if the sauce is too stiff. Serve immediately, dividing the rest of the crisp guanciale between the plates.

Linguine con zucchine
Linguine with zucchini, egg, and Parmesan

We make this a lot, since, as you may or may not have gathered, we are creatures of habit, especially when it comes to lunchtime pasta. The principle is similar to that of classic carbonara, and like carbonara, it is simple, but finding that point where the eggs are creamy but not scrambled does take a bit of practice. You could of course use spaghetti, but I love linguine here. Its strands, like flattened spaghetti (a similar shape to the strips of zucchini) have a way of wrapping themselves around your tongue in a most over-familiar way—after all, _linguine_ does mean "little tongues."

serves 4
1 small white onion or 4 scallions
10½ ounces zucchini
¼ cup extra-virgin olive oil
salt
about 1 pound linguine
2 whole eggs, plus 2 extra yolks
1 cup grated Parmesan
freshly ground black pepper
a few basil leaves

Bring a large pot of water to a rolling boil. Thinly slice the onion and cut the zucchini into 2-inch-long, 1/16-inch-thick strips. In a large frying pan, warm the olive oil over medium heat, then cook the onion and zucchini gently with a pinch of salt, turning them regularly with a wooden spoon, until they are very soft and tender—about 10 minutes. Remove the pan from the heat.

Add salt to the boiling water, stir, then add the linguine, fanning it out and using a wooden spoon to gently press and submerge the strands. Cover the pot until the water comes back to a boil, then remove the lid and continue cooking until the linguine is al dente (check the cooking time on the package and start tasting at least 2 minutes earlier).

While the pasta is cooking, in a largish bowl, whisk together the eggs, extra yolks, cheese, a pinch of salt, and plenty of black pepper. During the last minute of pasta-cooking time, put the frying pan back on the heat to warm both the fat and vegetables. Drain the pasta, reserving a cup of the cooking water. Add the pasta to the frying pan, stirring so it tangles with the zucchini strips. Remove from the heat and add the egg-and-cheese mixture and a little cooking water. Using a wooden spoon, mix everything together vigorously so that each strand is coated with a creamy sauce, adding a little more cooking water if the sauce is too stiff. Tear the basil and add it to the pan. Serve immediately.

Pasta e broccoli
Pasta and broccoli

My grandma Roddy would have approved of this recipe, the cooking of the broccoli at least, which should be boiled until it is soft—none of this al dente business, the mere thought of which gave my grandpa heartburn.

A much-loved dish in Rome, *pasta e broccoli* is often made with *broccolo romanesco* (romanesco cauliflower), a curiously beautiful, lime green vegetable with intricate clusters of closely packed florets that one of my books describes as architectonic spirals, and another as the aggressively brassièred breasts of Madonna in her Boadicea phase. Cooked romanesco has the texture and feel of good, creamy cauliflower but the taste of broccoli.

Once cooked until very tender and collapsing at the edges, you sauté the romanesco—or broccoli—in plenty of extra-virgin olive oil in which you have gently cooked a crushed clove of garlic and a little chile. Meanwhile, the pasta is cooked in the sweetly vegetal water you have just lifted the romanesco from, then lifted into the sauté pan, where the collapsing vegetable, oil, and starchy water clinging to the pasta combine to form an almost creamy sauce. It's not very traditional, but I like to add a handful of grated pecorino or Parmesan to the romanesco pan at the same time as the pasta, which helps the ingredients meld together even more beautifully. Romanesco is best, but I have made successful versions of *pasta e broccoli* with ordinary broccoli, purple-sprouting broccoli, and cauliflower.

serves 4
1 large head romanesco cauliflower or broccoli
salt
2 cloves garlic
1 small red fresh or dried chile
6 tablespoons olive oil
14 ounces short pasta, such as penne or rigatoni
⅓ cup grated pecorino or Parmesan, plus extra to serve

Pull away the tough outer leaves, cut away the hard stem, and break the romanesco or broccoli into small florets. Bring a large pot of water to a fast boil, add salt, and stir, then add the florets. Cook for 6–8 minutes, or until tender, which will depend on how fresh the romanesco is. Use a slotted spoon to lift the florets into a colander.

Meanwhile, peel and gently crush the garlic with the back of a knife and chop the chile. Heat the olive oil in a large frying pan, add the garlic and chile, and cook gently until the garlic is lightly golden and fragrant. Do not allow the garlic to brown or it will be ruinously bitter. Remove the garlic.

Bring the same water you cooked the romanesco in back to a fast boil and add the pasta. While the pasta is cooking, add the romanesco to the frying pan and stir so that each floret is glistening. Add salt, stir again, and mash the florets gently with the back of a wooden spoon so they break up. Either drain the pasta, saving some of the cooking water, and tip it into the romanesco pan, or better still, use a slotted spoon to lift the pasta into it. Throw over the Parmesan or pecorino and stir vigorously so that the pasta mixes with the romanesco. Serve immediately with more cheese.

La Torricella

The best time to go to trattoria La Torricella is on Friday for lunch. It isn't essential that you book, especially if you're there before one o'clock. That said, if you happen to be in the area, you could put your head round the door an hour or so beforehand and reserve a table. From April to October, ask to sit outside. I like the third table up from the door, the one in front of the owner Augusto's bike that is always leaning against the wall.

It took us a few years to get to La Torricella, even though it's local and we'd heard plenty of good things about it, especially its *moscardini* (floured and fried tiny octopuses). We eventually walked the couple of hundred yards or so across Testaccio on a Saturday night and lucked upon an outside table. First impressions were good, which was much to do with the ordinary charm of the place with its row of tables under a canopy in a quiet backstreet of Testaccio, and the all-permeating sense of family, both serving and being served. There was also the promise of fried fish and broad grin-sized wedges of lemon. Wine and water arrived immediately, but then service erred on the slow and brusque side; the last portion of *moscardini* was delivered to the table next to us and the food, although competent, was brusque too. On another occasion, with other people, these things might not have been forgiven, but that night they were—after all, it was Saturday and we'd arrived late. The following Friday we came back for lunch and over a bowl of octopuses and two near-perfect plates of spaghetti with clams, the brusqueness was forgotten, and we've been coming back since.

Friday lunchtime is the time to go because the curved glass-front fish counter just inside the door is filled generously. Augusto has negotiated with Mauro (his *pescivendolo*) until the veins throb in his throat, knowing that Friday is the day on which Romans traditionally eat fish. They do on Saturdays too, so overestimating isn't possible. While you're inside, glance to see if there's anything on the cart next to the fish counter; a full bowl of pink-tinged octopus salad, perhaps a tray of just-baked fish and potatoes, at the

right time of year a plate of braised, sultry olive-green artichokes, their stalks pointing skyward.

Order Acqua di Nepi, a naturally sparkling water from a town near Rome, and unless you really want to navigate the wine list, a bottle of the house wine, a functional Frascati that is more than fine with the food. You will be brought a single printed sheet of the day's specials, which are more or less all fish. There's also a full trattoria menu of all the Roman classics you can ask to be brought. However, my advice is to stick to fish—after all, it is Friday. The menu changes from day to day but there are some fixtures: for antipasti, the *moscardini,* for example, or *bocconcini di merluzzo* (bites of battered cod), and—my favorite—*alici fritti* (fried anchovies). Pasta is always a safe bet at Torricella, particularly the gnocchi or spaghetti *alle vongole*, and linguine with *astice* (male lobster). Two antipasti and two pasta dishes is normally enough for us. If we're still hungry we share a *secondo*, usually some grilled fish or the *paranza* (mixed fried fish) that comes with nothing more than a fat piece of lemon.

While you are eating, the tables will fill steadily with a reassuringly mixed crowd: several older couples, the real regulars; a large family group, who could well be from the block opposite celebrating a birthday or graduation; a group of suits profiting from

the fact that their meeting is on Friday; another group of students from the university; next to them a table of tourists who have been given good advice. By two o'clock the place should be quietly lively, and Augusto content.

Generally, we don't have dessert at La Torricella, preferring to walk up the road to the *gelateria*. But if we do, it's usually gelato with tiny wild strawberries, the sweetness of which demands an espresso straight afterward. If I know I can have a doze I might also have a homemade *genziana*, a shudderingly good, herbal Amaro, which my grandma Roddy would have said puts hair on your chest. The bill was reasonable, you might think to yourself as you walk through the by now quiet streets of Testaccio toward the main piazza, or up onto the Aventine hill, where you find a bench and watch the world go by.

Spaghetti alle vongole
Spaghetti with clams

The best clams for *spaghetti alle vongole* are *vongole veraci*, or Manila clams, which look like exquisite fluted stones streaked with white, gray, and brown that have just been lapped by the sea. But you can also use other small clams. To my mind, *spaghetti alle vongole* cooked well is the most perfect dish, the liquor of the clams like the sweet essence of the sea mixing with the garlic-and-chile-scented olive oil to create a seductive sauce for the pasta, which in turn provides a silky weave to ensnare the fleshy clams. I fell in love over a plate of *spaghetti alle vongole*. I also realized I quite liked the man I was eating with and we decided to give it a go.

As much as I like *spaghetti alle vongole* at La Torricella and our favorite beachside place in Fregene (the beach itself is no great shakes, but the trattoria is excellent), I like it most at home. This is because I buy the best *vongole* and we eat about 2 pounds of clams between two. A friend disagrees with this, saying that too many clams, like too many raisins in the raisin bran, spoils the treat, the proportions being all important. I, however, think that about 2 pounds of clams for 10½ ounces spaghetti are perfectly reasonable proportions.

I am set in my ways about my technique, as I have found a method that really works for me. It's important to be organized, since although it's a simple dish there are a couple of moves that require planning, most notably the draining of the broth. Two sets of hands are useful, one to cook the clams, drain, and cook again, the other to pick the flesh out of the shells. Read the

instructions carefully before you start, and arrange your pans and sieves accordingly.

Some marinated anchovies to begin, a bottle of Sicilian white, *spaghetti alle vongole*, and nothing to do for the rest of the afternoon, and I am an extremely happy woman.

serves 2 greedy people who love clams
(you could increase the pasta to about a pound to feed
4 people, although I'm not sure why you'd want to do that)
2¼ pounds clams, cleaned
5 tablespoons olive oil
2 garlic cloves

½ cup white wine
10½ ounces spaghetti
1 small red chile or a pinch of red pepper flakes
1 tablespoon finely chopped flat-leaf parsley

Sit the clams in a sink full of salted cold water for at least 2 hours. Drain and rinse them well, discarding any that are open. Bring a large pan of well-salted water to a fast boil.

In a large, deep frying pan or sauté pan with a lid, warm 2 tablespoons of the olive oil over medium-low heat, add a peeled and crushed garlic clove, and cook gently until fragrant. Add the clams and wine, cover the pan, and cook over lively heat, shaking the pan from time to time, until all the clams have opened (discard any that don't).

Use a slotted spoon to lift the open clams from the pan into a bowl, then drain the clam broth through a very fine sieve and set aside. Rinse and dry the pan. Choose 25 or so of the nicest clams and set them aside in their shells, then pick out the flesh from the rest of the clams and set the meat aside too.

Put the spaghetti in the by now boiling water and check the cooking time on the package; start tasting it 2 minutes earlier. Back in the frying pan, heat 2 more tablespoons of the olive oil and gently cook the second peeled and crushed garlic clove and the chile until fragrant. Add the clam broth and let it bubble and reduce for a few minutes before adding the reserved clams in their shells and cooking for a minute or so more.

Once it is al dente, drain the pasta, reserving a little of the cooking water; add it to the clams and stir well. Add the parsley and remaining tablespoon olive oil, stirring so that each strand of spaghetti is coated with broth. Divide between 4 plates, making sure each one has its fair share of clams.

Fettuccine al ragù
Fettuccine with rich meat sauce

Just the thought of making ragù makes me happy, not least because if you're adding a glass of wine to the pan, it would be careless not to have one yourself.

This is the recipe I began making long before I came to Italy, and it has resisted all the fist-thumping Roman and southern Italian influences in my cooking life. It takes inspiration from Elizabeth David and her interpretation of a traditional Bolognese ragù:

that is, a rich, slowly cooked meat sauce made with olive oil and butter, given a blush of color from just a tablespoon of tomato puree, depth from red wine, and soft edges from the milk. Its rich, creamy, yet crumbly consistency can come as a bit of a surprise if you're used to redder, tomato-rich ragùs. Rest assured, it's glorious, irresistible stuff. Like most braises, it's infinitely better the next day. I almost always make a double quantity, half to eat with fettuccine (fresh if I am in the mood) and a dusting of Parmesan, the other half in rather more English style.

I have adopted the Bolognese habit of sprinkling the grated Parmesan over the pasta before adding the sauce; the cheese, which melts in the warmth, seasons the pasta deeply and helps the sauce cling to it beautifully. This mixing is best done in a serving bowl, which you can then bring proudly to the table along with a bottle of good Soave.

serves 4 generously
1 white onion
1 carrot
1 celery stalk
2 ounces pancetta or unsmoked bacon
3 tablespoons extra-virgin olive oil
4 tablespoons butter
1 bay leaf
14 ounces ground beef
10½ ounces ground pork
¾ cup red or white wine
1 tablespoon tomato paste dissolved
   in 6 tablespoons warm water
salt and freshly ground black pepper
⅔ cup whole milk
1 pound egg fettuccine, tagliatelle, or farfalle, ideally fresh
   (pages 152–157), but best-quality dried if not
5 tablespoons grated Parmesan

Finely chop the onion and carrot along with the celery and pancetta. Some people like to do this in a food processor. In a large, heavy-bottomed saucepan or deep frying pan with a lid, heat the olive oil and butter, add the vegetables and pancetta with the bay leaf and cook over low heat until they are soft and fragrant and the pancetta has rendered much of its fat and is starting to color. This will take about 8 minutes.

Increase the heat slightly, then crumble the ground meat into the pan and cook, stirring pretty continuously, until the meat has lost all

its pink color and has browned evenly. Add the wine, turn up the heat, and let it evaporate for a couple of minutes before adding the tomato. Simmer, covered, over low heat for 30 minutes, by which time the sauce should have deepened in color and have very little liquid. Add a teaspoon of salt, lots of black pepper, and a little of the milk. Cook slowly, covered, for another hour over low heat, every so often lifting the lid and adding a little of the milk until it is used up. The sauce should be rich and thick with no liquid, but not dry either, so keep a careful eye on it.

When you're ready to eat, bring a large pot of water to a fast boil and, if it isn't already hot, gently reheat the ragù. Warm a serving bowl. Once the water has come to a fast boil, add salt, stir, gently drop in the pasta, and cook, stirring every now and then, until it is al dente. For fresh fettuccine or tagliatelle this will only take a few minutes, but farfalle will take slightly longer. For dried pasta, check the timing on the package and start tasting 2 minutes earlier. Drain the pasta and turn it into the serving bowl (reserving a little pasta-cooking water), sprinkle over the cheese, then add the sauce. Stir carefully, lifting the pasta from below with two wooden spoons, so it is well coated with sauce. If it seems a bit dry, cautiously add a little of the reserved pasta-cooking water and toss again. Serve.

Shepherd's pie (of sorts)

This is a dish in which my two food worlds collide, and one that may well make purists in Italy and England shake their heads. It consists of a good inch of my Bolognese ragù in the bottom of an ovenproof dish, topped with 2 inches of very buttery mashed potatoes. The combination of deeply flavored meat sauce, which is thick enough to behave, topped with mashed potatoes forked into peaks and then baked until golden, is superb. I should note that this is the only occasion on which Luca, who is always an enthusiast at the table, has actually banged his fork down and shouted, "More!" A few buttered peas are nice, as is a glass of Soave.

Making fresh pasta

When I was little, I was often given flour and water to play with while my mum cooked. At first I was happy simply to combine the two ad hoc and make an unctuous, sticky mess on the burgundy plastic cloth that protected the kitchen table from three boisterous kids. But I soon realized that real satisfaction was to be gained by mixing just enough of each, then patiently working and kneading them into a soft, pliable dough. I would then roll or simply pinch and twist the dough into shapes. I was making pasta.

As an adult, I avoided making pasta for years, fearful of something I imagined to be mysterious and difficult, especially for someone without even a drop of Italian blood or Latin sway to the hips. It took lessons with my friend Paola to remind me that making pasta is essentially simple, that it's about mixing enough flour and liquid, be it water or egg, to make a rough dough, neither too sticky nor dry, then practicing, finding your own moves and kneading rhythm to transform the rough dough into a soft, elastic one— exactly what I had done so instinctively as a child.

When it comes to fresh pasta, there are two basic doughs: flour and water and flour and egg. The principle is the same for both: the ingredients are combined, kneaded rigorously, and then left to rest (which is important) before being rolled by hand or machine, cut, folded, filled, twisted, or twirled into shapes. Everyone will tell you that you begin with a mountain of flour, then use the back of a fist to swirl the mountain into a deep crater or volcano into which you break the eggs or pour the water. Most people will tell you to swirl the water or break the eggs with a fork and begin incorporating the

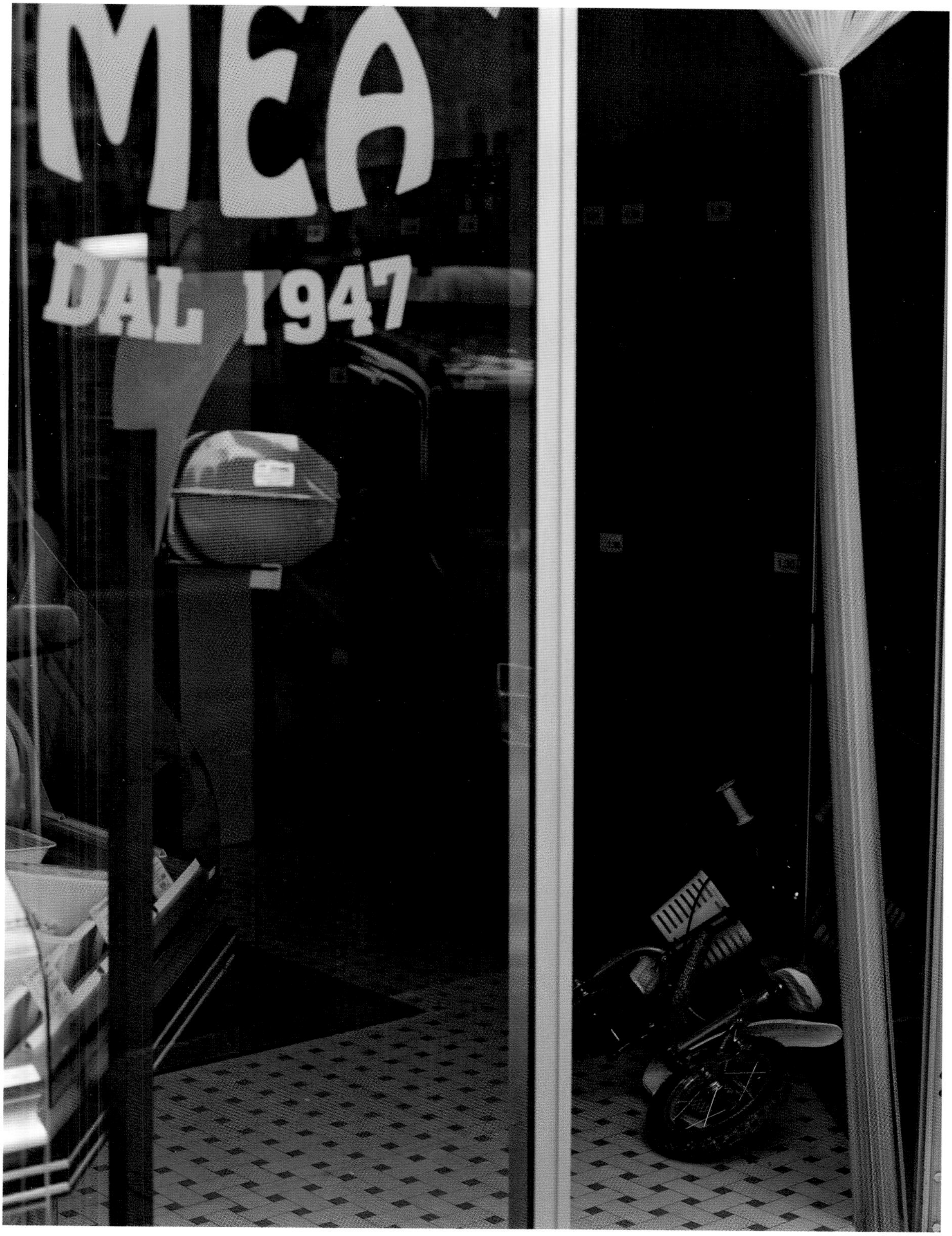
MEA
DAL 1947

flour into the liquid before using your hands to bring the two into a crude mass. As for kneading, beyond the guidance for pushing, folding, and rotating the dough that I will describe shortly, the advice is mostly to practice: making pasta is all about feel and experience. Kneading it requires strength and persistence, but once you find the steady, rocking rhythm of pushes and folds, the sway of the hips, and start to feel the transformation from rough, crude dough into a smooth, silky one, your effort is repaid richly.

I am reluctant to give precise times for how long you should knead, as I think they can be off-putting if you are just starting out. Let's just say that the minimum is 8 minutes and the maximum is whenever the dough feels soft and silky. I suggest you find a couple of quiet afternoons and some nice music to do a bit of experimenting.

Pasta all'uovo
Fresh egg pasta

makes enough for 4
**3¼ cups Italian 00 flour or King Arthur Italian-style flour,
  plus extra for dusting**
4 large eggs

Sift the flour into a broad mountain on a wooden board or work surface. Using the back of your fist, gently swirl a deep, wide crater into the center of the mountain. Break the eggs into the crater. Using a fork, pierce the yolks, then swirl the eggs and use the fork to start incorporating the flour into the eggs (the edges of the crater will stop the eggs from escaping). Once the eggs are absorbed, use your hands to bring the rest of the flour into a sticky, messy dough. Keep working the dough until all the flour is incorporated and you have a neat-ish ball and clean hands and work surface.

The kneading. Glance at the clock, put on some music, and place the dough on a work surface. Place the heels of both hands on the dough. Using your body weight, push the dough forward with one heel and then the other, folding the edges over as you go and turning the dough a quarter turn every few pushes. Find a strong but easy rhythm and continue kneading like this for at least 8 minutes, during which time the dough will transform from a rough ball into a firm, smooth, silky ball of dough.

The rolling. Allow the dough to rest for 30 minutes, covered with a clean tea towel, or simply on the work surface with a bowl inverted over the top. Once rested, you can move on to the next stage, which for the purposes of the recipes in this book is rolling into sheets (*le sfoglie*), which you can do by hand, or by using a hand-cranked machine that clamps to the table. You're going to cut the dough into 8 pieces, so mark it lightly with the blade of a knife so as to identify the pieces, but cut away only one and re-cover the rest of the dough to stop it from drying out. Set the rollers of your pasta machine to setting 1 (the widest). Flatten the lump of dough into a little patty, then send it through the rollers, cranking the machine with the other hand. Fold both ends of the dough in and over each other, like an envelope, and pass the dough through the machine again. Repeat with the other 7 pieces. Set the machine to setting 2 and pass all the pieces of dough through twice in the same way. Lay each freshly rolled piece on a floured board while you pass the others, and keep working like this, increasing the setting each time, until you reach the penultimate setting. You'll finish up with 8 narrow *sfoglie* (sheets) of pasta, all ready to cut.

   The cutting. For the recipes here, you'll need to make fettuccine (flat noodles), *quadrucci* (little squares), and farfalle (butterflies). The remnants and odd bits left over are your *maltagliati* (badly cut pieces), which can be frozen at first on a tray, and then in a bag, until you have enough for a soup. You can also use the *sfoglie* to make filled ravioli and lasagne.

Fettuccine

Lay the pasta sheet on a lightly floured board, dusting the sheet lightly with more flour, and then rolling it loosely into a flat roll about 4 inches wide. With a sharp knife, slice the roll at ¼-inch intervals. Save any odd bits for *maltagliati*. Once cut, gently fluff the fettuccine with your fingers and allow them to fall into loose little piles on the board until you are ready to use them.

Quadrucci

These are little squares, which is one of our absolute favorite shapes
at home. Vincenzo, who is usually a stickler for matching shape to
dish, would happily break the rules and have these in all the *minestra*
recipes. I learned to make *quadrucci* by watching the ladies in the *pasta
all'uova* shop in piazza Testaccio, their confident hands and impressive
blades a formidable combination. You begin as you would when making
fettuccine, by laying the pasta sheet on a lightly floured board, dusting
the sheet lightly with more flour, and then rolling it loosely into a flat roll
about 4 inches wide. With a sharp knife, cut the roll at ¼-inch intervals
to make fettuccine, keeping the pieces together, then rotate the roll
and cut it in the other direction, so as to make little squares. Save any
odd bits for *maltagliati*. Once cut, immediately fluff, lift, and separate
the *quadrucci* so they don't stick. Leave them spaced out on a board,
covered with a clean tea towel, until you are ready to use them.

Farfalle

Use a sharp knife or pasta cutter to cut the pasta sheet into ¾-inch
noodles as for thick fettuccine, then into rectangles about 1½ inches
long. Pinch each piece hard in the middle so that they resemble
butterflies or bow ties. Leave them spaced out on a board, covered
with a clean tea towel, until you're ready to use them.

Ravioli di ricotta e spinaci
Ricotta and spinach ravioli

The first time I attempted ravioli I ignored every bit of advice I'd ever given myself and made them in a rush, in my insufficient kitchen, for guests, as part of a complicated lunch. Needless to say, it was not a pleasant experience. The handle of the pasta machine kept flying across the kitchen, the filling was too wet, the dough was too dry, half of them burst in the pan, and even though everyone was very nice about my first attempt—although not nice enough to have seconds—I swore I would never make them again.

It took me a few years, but I did try again, on an ordinary day, when it was only us and if everything went wrong again we knew we could always go out for lunch (which we didn't).

You need a decent work space, which for me means the kitchen table, onto which the pasta machine clamps nicely. Two sets of hands are useful, too, one to roll and the other to fill, press, and cut. My other advice is to make sure you squeeze as much water as you can from the spinach, and to press firmly between the mounds. A wheeled cutter is useful, although not essential. Have a clean tea towel laid out ready—in my case on top of the washing machine— on which you can put the finished ravioli.

A few years on, ravioli are one of my favorite things to make. I still can't make them in a rush or for more than 6 people, and they still occasionally burst in the boiling water, but not very often. I like them with quite a lot of melted butter and sage and a glass of aromatic white wine like Greco di Tufo, which holds its own against the sage.

serves 4
7 ounces spinach
1⅓ cups best-quality ricotta, ideally made from sheep's
   milk, drained
¾ cup grated Parmesan, plus 3 tablespoons to serve
a little grated nutmeg (optional)
1 quantity egg pasta (page 155), cut into manageable
   lengths (about 4 inches wide)
7 tablespoons butter
8 small sage leaves

Rinse the spinach, then cook it in a hot pan, covered, with just the water clinging to the leaves, until it has wilted. Drain the spinach well, then squeeze as much water as possible from it. You'll be left

with a tiny ball. Roughly chop the spinach and then mix it in a bowl with the ricotta, Parmesan, and grating of nutmeg, if you are using it.

On a work surface dusted lightly with flour, lay out the pasta sheets. Using a teaspoon, put an acorn-size mound of the ricotta-and-spinach mixture at 1¼-inch intervals until you get halfway along each strip of pasta. Fold the pasta sheet over to cover the heaps of filling and press it down around them, then firmly press your fingertips between the mounds to seal them. Cut the ravioli apart with a wheeled cutter, then place them on a clean tea towel or flour-dusted tray, making sure they don't touch each other or they will stick.

To cook the ravioli, bring a large pot of water to a fast boil, add salt, stir, and then carefully drop the ravioli into the pot a few at a time. Depending on the thickness, ravioli takes anywhere from 5–8 minutes. Test for doneness by eye, pinching the (hot) edge of the pasta and tasting. Keep an eagle eye out and don't leave the pasta unattended.

While the pasta is cooking, melt the butter in a small saucepan or frying pan over low heat. Increase the heat and add the sage leaves. When they begin to change color, which should take about 1 minute, remove the pan from the heat and keep warm.

Once cooked, lift the ravioli from the water with a slotted spoon or spider strainer directly onto a warm serving dish. Sprinkle with Parmesan, pour over the butter and sage, and serve immediately.

Gnocchi di patate
Potato dumplings

Gnocchi are little dumplings; the word comes from a northern Italian dialect and means "little knots." They can be made from flour or bread crumbs with the addition of potatoes, vegetables, or ricotta, or a mixture.

In Rome, it's traditional to eat potato gnocchi on Thursdays. Press your nose up against a misted-up windowpane or peer round the door of any traditional trattoria on any given Thursday and you will almost certainly see _gnocchi di patate_ or _gnocchi del Giovedi_ chalked up on the blackboard. Peer persistently, and you might well catch sight of the gnocchi being whisked from kitchen to table:

steaming bowls of small, pale dumplings, forked on one side, thumb depressed on the other, sitting nonchalantly in a simple sauce.

To add eggs, or not to add eggs: that is the question. In Rome the answer is resolutely yes. Eggs are mixed with *farinose* (floury) potatoes and a generous amount of flour, which produces stout, well-bound, and thus well-behaved gnocchi, the kind that can withstand a rowdy, rollicking boil in an equally rowdy trattoria kitchen. The general Roman consensus seems to be more or less 2¼ pounds potatoes, 2 whole eggs, and 3¼ cups flour, give or take the odd very strong opinion.

serves 4

**about 1¼ pounds russet potatoes,
   ideally 3 or 4 equal-size ones**

1 egg

**scant 2½ cups Italian 00 flour or King Arthur Italian-style
   flour (you may not need all of it)**

Scrub, but don't peel, the potatoes. In a large pan, cover the potatoes with cold water, bring to a boil, and cook until they're tender to the point of a knife. Drain and then return them briefly to the pan over very low heat for about 30 seconds so that they dry out.

Once the potatoes are cool enough to handle, peel them, and while they are still warm, pass them through a potato ricer or food mill into a heap on a work surface. Make a crater in the center of the pile, break the egg into the crater, and then, using your fingertips, work the egg into the potato. A wonderfully sticky job.

Sift the flour into a bowl and then tip half of it over the potato-and-egg mixture. Work the flour into the mixture with your fingertips, adding more flour and working until you have a consistent, soft dough that comes away from your hands and the board. The amount of flour you need will vary.

Divide the dough into 6 pieces and, on a lightly floured board, roll each piece into a slim log about ¾ inch wide. Cut the log into pieces as wide as they are thick, then gently press each piece with the back of a fork to give it the ridges that will later collect sauce. Cover the gnocchi with a clean tea towel until you're ready to cook them.

Gnocchi di patate con ragù con le spuntature
Potato gnocchi with pork rib ragù

Spuntature (rib tips) are cut from the end of the spare ribs, and are made up of flexible cartilage rather than bone. It's this cartilage that makes this dish of ribs braised with tomato so unctuously good, because it thickens the sauce. It's sometimes served with pasta, but best of all with potato gnocchi for what would be called _un piatto unico_ (a single dish), the deep red sauce coating each gnocchi and the ribs waiting to be picked out with your fingers. I also like it as a main dish, perhaps with good sausages too, with rice or plain boiled potatoes.

serves 4
1 large white onion
3 tablespoons extra-virgin olive oil
14 ounces short pork ribs, trimmed of fat
1 (28-ounce) can plum tomatoes, chopped or milled, or passata
salt and freshly ground black pepper
1 quantity potato gnocchi (page 160)

Dice the onion. Warm the oil in a deep sauté pan or heavy-bottomed frying pan over medium heat and add the onion and ribs. Fry the ribs gently for about 20 minutes, turning them regularly until they are light brown on all sides.

Add the tomatoes, a good pinch of salt, and some black pepper. Cover the pan and leave it to simmer gently over low heat, stirring every now and then, for 1 hour, or until the sauce is richly flavored, thick, and the meat tender. Keep the sauce and ribs warm.

To cook the gnocchi, bring a large pot of well-salted water to a fast boil. Warm a large shallow serving dish and make sure you have the warm sauce and ribs and a slotted spoon at the ready. Drop the gnocchi into the boiling water. As soon as they bob to the surface, which will take a matter of minutes, scoop them from the water with the slotted spoon and into the serving dish. Spoon over the sauce, tossing the gnocchi gently to coat, arrange the ribs over the gnocchi, and serve immediately, dividing the gnocchi and ribs between the plates. The ribs are served whole, and should be picked out and eaten with fingers.

3
MEAT & FISH

The Other Quarter

Grilled lamb chops

Broiled pork chops with fennel and juniper

Sautéed beef with arugula and Parmesan

Veal rolls with prosciutto and sage

White beans with sage and sausages

Boiled beef and carrots

Meatballs in tomato sauce

Beef rolls in tomato sauce

Sausage and cabbage cake

Braised veal with celery

Chicken with tomatoes and sweet red peppers

Chicken or rabbit, hunters' style

Roast lamb with potatoes

Porchetta

Roman-style tripe

Oxtail with tomatoes and celery

Tongue with green sauce

Whole fish baked in the oven or grilled

A pot of mussels

Salt cod with tomatoes, raisins, and pine nuts

Miriam's sea bream baked with potatoes

Beef simmered with carrots and celery until it's so tender you can serve it with a spoon; slow-roasted lamb with roast potatoes; oxtail braised slowly until it falls from the bone; boiled tongue sliced thinly and tucked into sandwiches. I could be talking about the food of my northern English family, but I'm actually talking about some of Rome's most traditional meat dishes.

At first, living and cooking in Rome was all about the discovery of things that seemed entirely different. I wanted to understand how Romans mix garlic, rosemary, chile, and white wine in the most seductive way that clings to lamb and chicken and rabbit; to discover the key to simmering meatballs and rolls of beef until they are plump in rich, smooth tomato sauce; to learn to fry meat with sage or rosemary until it's so tantalizing you grab it while it's too hot. I bought myself two wide pans, like the ones I could see through the window of the trattoria backing onto our courtyard, and I began.

As I stayed longer and tasted more, I realized that amid the different and new there was also something extremely familiar. I saw that Roman *lesso* is not just similar but almost identical to the boiled beef my auntie May made in the back kitchen of my grandmother's pub in Oldham; that roast lamb with burnished potatoes here is very like roast lamb there; that boiled tongue is as delicious with *salsa verde* as it is with a dab of English mustard; that English northerners and Romans alike know that tripe is tripe and can be plain delicious. Cooking meat in Rome wasn't just about discovery, it was about the rediscovery of the dishes of my childhood, or some of them at least. I was reminded of something I'd once read: that cooks inherit a food tradition, or choose to follow one, or both. My inherited traditions were those of my northern English family; the ones I chose to follow were those of the city I found myself in—Rome. It was in cooking meat that the two seemed to meet, or rather collide, in a small, breeze-ventilated kitchen in Testaccio.

Good Roman cooking, like any good, popular cooking, is homely and rooted in tradition. It is simple and, unlike me, unpretentious. It makes virtue out of necessity and makes things taste as good as they possibly can. These characteristics are particularly apparent when it comes to meat, which is cooked simply and resourcefully, making a little go a long way and letting nothing go to waste. This part of the book is about these discoveries, the not-so-secret revelations of garlic and chile, the tomato sauce and the strategically placed sage leaf. It's also about the rediscoveries, the dishes I wanted to make because in some way they reminded me of home—after all, food is about making connections—but most of all it is about the way I like to eat.

It's nine o'clock on a Tuesday morning and I've drunk too much coffee. The man in front of me, who must be in his late seventies and reminds me of my uncle Frank, slight and spritely with a cigarette pinched between thumb and index finger, is buying three *etti* (300 g) of tripe. Roberta folds the pale honeycomb pieces into a clear plastic bag, which she then spins and knots. To my right, a woman I recognize from the pharmacy, and who seems undressed without her white coat, is buying liver and veal for *spezzatino*. "Everyone is home for dinner," she notes, "so give me enough for six." At the other end of the long counter, Mauro is serving a woman sausages and rib tips (Romans call them *spuntature*), which I imagine will be cooked together for a rich stew. As I wait in front of folds of tripe and dark red swathes of liver, the blows of the cleaver and slow grind of the meat grinder fill out the hiss and clatter of saucers from the bar nearby. Luca balances on the lip at the bottom of the counter. He peers through the glass, his breath leaving a tiny cloud, and whispers, "*meat*."

My butcher's shop, Sartor, began life as a chair in the open market from which Mauro's grandmother sold chicken and lamb. Eighty-five years later, the stall is one of the most significant in the market. The family have more or less set positions behind the double-fronted glass counter: father Mauro at the far left manages the pork and lamb; Roberta, his wife, handles birds and rabbit; their eldest son, Daniele, who is unmistakably his parents' son, with his mother's smile and his father's slant to the eye, oversees the beef. Enrico is usually at the far end with the veal. He isn't family but almost is, having worked there since the day when, 26 years ago and at age 14, he refused to go to school, and Roberta appeased his distraught mother by giving him a chance. They are all good butchers and good people. They are skilled, courteous, and have seemingly nothing to hide, so are only too happy to share their knowledge, to explain why and how.

It was Mauro who first served me more than nine years ago when, having just moved into my new flat right next to the old market, I visited the stall for the first time to buy a lamb chop. He sized me up politely but quizzically, anticipating a miscommunication. I confirmed his suspicions by uncertainly repeating the word I had looked up in the dictionary three times: "*Costolette. Costolette. Costolette.*" On the third attempt he understood. "*Solo una?*" ("Just one?"), he said, holding up his index finger. "*Si,*" I said, returning the gesture, which made me feel even more feeble. A woman next to me

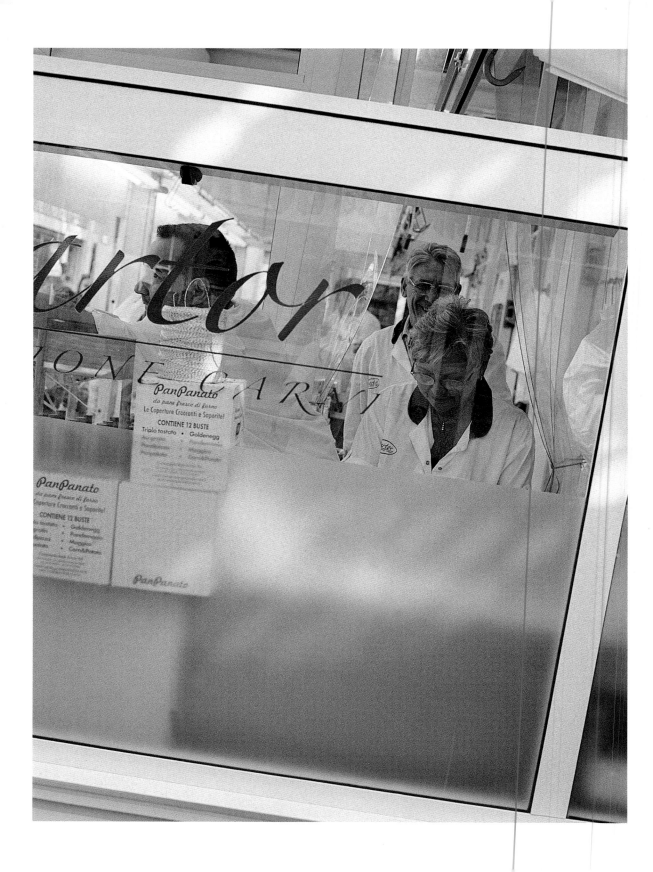

was engaged in some serious shopping, on the counter before her a mound of neatly wrapped packets. "*Solo una*," Mauro repeated, just before his cleaver hit and then flattened the meat against the thick wooden board—*thwack*. At which point I understood his insistence: the chop, or rather cutlet, was tiny, a mouthful of pink flesh attached by a seam of fat to a slim rib. From where I was standing I imagined that, once cooked, I could eat three, four, five even, given the amount of packing and unpacking I had done that day. But it was too late, I couldn't remember one useful word. "*Si*," I said and Mauro handed me my small parcel. "*Mangiano poco, queste donne Americane*," ("they eat little, these American women") he said, and everybody laughed as if I had proved a point. I wanted to tell them I was English and could eat 10 of his *costolette*.

Agnello alla scottadito
Grilled lamb chops

More than 3,000 years ago, the very first Romans were shepherds. Sheep grazed in this part of the city until 150 years ago, despite edicts forbidding them within the ancient city walls. Lamb, mostly very young suckling lamb (*abbacchio*), is still a Roman favorite, especially at Easter time, when it's roasted with potatoes, braised with rosemary and garlic, or its cutlets are dipped in bread crumbs and then fried until golden, or grilled *scottadito:* so hot that they burn (*scotta*) your finger (*dito*).

It's rare to find such young lamb outside Rome, so the following recipe, although inspired by the Roman *abbacchio alla scottadito*, is appropriate for small lamb chops, the kind I find (and miss) in England. The chops need to marinate in olive oil, salt, pepper, and rosemary for about an hour before being cooked on a very hot grill for a few minutes on each side. If you want to burn your fingers, you need to grab the chops as soon as they come out of the pan, which means having warm plates, people, and filled wineglasses at the ready. In Rome, lamb cooked this way is usually served with nothing more than a wedge of lemon. I also like new potatoes and a big spoonful of the glorious green sauce that is *salsa verde*.

serves as many as you like
2 small, ¾-inch-thick lamb chops or cutlets per person
salt and freshly ground black pepper
a sprig of rosemary, chopped

extra-virgin olive oil, to marinate
boiled new potatoes and salsa verde (page 268), to serve

Put the lamb chops in a shallow dish, season with salt and pepper, add the rosemary and a good amount of olive oil, and leave the chops to marinate, turning them from time to time, for 1 hour.

Heat a grill pan or frying pan until it is very hot, then grill the chops, without pressing them down, for 3 minutes on one side, then 3 on the other, by which point they should be burnished on the outside but tender and pink inside. Lift onto a warmed plate and serve immediately.

A plain broiled fat pork chop has long been a favorite in both
England and Italy. The pork has to be good: Gloucester Old Spot or
Tamworth back in England, or *cinta senese* in Italy, the black pig with
the white stripe that my pork butcher has from time to time. If I'm
not broiling them plain I like to marinate the chops in a mixture of
fennel and crushed juniper berries, an idea from Elizabeth David's
book *Italian Food*, which, far from being overpowering, is extremely
companionable. The gentle aniseed from the fennel and the spicy
woodiness of the juniper are flavors I seem to use more and more
these days.

It's a tidy dish to make, in that you marinate the chops in a
shallow ovenproof dish that can be put straight under the broiler
and then brought to the table. The chops need nothing more than a
green or bitter leaf salad, some fresh bread to mop up the juices
and a glass of red wine with good tannins and a spicy nature, such
as a Cirò from Calabria.

serves 2
a small bulb of fennel with fronds
1 garlic clove
4 juniper berries
salt and freshly ground black pepper
extra-virgin olive oil, to marinate
2 large pork chops

Chop the fennel and garlic and crush the juniper berries. Put them
in a shallow ovenproof dish and season with salt and pepper. Pour
over a good amount of olive oil. Put the pork chops in the dish and
leave them to marinate for 3 hours, turning them from time to time.

Preheat the broiler to high. Slide the dish under the broiler and
broil the chops for about 20 minutes, turning them at least twice.
In the absence of a broiler, you can also roast them at 400°F in the
oven, turning them twice (you won't get the same golden color, but
they still cook beautifully). Once cooked, bring the dish to the table
and serve the chops from it, spooning over some of the juices. Mop
up the remaining juices with bread.

Straccetti di manzo con rughetta e Parmigiano
Sautéed beef with arugula and Parmesan

A *straccio,* which comes from the verb *stracciare* (to rip), was traditionally a rag cloth made from old clothes or sheets. I have inherited my granny's and mum's fetish for rags: old T-shirts for the windows, a silk shirt streaked with Rioja for polishing, threadbare cotton sheets ripped into squares for everything else. Today the word *straccio* is also used for kitchen cloths, particularly the coarse cotton ones for the kitchen floor. *Straccetti* are little rags, so to make *straccetti di manzo* you rip very thin pieces of lean beef into rag-like pieces, rub them with olive oil, and cook them swiftly in a hot pan until they curl and shrink and look even more like old rags, but taste anything but, especially when eaten with arugula and curls of Parmesan cheese.

Pan-fried beef, apart from being beefy, has a salty, umami-ish quality, and good Parmesan does too, which makes them a charismatic pair, especially when placed on a grass-green weave of peppery arugula leaves, the juices from the pan providing

the dressing. I love the way the arugula begins like a teenager, offering resistance and kick, but then as the warmth of the beef sets in and you muddle everything with your knife and fork, the leaves start cooperating enough to wrap themselves around the rags of beef, catching warm curls of cheese as they go. By the time you reach the last few mouthfuls you're torn, a bit like when you approach the last pages of a good book: a greedy gallop to the finish, or a rein-in to savor every last bit? The last few leaves should have collapsed into a pile to be scooped up with your fingers. It's ridiculously delicious food, and fast too, which makes it one of my favorite speedy solo suppers after toast, butter, and anchovies.

serves 2

10½–14 ounces lean steak, such as rump, very thinly sliced with the grain (I ask my butcher to do this, or you can freeze it to help you slice it very thinly)
extra-virgin olive oil, for marinating and cooking
salt and freshly ground black pepper
a bunch of arugula
Parmesan, to serve
lemon wedges, to serve

Tear the steak into smallish pieces (rags) and put them in a bowl. Pour over a couple of tablespoons of olive oil, season with salt and pepper, toss well with your hands, and leave to sit for 5 minutes. Meanwhile, wash and dry the arugula and divide it between 2 plates.

Warm 1 tablespoon olive oil in a frying pan over medium-high heat, add the beef and the oily juices from the bowl, and sauté briskly until it is just colored, but still a little pink in places, which will take a matter of seconds. Divide the meat between the plates, spooning over any juices, then use a vegetable peeler to pare curls of Parmesan over the beef and arugula. Pour over a little more olive oil if you think it needs it, and serve with a wedge of lemon.

Saltimbocca alla romana
Veal rolls with prosciutto and sage

It's a wonderful thought that something could be so appetizing that it literally jumps from the plate into your mouth. This is the promise of *saltimbocca*, which literally means "jump" (*salt*) "in" (*im*) "the mouth" (*bocca*), an inspired combination of veal, prosciutto, sage, butter, and wine. Having jumped, the tender veal, salty prosciutto, musty sage leaf, and buttery sauce stop being so energetic and roll around the mouth instead.

The veal must be thin, and the prosciutto just slightly smaller than the veal. You pin the silvery-green sage leaf to the veal and prosciutto with a toothpick in much the same way as you would a brooch, which means that I often think, rather incongruously, of my grandmother, who was never without a brooch on her lapel. Traditionally, the veal would be dusted with flour, which thickens the sauce. I prefer not to dust, but you might like to. It is worth experimenting with both ways. If *saltimbocca* really is to jump and roll, I think it needs to be eaten almost immediately. The best *saltimbocca* I've made was for two people: four slices pinned, sautéed, and slid onto warmed plates on the table just steps from the stovetop. You need bread to mop up the juices and a glass of something dry, white, and—working on the principle that local food goes with local wine—from this part of Italy, such as a Marino or a Frascati.

The detail in the recipe and the hands in the pictures are Carla's, a woman from Testaccio whose market-shopping prowess I admired from a distance for years. We met officially at our fruit-and-vegetable stall, when she reprimanded me for asking for radishes out of season. She picked me up again at the butcher when I asked for a particular cut of veal, at which point I asked her how she made *saltimbocca*. The next day she invited herself into my kitchen to show me. It is her touches, the nicks around the edge of the veal, the split sage leaf, the pan dotted with butter, that make all the difference.

serves 2

4 slices veal, about 2¾ ounces each (they should be quite thin,
 about ⅛ inch; ask your butcher or pound them yourself)
salt and freshly ground black pepper
4 slices prosciutto
4 sage leaves
butter, for frying
about ½ cup white wine

Working with one slice of veal at a time, make 6 or so little nicks with a knife around the edge; this stops it from curling up as it cooks. Season with salt and pepper, place a slice of prosciutto on top, and attach a sage leaf with a toothpick or cocktail skewer. Carla notes that you can rip the leaf in half and pin two pieces, which distributes the distinctive sage flavor even better.

Dot a frying pan with butter. Once the butter foams, add as many slices of veal, sage-side up, as the pan can accommodate comfortably in a single layer. Fry for 2 minutes on one side, then turn it over and fry for 2 more on the other. Transfer to a warmed plate and fry the remaining slices in the same way, adding a little more butter if necessary.

Add another knob of butter to the pan, and once it has melted, add a little wine. While it bubbles and evaporates, scrape the meat juices into the buttery sauce. Serve each person 2 saltimbocca slices with a little of the buttery sauce.

Salsicce con fagioli
White beans with sage and sausages

This is perhaps my favorite dish for one of my favorite beans: small, creamy-white cannellini. The combination of beans, some whole and some reduced to a puree, scented faintly with bay and more intensely with sage, and good sausages is a particularly good one.

Although you can use ever-helpful and time-saving canned beans, it really is worth soaking and cooking your own beans for this dish. They not only have a better flavor and consistency, but

cooking your own also means you can add a couple of bay leaves to the pan, which lend a fragrant and piney note. It also means you have the benefit of the cloudy, starchy bean-cooking water, a little of which, along with the olive oil, gives the beans a creamy texture. It's important to fry the garlic and sage in plenty of olive oil. The cloves and leaves should sizzle gently in a coat of tiny bubbles until their scent rises fragrantly from the pan. If you come over for dinner there is a very good chance I will serve you this, made with dark *cinta senese* sausages. If you want to bring wine, a bottle of a Montepulciano d'Abruzzo would be nice.

serves 4

2¾ cups dried cannellini beans, soaked in plenty
of cold water for 12 hours
2 bay leaves
salt
8 good sausages
2 garlic cloves
6 tablespoons olive oil
6 sage leaves
freshly ground black pepper

Rinse the soaked beans, tip them into a large, heavy pan, add enough cold water to cover them by at least 3 inches, and add the bay leaves. Bring to a boil, then reduce the heat to a low simmer and cook until the beans are tender, which should take about 1 hour, but will depend on the age of the beans. Once the beans are cooked, stir in a generous pinch of salt and leave them to cool in their liquid. This can be done the morning or day before.

Grill or pan-fry the sausages. Peel and smash the garlic with the back of a knife. In a large frying pan or sauté pan, warm the olive oil and cook the garlic and sage leaves until fragrant and golden. Use a slotted spoon to ladle the beans from their cooking water into the pan and stir until the beans are warmed through and coated with oil. Transfer about one-third of the beans from the pan to a bowl, add a couple of tablespoons of their cooking water (save the rest for soup), and either mash them by hand or use an immersion blender to reduce them to a smooth paste, then return them to the pan. Taste and season with salt and pepper. Slice each sausage into 3 pieces, arrange 6 slices on a pile of beans, and serve immediately.

The connection

I grew up in Harpenden, a smallish town just north of London, which had six butchers. My mum, like her mum, was particular and demanded good meat with all the right credentials. So we traveled to the farthest one, Harbour Butchers on Southdown Road, of which I have hazy recollections: the sawdust on the floor, the not-unpleasant smell of fat, hooks against white tiles, Mr. Harbour's striped apron, and the glass cabin across from the counter where Mrs. Harbour sat and collected the money. We were encouraged to peer through the glass counter and our uneasy questions were answered with honesty while we kicked the sawdust. As much attention was given to a rib of beef or rack of lamb as to a cluster of kidneys or a few ounces of liver, and questions and advice were passed across the counter like wrapped packets of meat. Back home, the packets were unwrapped and more questions asked and answered. If Grandma Roddy was around, which she often was, she would remind us how lucky we were.

We didn't eat meat every day—far from it—but when we did I remember my mum cooking it with care. Lamb chops were trimmed and grilled for tea, a roast on Sunday provided sandwiches or a shepherd's pie on Monday, a chicken was roasted for supper and its remains were made into soup, and kidneys were fried and served on toast. Of course, among all this were also bad school lunches, bad meat, and bad butchers, as well as rejections and refusals passed contagiously among siblings: "I don't like tongue," I announced. "I don't like tongue either," said Ben. "I hate tongue," piped up Rosie. In fact, unlike me, Rosie really did hate tongue—most meat, actually—which is why she became a vegetarian at age 12 and has remained so ever since. But refusals aside, the foundations were laid: good quality, varied meat, but not too much of it, bought from a good butcher and cooked simply.

Perhaps even more vividly than my mum I remember Grandma Roddy, who although not a natural cook was a capable, thoughtful, and resourceful one. She (Phyllis) was a wiz at turning a few ounces of ground meat into tattie hash, at boiling and then pressing a tongue to be sliced warm with new potatoes or cold for sandwiches. I also remember Granny Alice cooking meat with her sister May in the kitchen at the back of her pub in Oldham, while shouting at my uncle Colin to "Put that cigarette out right now!"; a piece of braising steak and fat kidneys made into pies, a rib of beef for Sunday lunch around the pub tables, an oxtail made into soup, beef boiled with carrots until the meat was so tender you could almost cut it with a spoon.

Lesso o allesso
Boiled beef and carrots

Sergio reminds me of someone, only I can't remember who: a film star, a schoolteacher, the man at the garage two doors down? This fact has been niggling me for the past two years, ever since he opened what is now the third-best stall in the market, in my opinion, after my fruit-and-vegetable stall and my butcher. The idea is so obvious and brilliant that it seems extraordinary that nobody had thought of it before: to make traditional Roman dishes, like boiled beef, chicken with tomato sauce, boiled tongue with green sauce, or oxtail stew, and serve them in sandwiches. He has been lauded with prizes and praise but the best reward is the sure sign of decent grub in Rome: a constant and dedicated queue of students, workers, suits, journalists, locals, and tourists who wait patiently and impatiently for his sandwiches every lunchtime.

I find it almost impossible to order anything except his boiled beef sandwich, which might sound plain but is actually a wonderful thing consisting of beef cooked for hours with masses of aromatics until it is falling apart, tenderly squashed between a soft, flat roll that has been dipped in meat broth. It is elemental, visceral, satisfying food, best eaten sitting on a bench in the sun looking up at the urban wilderness capping Monte Testaccio. When people visit me in Rome and I take them to all my most trusted places (Cesare, La Torricella, La Gatta Mangiona), I also take them here, and it's often the place they talk about most. What's even more fitting is how similar this boiled beef is to the one made by Grandma Roddy and Auntie May, who coincidentally also served sandwiches to hungry and particular regulars at the pub. Their beef, though, wasn't destined for sandwiches, but for a warm plate with a few boiled potatoes, which you would mash with the back of your fork so they provided a bed for the meat broth and a soft partner for the meat.

The recipe that follows is a hybrid of the two, and can be served both ways: for lunch and dinner with carrots and boiled potatoes, and the next day, when the beef is even better, served as Sergio does, stuffed in a bread roll that you have dipped in the broth and with a very cold beer.

serves 4 for lunch, with leftovers for 2 sandwiches

3¼ pounds beef brisket in one piece
a bunch of flat-leaf parsley
3 celery stalks, chopped into large pieces
8 carrots
6 small onions
2 bay leaves
3 black peppercorns
salt

Put the meat in a pan large enough to accommodate it with all the vegetables and cover it with cold water. Bring to a boil, skim off any scum that rises to the top, and add the parsley, celery, one of the carrots, one of the onions, the bay leaves, peppercorns, and a big pinch of salt. Reduce the heat to a very gentle simmer and cook for about 4 hours.

After 3 hours, add the rest of the onions and carrots. After about 3½ hours, prod the meat with a knife to see how it's doing; it should be very tender. Check the vegetables too, which should be soft; if they feel done before the meat is, remove them and keep simmering the meat very gently.

To serve it with potatoes: since the meat is best kept in its broth, I would serve it up on warmed plates in the kitchen, giving everyone a couple of slices of beef (it won't cut neatly), a couple of carrots, an onion, some plain boiled potatoes, cooked separately, and a ladle of broth.

To serve it in sandwiches: gently reheat the meat in a smaller pan with some of the broth. Once the meat is just warm, split open a bread roll, spoon a little broth on one side, lay over a couple of raggy slices of beef, season with salt, put on the lid, squash into manageability, and eat.

I have a collection of essays by the Italian food writer Massimo Montanari called *Let the Meatballs Rest*. In the introduction he describes making meatballs in the kitchen one evening from boiled meat, bread crumbs, eggs, and salt and pepper, shaping them and then arranging them on a plate. He goes on to describe how Marina, to whom we are not introduced any further, suggests leaving the meatballs to rest for two hours, during which time they firm up and the flavors are thoroughly combined.

Leaving the meatballs to rest, it occurs to him, is similar to what takes place in our mind when we work out an idea. Ideas, he proposes, are the results of various ingredients, of suggestions, reflections, experience, and encounters that come together and form a new thought. We can, of course, act upon this thought immediately, but it's more useful to let the newly mixed ingredients rest, to become blended and firm up. "The resting of meatballs," he says, "is like the resting of thoughts: after a while, they turn out better."

Polpette al sugo
Meatballs in tomato sauce

I like making meatballs nearly as much as I like eating them. The forgiving proportions, the easy squish and squash of it all, the fact that mixing and molding the balls requires only half of your attention, allowing the rest to wander off somewhere else, a kitchen conversation or another episode of *Desert Island Discs*, perhaps.

I like a mixture of pork and beef, half and half ideally, but any proportions will do. I also like the addition of bread crumbs soaked in milk for precisely the reason that some people don't like the addition of bread crumbs soaked in milk: they give the meatballs a slightly bready plumpness. I sometimes add an onion cooked gently in olive oil, which lends a nice savory dimension, but it is a step easily omitted and one pan less to wash if so. Parmesan, in my opinion, is crucial, as is finely chopped parsley, mint if I have some, and a grating of nutmeg.

Baking the meatballs in the oven for 10 minutes is a fairly recent habit to which I am now pretty devoted. The meatballs cook more evenly and don't break up, are leaner, and poach better in the sauce, although I'm not sure Vincenzo's *nonna*, who makes the best *polpette* in the village, would agree. You can fry them if you wish. I make small meatballs to serve with spaghetti, a gastronomic sin to some Italians, although not the ones I have dinner with. I serve larger ones alone with bread or alongside mashed potatoes or rice, ideally with a glass of Sicilian red wine. I usually double this recipe and freeze half the meatballs on a baking sheet and then, once solid, freeze them in bags of six.

makes 12–15
1⅓ cups fresh bread crumbs, preferably from stale bread
¼ cup milk
14 ounces ground beef
7 ounces ground pork, or a fat sausage
1 egg
⅓ cup grated Parmesan
a grating of nutmeg
2 tablespoons finely chopped flat-leaf parsley and mint
salt and freshly ground black pepper

for the sauce:
2 (14.5-ounce) cans plum tomatoes
1 garlic clove
3 tablespoons olive oil
2 bay leaves

Preheat the oven to 425°F and grease a baking sheet. Put the bread crumbs in a small bowl with the milk and leave it for 10 minutes, or until the bread absorbs the milk. Mix together all the ingredients for the meatballs and season with salt and pepper. Using your hands, mold the mixture into roughly 1½-ounce balls if you are eating them alone or with mash or rice, or ¾-ounce balls for eating with pasta (you could weigh the first one to get an idea). Put the balls on the prepared baking sheet and bake for 15 minutes for big ones or 8 minutes for small ones, turning them once, until they are just starting to brown. Alternatively, fry the *polpette* in a sauté pan in a little olive oil, turning them carefully until evenly browned.

Meanwhile, make the tomato sauce. Coarsely chop the tomatoes or pass them through a food mill. Crush the garlic with the back of a knife. Heat the oil in a large, deep frying pan, add the garlic, and cook gently over low heat until the scent rises up from the pan. Add the tomato and bay leaves and simmer for 15 minutes, stirring and breaking the tomatoes up further with the back of a wooden spoon, until the sauce is thick. Season with salt and pepper, then add the meatballs and cook them in the sauce for a further 15 minutes.

Serve alone with bread on the side, or with mashed potatoes or rice. If you are serving them with pasta, transfer the meatballs from the sauce with a slotted spoon to a warm plate. Mix the sauce with cooked drained spaghetti in a wide bowl, then dot with the meatballs and serve.

Involtini al sugo
Beef rolls in tomato sauce

The word *involtino* comes from the verb *avvolgere* (to wrap) and the suffix -*ino* means little, so literally translated it means "little packet or parcel." The technique is not dissimilar from swaddling a baby: roll, tuck, roll (if your baby is willing, that is, which mine wasn't—while the other babies in the maternity ward were wrapped into contented little parcels, Luca assumed a star position and bleated until he was bright red and the wrapping stopped).

Involtini can be made with slices of meat, fish, or vegetables. Regional variations are infinite, as are the dialect terms to describe them. In Rome, *involtini* are usually made with beef, and most trattorias have *involtini al sugo* on the menu. For years I overlooked them dismissively, until on a friend's recommendation I ordered them at Cesare, a trattoria I'd also walked past dismissively until it was recommended by the same friend, and has since become a favorite. At Cesare the *involtini* are classic: slices of beef and possibly prosciutto wrapped around a tidy bundle of carrot and celery batons, secured with a toothpick and simmered until tender in tomato sauce. They are small, so you are served three. At another favorite trattoria, La Torricella, you are brought one large solitary *involtino,* which also has a layer of prosciutto. In both places they are quietly delicious. I generally make small rolls at home, as they seem easier to simmer to the point of extreme tenderness that's so desirable.

Sometimes, in keeping with the one-preparation-two-courses principle, I use the mahogany-red, meaty sauce to dress some pasta, then we have an *involtino* or two as a separate second course. Other times we have *involtini* with mashed potatoes, which provide a bolstering and buttery foil to the tender beef, savory bundle, and richly flavored sauce. Like most braises, *involtini* are better after having sat for a few hours, and better still the next day.

serves 4 (2 each, with 2 extra to argue over)

1 large carrot
1 large celery stalk
10 (⅛-inch or so) slices of beef (rump or chuck are ideal)
salt and freshly ground black pepper
2 (14.5-ounce) cans plum tomatoes
3 tablespoons extra-virgin olive oil
½ cup white wine or red wine

Cut the carrot and celery into extremely thin batons that are roughly
the same length as the beef slices are wide. Take a slice of beef, lay
it flat on your work surface, and season it with salt and pepper. Place
a bundle of carrot and celery at the bottom of each beef slice and
roll the beef around the batons, tucking the sides in if you can, until
you have a neat cylinder. Secure the roll with a toothpick along its
length.

Coarsely chop the tomatoes or pass them through a food mill.
Warm the olive oil in a heavy-bottomed frying or sauté pan. Add the
beef rolls and cook them, turning as needed, until browned on all

sides, which will take about 6 minutes. Add the wine to the pan and increase the heat until the wine sizzles and evaporates. Add the tomatoes and stir and nudge the rolls so that they are evenly spaced and well coated. Reduce the heat to medium-low and cook the rolls, partly covered, stirring gently and turning them a couple of times, until the meat is cooked through and tender. This will take 1½–2 hours. Add a little more wine or water if the sauce seems to be drying out too much during the cooking. Let the rolls rest for at least 15 minutes before serving with a spoonful of sauce.

Sausage and cabbage cake

We call this the "majestic oak-tree cabbage and sausage cake" at home. When you turn it out, the cabbage leaf at the bottom becomes the top and its thick rib looks like the trunk and its veins like the branches of an oak tree. The recipe is from one of my favorite chefs, Rowley Leigh, by way of my brother, and has been an unfailing favorite in this Roman kitchen ever since I first made it for the blog four years ago. It's unfailing, too, in its ability to make me think, "What a brilliant idea!"

You need a handsome savoy cabbage, from which you pick seven of the nicest leaves, blanch them, and use them to line a suitable dish. After that, it's all about layers of boiled, buttered, chopped cabbage and sausage meat. You can add a scant sprinkling of fennel seeds too, if you like, as fennel and sausage get on like a house on fire. Be careful as you invert the cake onto the serving plate, as there will be hot, buttery juices. After admiring your tree, it's hard not to marvel at each neat slice too, with its pleasing stripes of green, pink, green, pink, green. I like a big slice of tree cake with buttery mashed potatoes, a dab of strong mustard, and a glass of aromatic white wine like Greco di Tufo from Campania. It's also good with a simple tomato sauce.

serves 6

1 large savoy cabbage
2 tablespoons olive oil
½ teaspoon fennel seeds
salt and freshly ground black pepper
1½ tablespoons butter
about 1 pound very lean, well-seasoned sausage (without casings)

Remove 7 of the largest, handsomest outer leaves (discard any that are discolored or damaged) and wash them carefully. Bring a large pot of salted water to a boil and add the chosen leaves. Wait for the water to come back to a boil, then blanch the leaves for 2 minutes. Use a slotted spoon to remove the leaves and drain in a colander in the sink, rinsing with very cold water to fix the color. Drain them well and spread them out flat to dry thoroughly on paper towels. Set them aside.

Cut the rest of the cabbage into quarters and bring the same water back to a boil. Cook the cabbage quarters in the boiling water for 5 minutes, by which time the leaves should be tender but the stems still firm. Drain the cabbage, rinse with cold water, drain again, and squeeze out any excess water. Cut away the hard central stem and separate the leaves into a bowl. Dress them with olive oil and fennel seeds and season with salt and pepper.

Preheat the oven to 350°F and grease an 8-inch round shallow ovenproof dish with half the butter. Choose the largest and best-looking leaf from the 7 you have set aside and place it in the bottom of the dish. It should cover the base and come up the sides. Arrange the other 6 leaves so that they cover the sides of the dish, fanned out, overlapping a lot and hanging over the edges.

Using a third of the seasoned cabbage, make a layer at the bottom of the dish and cover with half the sausage, pressing it down so it molds into the dish. Repeat the process, ending with a third layer of cabbage leaves. Press everything into the dish. Fold and bring in the overlapping leaves to cover the top and make a neat packet. Dot with the remaining butter and bake for 1 hour.

Remove and allow the cake to stand for 5 minutes before inverting a serving plate on top of the baking dish and turning out the cake. Be careful, and do this over the sink, as there will be hot juices.

Spezzatino di vitello
Braised veal with celery

My former actress self would have been mortified to hear that she was going to end up teaching English to children through music and theater. Fortunately I left her behind at the airport nine years ago, so she will never know how much I enjoy singing a pseudo-folk version of "Eensy-Weensy Spider" to three-year-olds on a Wednesday morning in the park. The pseudo bit is me and the folk bit is Diego, the man whose guitar keeps me in tune, and who talks me through how to cook braised veal with celery as we walk across the park after a lesson.

I think this dish sums up much about Roman cooking: it's simple, clever, homely, rooted in popular tradition, and really sensual. A good pan with a tight lid is important, as the veal needs to simmer very gently. I like the way the veal seizes slightly at first but then, given time, the influence of the wine and veal juices and a little more hot water if the pan seems to be getting dry, relaxes into tenderness. In Rome, potatoes, root vegetables, and peas are often added at an appropriate point in the cooking process, making a satisfying whole. I prefer the veal just with celery, and either served alone with bread to mop up the juices or (predictably) with mashed potatoes.

serves 4
1½ pounds braising veal, such as shoulder
1 onion
6 celery stalks
4 tablespoons extra-virgin olive oil
1 cup white wine
salt and freshly ground black pepper

If your butcher has not already done so, cut the meat into 2-inch cubes. Dice the onion and slice 1 celery stalk crosswise. In a large deep sauté pan or casserole dish with a lid, heat the olive oil. Add the onion and celery and cook for 1–2 minutes, until softened. Add the meat, increase the heat, and brown it on all sides.

Add the wine and let it sizzle for a minute or so, then cover the pan, reduce the heat, and leave the meat to simmer gently for 1½ hours. Meanwhile, chop the remaining celery into 2¾-inch lengths and add them to the pan after 45 minutes. Keep checking the pan; if at any point it seems dry, add a little boiling water. It's ready when the meat is extremely tender, the celery is soft, and the liquid has reduced to a tasty and thick gravy.

Pollo alla romana con peperoni
Chicken with tomatoes and sweet red peppers

The front door of my first flat in Testaccio opened onto a narrow walkway suspended over an internal courtyard. The courtyard itself was a sort of vortex that drew in the scents and smells from the bakery and trattoria on the first floor, then spun them upward, past 28 apartments on five floors, and into the Roman sky. In the morning it was the scent of bread and *pizza bianca* that swirled past our third-floor flat, mingling amicably with coffee smells gathered from the morning pots brewing in flats on the first and second floors. At about ten o'clock, the trattoria occupying the lower right-hand corner of the building began preparations for lunch. Often the smell was of boiled greens: vegetal, vaguely sulfurous and reminiscent of school. It seemed sent purposely to challenge any romantic illusions about Italy I might be harboring while leaning over the balcony. Then, as if to make up for the intrusion, there would be the scent of frying pancetta, garlic and rosemary in olive oil, or better still, the sweet waft of red peppers simmering for what I imagined was *pollo alla romana con peperoni.*

Traditionally, the chicken and tomatoes are cooked in one pan and the peppers in another, and then they are united to create this glorious, classic Roman dish. Simpler, marginally lighter, and I think nicer (which could be construed as Roman gastronomic blasphemy) is this version, in which you roast the peppers in the oven, or, if you are brave enough, char them over a flame on the stovetop. Once the chicken is tender and the tomato sauce is thick, you add the red peppers torn into strips, cook it for a little while longer, then let everything sit for at least an hour so the flavors can get acquainted with one another. Its depth of flavor and smoky complexity never fails to please me. It's a summer dish in Rome, and since most Romans are convinced that they can't digest peppers after three o'clock, it's eaten for lunch, and usually warm rather than hot so that the flavors are at their most sultry. Bread is provided to mop up the juices, along with a glass of young, flavorful red like Cesanese from Lazio. I also like it for supper with mashed potatoes, rice, or couscous.

serves 4

3 tablespoons olive oil
2 ounces pancetta, diced (optional)
2¾ pounds chicken, either a nice plump whole chicken cut into 8 pieces, or chicken thighs

salt and freshly ground black pepper
½ cup dry white wine
1¼ pounds canned plum tomatoes with their juice,
   or fresh tomatoes, peeled
1 plump garlic clove (optional)
a sprig of rosemary
4 large red peppers

Heat the oil in a large, heavy-bottomed casserole dish or deep sauté pan, add the pancetta, if using, and cook until it renders its fat.

Add the chicken pieces, skin-side down, and cook until the skin forms a golden crust, then turn them over and brown the other sides.

Season with salt and several grindings of black pepper, add the wine, and let it bubble away until most of it has evaporated. Meanwhile, coarsely chop the tomatoes, gently crush the garlic with the back of a knife, and roughly chop the rosemary. Add them to the pan, stir, and cook, covered, over moderate heat. Keep an eagle eye on the pan for the first 10 minutes, stirring every now and then to prevent sticking. Once everything has gotten going, half cover the pan and cook for another 45 minutes, or until the tomatoes have reduced into a dense, rich sauce and the chicken is tender. If at any point the sauce seems too thick, add a little water.

While the chicken and tomatoes are cooking, preheat the oven to 400°F. Roast the peppers for about 45 minutes, turning them every now and then, until they are soft, blistered, charred, and floppy, at which point tip them into a bowl and cover it tightly with plastic wrap. Leave them to steam for 10 minutes, by which time the skins should be easy to peel away. Discard the skins, seeds, stem, and pith. Cut or tear the peppers into thick strips and stir them into the chicken. Cook over low heat for another 5 minutes so that the flavors have a chance to mingle.

Allow the pan to sit for about 15 minutes, or better still for an hour or several. You can serve it at room temperature or reheat it over low heat until warm, but not hot.

Pollo o coniglio alla cacciatora
Chicken or rabbit, hunters' style

If I go to Bar Barberini at about four o'clock, there's a good chance I will meet Donato, the affable cook and manager of Volpetti Più, the canteen-like *tavola calda* (café) where we have our lunch one day most weeks. Standing at Barberini's sickle-shaped bar, with the clatter of cups and hiss of the espresso machine in the background, Donato has explained exuberantly how he makes lasagne, *pasta e ceci*, batter for *fritti* and—most important—his excellent chicken or rabbit *alla cacciatora* (hunters' style).

Unlike other versions of this dish, which include tomatoes, onions, and red peppers, Donato's is extremely simple and fragrant. Very good chicken or rabbit is browned and then simmered until tender with white wine and finely chopped rosemary, chile, and garlic, and the dish is finished with a tablespoon of vinegar and some black olives. Just the thought of preparing this dish makes me happy, not just because any dish that requires a glass of wine for the pan requires one for the cook, but because of the roaring scent of garlic and rosemary rising up from the cutting board, the golden crust on the meat, the *whoosh* the wine makes as it hits the hot pan, and the warm scent that fills the kitchen as the dish bubbles away. The vinegar may sound like an odd addition, but it works beautifully by sharpening the edges of the dish, making it bolder and more defined. It is, of course, optional, as are the olives.

It's impossible to give precise timings, since so much depends on the meat. My butcher Roberta, who rather reassuringly makes her chicken and rabbit *alla cacciatora* in much the same way as Donato, notes that a cage-raised animal will cook in almost half the time of a free-range one. She also notes that while the meat is cooking you must make sure that both the pan and cook have enough wine, and scrape the meat juices every now and then from the bottom of the pan into the gravy, which should coat the pieces.

As for the wine, more often than not I use a white wine from the Marche region of Italy called Verdicchio dei Castelli di Jesi, which is dry and fragrant and works well, both in the dish and for drinking with it (if the cook hasn't finished the entire bottle, that is). I generally serve it with a green vegetable, fine green beans being a favorite, or a green salad and some bread for mopping up juices.

serves 4
1 (3¼–4½-pound) chicken or rabbit
5 tablespoons olive oil
2 garlic cloves
1 chile pepper, or 1 teaspoon red pepper flakes
a sprig of rosemary
1 cup white wine, plus extra if needed
salt and freshly ground black pepper
1 tablespoon red wine vinegar
a handful of pitted black olives

Cut the chicken or rabbit into 12 pieces (I ask my butcher to do this). In a deep sauté pan or casserole dish with a lid that's large enough to fit the meat in a snug single layer, warm the olive oil over medium heat. Add the meat pieces, skin-side down, and cook until the skin forms a golden crust, then turn them over and do the same on the other side. This will take about 20 minutes.

While the meat is browning, very finely chop the garlic, chile, and leaves from the rosemary sprig. Once the meat has browned, sprinkle in the chopped garlic, chile, and rosemary, pour over the white wine, season with salt and pepper, cover the pan, and turn the heat down to low. Cook the meat, turning from time to time, until the thighs feel very tender when prodded with a fork and the meat is surrounded by a thick gravy. This will take anywhere from 45 minutes to 1¼ hours, depending on the chicken (or rabbit). If the pan seems dry, add a little more wine. In the last minutes of cooking, add the vinegar and olives, stir, and divide among warmed dishes.

Abbacchio al forno con le patate
Roast lamb with potatoes

In my family we weren't religious about traditional Sunday lunch in the way that many people were. We were just as likely to be eating tagine and couscous or a Greek spinach pie with whole eggs in it. However, when Granny Alice or Mum did cook a traditional roast, it was greeted with a hungry roar of approval. Everyone else's favorite was roast beef and all the trimmings, but mine was a shoulder of English lamb with roast potatoes. Especially when it was cooked by Alice, my mum's mum and my second namesake.

We English are mocked for our plate piling and sea of gravy, especially on Sundays. Granny Alice, however, was not a fan of such plate chaos. She served her lamb generously but simply: a few slices of meat with some crisp and golden potatoes beside it, a spoonful of the juices from the bottom of the pan over the top. Alice would have approved of lamb in Rome, because that's precisely how it's served, usually on Sundays and festive days here. The lamb is much younger, often a small *abbacchio* or suckling lamb. A slim leg with ribs and kidneys attached is perfumed with fresh rosemary and garlic, then cooked in a slow oven with pieces of potato anointed with *strutto* (lard) or olive oil until they are golden and crisp, and the meat is tender and falling off the bone.

serves 4
4½ pounds whole young leg of lamb
3 garlic cloves
several sprigs of fresh rosemary
a slice of lard or 4–6 tablespoons extra-virgin olive oil
salt and freshly ground black pepper
2¼ pounds potatoes

In Rome, they slash the leg of lamb deeply, without cutting through it entirely, to create thick slices. If I have a larger leg, though, I simply make tiny slashes. Place the lamb in a roasting pan large enough to accommodate it with the potatoes. Slice the garlic and break the rosemary into small sprigs. Rub your hands with lard or olive oil, then massage the lamb generously, inserting the slivers of garlic and rosemary into the slashes as you go. By the time you've finished, the lamb should be glistening and scented with garlic and rosemary.

Smear a little lard or oil on the base of the roasting pan, then place the lamb skin-side down in the pan. Season with salt and pepper and leave to rest for 30 minutes or so. Preheat the oven to 350°F.

Cut the potatoes into quarters, rub them with lard or olive oil (hands are best for this), then arrange them around the lamb. Season the potatoes with a little salt. Slide the lamb into the oven. Cook for about 1 hour, basting every so often and turning the leg twice, or until the meat is very tender when prodded with a fork. Very young lamb might need less time and older lamb may need more. Some people like to pour a glass of white wine over the lamb halfway through the cooking time, although in this case I don't, as it tends to make the potatoes soggy. Leave the meat to rest, covered loosely with aluminum foil, for at least 10 minutes, then serve in thick slices with a potato or two and a spoonful of the sticky juices from the bottom of the pan.

The other butcher

The first time we drove across Rome to Bottega Liberati, it felt like a betrayal, a clandestine visit to another butcher. As comeuppance, we got lost twice near Caffarella Park, then caught up in a one-way system that took us back onto the congested Toscolana. Our car, a tin-can Fiat Panda, overheated, as did we. *It'd better be worth it,* we both scowled while Luca howled.

It was. The distinctive double-fronted shop on an ordinary street in south Rome is extraordinary, a beacon for butchery and good food. Father and son Emilio and Roberto Liberati know the origins of every single animal, all of which are organic, and they make butchery look like an art, which of course it is. Congestion and betrayal were quickly forgotten. We were here for *porchetta*.

Porchetta is a large, boneless pork roast typical of Lazio, most notably Ariccia in the province of Rome. The body of the pig is gutted, deboned, and arranged carefully, then seasoned generously with salt, garlic, black pepper, rosemary, and other herbs before being rolled into a log, usually about a yard long, tied, and roasted slowly. It is then served in thick slices, usually sandwiched between two pieces of chewy *pane casareccio* (home-style bread). Made well, porchetta is utterly delicious, the rolled meat swirled with thick swathes of fat, both of which are deeply seasoned, with dark gold skin crisp enough to cut your lip. It's also ubiquitous: most towns and cities have a stall, usually a semipermanent truck with a hatch, awning, and possibly a cluster of plastic chairs at which to sit and eat your sandwich. Porchetta trucks are fixtures at every festival, fair or village *sagra* (local fête), parked in the middle of the benign pandemonium and providing an option for supper. Ubiquity means questionable quality, so you have to be picky about where you buy porchetta. We have several trusted stalls and shops, the best being Il Norcino Bernabei, a drive away in Marino, the home of Vincenzo's oldest friend, Paola. We eat our porchetta panini with cold beer, then wander to see the Fontana dei Quattro Mori.

But back to Bottega Liberati and that first visit. Roberto had prepared the porchetta meat for us, a piece significantly larger than Luca, who was running around the shop. I was slightly overwhelmed by the size. Roberto, a butcher and a gentleman, noted this and offered to sell us only a section, but my inability to say, "Yes, actually it is three times bigger than I imagined," means we were soon heaving a 29-pound porchetta into the trunk, which sagged like a crestfallen dog. Our job was to drive the porchetta across Rome and deliver it to Chris, a friend and chef who was going to season it, roll it, tie it, and cook it in a professional oven for a lunch two days later. The plan was that I would observe the process and then write about it for the book—a plan that fell at the first hurdle because I didn't end up being able to watch the seasoning, rolling, and roasting. I did help eat the porchetta that Chris cooked masterfully, but I quietly shelved the recipe for the book.

A few months later, however, we returned to Liberati, getting caught in the one-way system again for posterity, to watch Roberto prepare a smaller 6½-pound piece of pork. He cut away the ribs from a piece of belly, pulled away certain sections of fat, and trimmed the piece of skin that he would roll back over the pork. He then put a small piece of fillet in the center and seasoned the pork generously with salt, chopped garlic, rosemary, chile, black pepper, and a dusting of fennel pollen, rolled it up, and tied it with string at ¾-inch intervals.

This time I roasted it in my tin-can oven at 325°F for 4½ hours, which meant sliding it into the oven while I ate breakfast. By eleven o'clock, two neighbors were peering through the (open) front door to ask if they were invited. By twelve o'clock we had possibly one of the best roasts I've ever cooked: a burnished roll that sat resting until we ate it cut into big, shaggy slices, the meat in shades of pink and brown swirled with soft, seasoned fat. The next day, the porchetta was every bit as good cold, the meat firmer and the fat in opaque swathes, stuffed into sandwiches with lettuce and mustard.

The next day I told Mauro, my usual Testaccio butcher, somewhat sheepishly about my visits to another butcher for porchetta. The admission was met with both disapproval and approval. "*Come era?*" ("How was it?") he asked. "*Veramente buono*" ("Really good"), I told him. "*Allora, va bene*" ("Well then, that's OK"), he replied before thwacking a lamb chop, and that was that.

Porchetta

Advice about porchetta is plentiful, but this recipe is based on the
one Roberto Liberati prepared for me, and inspired by the porchetta
I've eaten at Il Norcino in Marino. The pork should be the very best
you can afford. You need to enlist your butcher and ask him (or her)
to prepare you a boneless porchetta cut, which is the belly with the
ribs removed and attached to the loin, or a rectangular piece of pork
belly and a pork loin.

    Fennel pollen, with its sweet-citrus and licorice-like flavor, is
an ingredient traditionally foraged, therefore free. Nowadays it

has become rather fashionable and very expensive, which I think negates the beauty of it. If you can't find it easily and at a reasonable price, best to spend your money on fantastic pork and use ground fennel seeds instead, which have the similarly distinctive flavor that works so beautifully with pork. To drink, you want acidity, bubbles, and a strong flavor: a very dry Franciacorta or Lambrusco would be lovely.

serves 6 generously, with leftovers for sandwiches
1 (6½–9-pound) porchetta joint
salt
1 teaspoon black peppercorns, crushed
1 teaspoon red pepper flakes
2 tablespoons chopped rosemary
2 garlic cloves, finely chopped
1 tablespoon ground fennel seeds
  or fennel pollen, if you can find it

Bear in mind that the porchetta needs to rest, once seasoned, for at least 12 hours, and then come back to room temperature before roasting.

Place the pork skin-side down on a clean work surface, season it generously with salt, then massage the salt into the flesh with your fingertips. Sprinkle over the black pepper, red pepper flakes, rosemary, garlic, and fennel. If you are using a loin, place it about 2 inches from one end. Roll the porchetta up as neatly and tightly as possible. Tie it at ¾-inch intervals with kitchen twine. Prick it all over with a trussing needle or the tip of a very sharp knife. Cover the pork, first with wax paper, then with foil, and leave it to rest for at least 12 hours in the fridge.

Remove it from the fridge at least 1 hour before roasting and preheat the oven to 325°F. Use a clean, dry dish cloth to pat the meat very dry and put it on a rack over a large baking sheet. Slide the pork into the middle of the oven and roast for 4½ hours. For the last half an hour, crank the oven up to maximum to crisp the skin, so that it almost ruptures into deep golden crackling. The meat inside will be soft and succulent. Leave the meat to rest, uncovered, for at least half an hour before eating.

The other quarter

To understand something of Testaccio and its *mattatoio* (slaughterhouse) is to understand something of Roman food, and therefore part of the story of Rome. The area itself has been associated with food trading since ancient Roman times, when it was a port and sprawl of warehouses. In fact, Testaccio takes its name from the Monte dei Cocci that rises somnolently at the bottom of the wedge, an extraordinary 115-foot-high, 650-yard-round mound of broken but neatly stacked amphorae dating from the second century. It is now the hub for a cluster of nightclubs that burrow into its base, which means that at night the ancient amphorae jolt in time to drum and bass, Latin jazz, and '80s disco, the ancient and the everyday colliding with almost banal ease.

Until it was developed in the late nineteenth century, Testaccio was an open space, dotted with ruinous clues to its ancient significance and vines producing wine grapes for industrious Romans. It was common land for common people to wander, idle, eat, drink, and during carnivale: wreak havoc. In the 1870s, when Italy was unified and Rome became the capital, a zoning plan turned the former port and open space into a quarter of public housing, factories, and the slaughterhouse. It was supposed to be the ultimate working-class neighborhood, where thousands of immigrants from all over Italy, attracted by the promise of work and the metropolitan lifestyle Rome had to offer, could live.

For the next hundred years the slaughterhouse was quite literally the bloody, beating heart of the quarter, providing work and meat for those who could afford it. The workers, of course, couldn't afford the meat (or much else, since poverty was endemic), but they were paid in kind with the bits nobody else wanted: the offal that made up a fifth of the animal's weight. It was this *quinto quarto* (fifth quarter) that the workers took home to their wives, and that local trattoria owners inventively and resourcefully turned into tasty, sustaining meals.

The uncompromising and distinctive *quinto quarto* cooking is a style that evolved through necessity but continued for posterity, flavor, and because the bits neglected became the bits selected, by some at least. It's a style of cooking that you still find in trattorias and homes: oxtail cooked slowly with celery, tripe with tomato sauce and dusted with pecorino, lamb's offal with artichokes, tongue with green sauce. These are dishes that merit attention, and for some of us a leap beyond misconceptions, squeamishness, and a possible moral crisis, because they are tasty and good, and because they tell a story. This is why they are as much a part (albeit a less frequent one) of this tiny, chaotic Roman-kitchen-of-sorts as freshly baked *pizza bianca,* battered squash blossoms, *pasta e fagioli, spaghetti al pomodoro,* braised beef, artichokes, curls of *puntarelle,* sweet tiny peas and fava beans, ricotta, sour cherries, sweet yeasted buns, strawberry-scented grapes, ugly hazelnut cookies that taste *buono,* and other good things.

My grandpa Gerry would have loved the next three recipes, and so would my grandpa John, even though the tomato with the tripe might have given him heartburn (but then most things gave him heartburn). All my grandparents knew the economic and gastronomic merits of offal, and that if you eat meat it is disingenuous and wasteful not to eat the whole animal. My brother does too; in fact, ever since I moved to Rome and started my blog, he has been pestering me for recipes for oxtail stew, Roman-style tripe, and tongue. Ben, these three are in no small part for you.

Trippa alla romana
Roman-style tripe

Good tripe from a good butcher, cleaned properly and cooked well, has a tender, bizarrely soothing succulence and fragrance that most meats don't even come close to. Three people I trust implicitly and admire when it comes to meat and offal (Fergus Henderson, chef Leonardo Vignoli from trattoria Cesare, and my butcher Roberta) are all champions of tripe. In Rome, tripe is simmered with tomatoes, scented with Roman mint, and dusted with *pecorino romano,* a dish that manages to be both elegant and workaday. I think it's the best introduction to tripe. It's vital you get well-sourced, honeycombed tripe that has been properly cleaned and precooked (unless of course you are prepared to do the preboiling yourself). The best thing is to talk to your butcher.

serves 4
about 1¾ pounds veal honeycomb tripe, cleaned
1 onion
2 slices pancetta
a small handful of mint leaves
1¾ pounds canned plum tomatoes or peeled fresh ones
3 tablespoons extra-virgin olive oil
½ cup white wine
salt and freshly ground black pepper
freshly grated pecorino, to serve

Wash the tripe thoroughly in hot water, drain it, and then plunge it into a pan of boiling water. Let it boil for a few minutes, then drain and allow it to cool enough to handle. Cut the tripe into pieces roughly ⅜ inch wide and ¾ inch long.

Finely dice the onion and pancetta and tear the mint leaves into 2 or 3 pieces if they are large. Chop, puree, or pass the tomatoes through a food mill. In a cast-iron or heavy-bottomed pan large enough to accommodate all the ingredients, warm the olive oil, add the onion, pancetta, and mint, and cook gently until the onion is soft and the pancetta has rendered its fat. Add the tripe, stir, and add the wine. Allow it to bubble for a few minutes. Add the tomatoes, stir, and bring to a slow boil, then reduce the heat to a simmer and cook, covered, for 20–25 minutes, or until the tripe is very tender but still has a slight chewiness. Season with salt and pepper, then serve with a dusting of grated pecorino.

Coda alla vaccinara
Oxtail with tomatoes and celery

Coda alla vaccinara is oxtail cooked in the style of the *vaccinari,* or "cow men," who butchered the animals, and it was born here in Testaccio. It's still one of the most typical and beloved *quinto quarto* dishes, and is served with matter-of-factness in most trattorias and home kitchens.

There are as many versions of *coda* as there are cooks who make it. Almost everyone agrees on the initial boiling of the pieces, then the all-important browning of the meat, which is fundamental to the final flavor. Most people agree on the inclusion of tomato, wine, and lots of celery, but additions like spices or chocolate, which serve to enrich it, are endlessly agreed and disagreed upon. At trattoria Agustarello, Sandro makes a deep, dark *coda* with pine nuts, spices, chocolate, and other secret ingredients. My other favorite *coda* is made by the generous and unsecretive Leonardo at trattoria Cesare, which is simple, with lots of tomato and celery, and very delicious.

If you have never cooked them before, I understand why cooking tails may make you uneasy. But the pieces come from your butcher in short chunks that look no different from ribs, and are just as straightforward to prepare. Oxtail requires time and patience, especially at the beginning: go slowly, letting each piece burnish, scraping up the brown bits stuck to the bottom of the pan and deglazing intently. Let the pan bubble quietly, topping it off with water if need be. I generally make it on Saturday afternoon for good friends I know are going to love it.

Cooked well, *coda* is one of the most luscious and sensual dishes, the tender, glutinous meat falling from the bones, with cartilage to nibble and marrow to suck. You begin with knife and fork, but after a while hands are best, the nobbles of bone making perfect handles. Working on the principle that what grows together goes together, serve it with a big red Lazio such as a Cesanese, or an Aglianico from Basilicata. You'll need lots of bread to mop up the sauce, a green salad to follow, and then chocolate cake.

serves 4

3 ¼ pounds oxtail cut into 2-inch pieces, trimmed of excess fat
1 large white or yellow onion
1 carrot
7 celery stalks
a few flat-leaf parsley sprigs, if you have them
5 tablespoons extra-virgin olive oil
salt
1 cup white or red wine
2 (14.5-ounce) cans plum tomatoes with juice
1 tablespoon tomato paste (optional)
⅓ cup pine nuts
⅓ cup raisins
freshly ground black pepper

First, cover the oxtail with cold water in a pan, bring it to a boil, and simmer for 15 minutes to remove some of the fat that will rise to the surface; skim it away diligently. Drain the oxtail and set it aside. Finely dice the onion, carrot, 1 celery stalk, and the parsley. In a large, heavy-bottomed pan or casserole dish, warm 3 tablespoons of the olive oil, add the vegetables, and cook over low heat for 8–10 minutes, or until soft. Remove the pan from the heat.

In a large frying pan, warm the rest of the oil over medium heat, add the oxtail pieces, in batches if necessary, and brown them for 12 minutes or so, turning them so they color evenly. As the pieces brown, add them to the vegetables and sprinkle with a little salt.

Return the casserole dish to medium heat. Once the pan is hot, add the wine and let it sizzle and evaporate for 5 minutes or so. Coarsely chop the tomatoes, then add them to the pan with their juices and another pinch of salt. The oxtail pieces should be submerged; if they're not, add a little water. Reduce the heat and

leave to simmer very gently for 3 hours, or until the meat is falling off the bones. Keep an eye on the pan, stirring it every now and then and adding a little more hot water if the liquid level is too low. If you're organized, you could keep a small pan of boiling water into which you have stirred a spoonful of tomato paste on the back burner to add as needed.

Meanwhile, cut the remaining celery into 1½-inch pieces and add them 40 minutes before the end of the cooking time. Add the pine nuts and raisins. Stir them until they're well coated, then continue cooking until tender. Taste and season with salt and pepper.

Lingua con salsa verde
Tongue with green sauce

My brother and I both lay claim to the family kitchen heirloom that is Phyllis Roddy's uncompromisingly named tongue press. (The press belonged to my great-grandmother Rachel, who was married to James, who smoked a brand of cigarettes called Three Castles, which had a picture of a boat called the *Saucy Rachel* on the packet.) As I write, the jet-black iron contraption is sitting in a box in Dorset, waiting to claim a place in Mum and Dad's new kitchen. It was in the bowl of this press that, for years and years, Phyllis curled a boiled cow's tongue, then wound down the lid and clamped the press to the table. A few hours later she would unclamp and release a cylinder of neatly pressed tongue that could be sliced and served with buttered bread, pickles, and ice-cold celery.

I understand why people are squeamish about tongue. After all, it looks—unsurprisingly—like a tongue. I am not, however, thanks to Phyllis and now nine years in Testaccio, where tongue is ordinary and appreciated, and cooked simply to delicious effect in a way which, in another nice stroke of kitchen symmetry, is not that different from how Phyllis did it. It is boiled with cloves and bay leaves and plenty of *odori*—carrots, celery, and parsley stems—until tender. Tasty, richly meaty, and with a pleasing firm texture, tongue is served hot, warm, or cold, and most often with *salsa verde* (green sauce). I also like it hot with mashed potatoes, or cold and sliced very thinly with beets, bread and butter, and a dab of English mustard.

> serves 4 with leftovers
> **1 beef tongue, about 3¼ pounds**
> **1 onion**
> **5 cloves**
> **1 leek, cut into 3 pieces**
> **1 carrot, cut into 3 pieces**
> **2 celery stalks, cut into 3 pieces**
> **2 bay leaves**
> **salsa verde (page 268), to serve**

Rinse the tongue, then put it in a large pan and cover it with water by at least 4 inches. Bring to a boil and remove any scum that rises to the surface. Add the onion, cloves, leek, carrot, celery, and bay leaves, reduce the heat, and simmer gently, making sure the tongue remains covered with water, for about 4 hours, by which point it should be very tender when prodded with the point of a knife.

Once the broth has cooled a little, lift out the tongue, peel it, then return it to the broth. Keep the tongue in the broth until you serve it, then slice it thinly and serve with a spoonful of salsa verde.

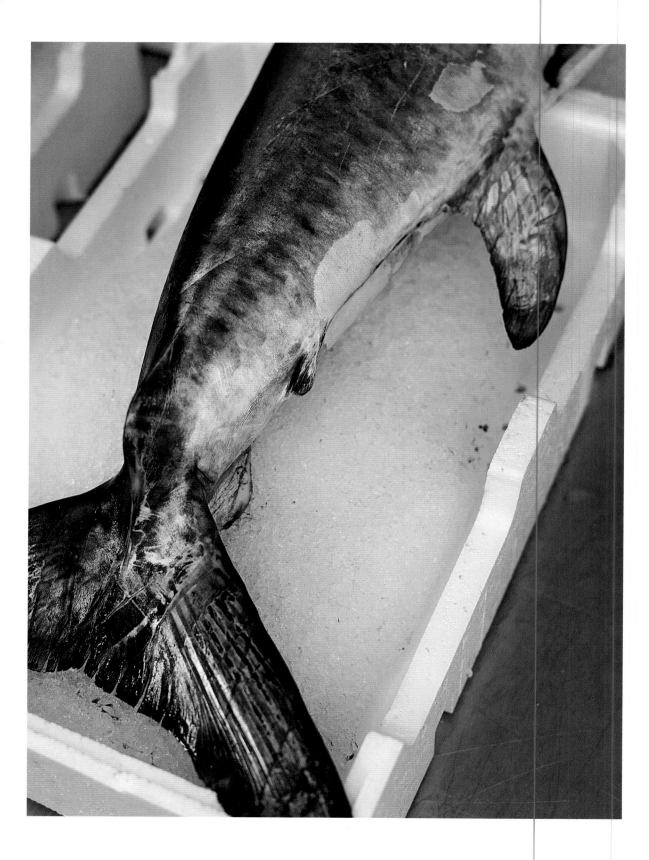

Unlike my butcher, to whom I have remained faithful for nearly ten years, I flitted between the fish stalls in Testaccio market for the longest time, distrustful and finding the wheeling and dealing altogether disconcerting and *fishy*. I felt I was missing some fish-negotiating gene. Things changed when the market moved two years ago, and the bright new structure illuminated what had seemed so mysterious and shady; they shifted again the day I asked Augusto, owner of the trattoria La Torricella, where he negotiates his daily fish.

We met early enough to see the porters unloading and wheeling carts piled ten-high with wooden crates filled with fruit and vegetables and white Styrofoam ones filled with fish. Augusto leaned his push bike against the side of a stand, a corner stall distinctive for its immodest signage emblazoned with the word Mauro, a blackboard promising "Fresh fish daily from Anzio," and nearby a trio of white plastic chairs around a card table. I had imagined introductions, but Augusto—who had clearly forgotten my name—simply raised a serious finger at Mauro and said, "*Trattala bene*" ("Treat her well"). Then we shook hands, which really did make it feel as if a fishy deal had been struck.

In Rome, as in much of Italy, for many people it is still traditional to eat fish on Tuesdays, which means that the fish is fresh from Monday's catch after the Sunday rest, and on Fridays, historically the day the Catholic church observed as lean—meaning no meat. The fish stall is at its most impressive and brightest-eyed on Tuesday and Friday mornings: anchovies shining like newly minted coins; tentacles of ivory octopus and pink-orange *gamberi* (shrimp); firm, slivery, and elegant *spigola* (sea bass) and mackerel; and the *palombo* (a type of dogfish) snaking across the ice. As at the bar and butcher, Luca hops up onto the ledge around the stall so he can get a better view of the pink-orange scorpion fish and a *pesce spada* (swordfish) almost as big as him, its sword pointing skyward, all the while trying to lick the ice.

I often buy anchovies, which are cheap, abundant, and tasty and historically a favorite in Rome, and mine too. We marinate them, bake them with a crust of bread crumbs, or flour and fry them until they curl. Other favorites are the beastly looking monkfish, mackerel, *orata* (gilt-head bream), *spigola*, and a deep-water fish with huge, orange-tinted eyes called *pezzonia,* which I bake in the oven wrapped in wax paper or—if it's warm enough to have the door wide open—cook in the grill pan on the stovetop.

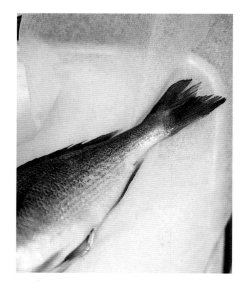

Pesce al forno o sulla griglia
<u>Whole fish baked in the oven or grilled</u>

I generally cook fish in the oven, the wax paper packet (*cartoccio*) puffing up proudly and allowing it to bake and steam at the same time. It emerges so incredibly moist that it makes up for the absence of charred, crisp skin. The paper also makes this an extremely neat supper, as the baking dish remains clean. The package can be opened at the table, the fish lifted onto a clean plate, and the bones wrapped neatly back in the paper and deposited on the drain board until someone volunteers to put them in the trash outside. Minimal

washing up all round: an important consideration in this house.

Apart from a barbecue overseen by my brother, Ben, though, my favorite way to cook fish is on the grill, the charred skin and direct heat imparting a distinct smokiness. Our kitchen is small, and the exhaust fan is enthusiastic but ineffective, so I only do it when it's warm enough to have the doors wide open. It's important that the fish is dry, which ensures a crisp, charred skin, and also to brush it with olive oil to prevent it from sticking completely (it will stick a little). I cook whole sea bass, red mullet, and sardines in this way, allowing about 14 ounces of fish per person, so one large fish or several small ones in the case of red mullet.

If the fish is really fresh, with bright eyes, red gills, and a smell not of fish but of the sea, it needs no additions or embellishments. That said, if you like you can tuck some parsley and a slice of lemon in the fish before wrapping it for the oven. I almost always serve baked or grilled fish with *salsa verde* (green sauce, page 268), a combination that never fails to give me table joy. New potatoes go well too, or braised fennel, a green salad, and a glass or three of Soave from Veneto; with grilled fish, perhaps a white from Etna in Sicily.

serves 2

1 (1¼–1½-pound) sea bass if you are oven baking, or 14 ounces whole fish per person if you are grilling, scaled and cleaned
1 lemon, sliced (optional)
a few sprigs of flat-leaf parsley (optional)
salt and freshly ground black pepper
olive oil, for brushing

To bake the fish, preheat the oven to 375°F. If your fishmonger hasn't cleaned the fish, do so by cutting it open from the head to the top of the tail, and pulling out and discarding the innards. Scrape away the scales from the fish with the edge of a sharp knife, then rinse it inside and out with cold water and pat it dry. Now—and this is important— leave the fish, ideally in a sunny spot, to dry completely.

Take a piece of wax paper large enough to wrap generously around the fish. Place the fish in the middle of the paper, tuck a couple of slices of lemon and a couple of sprigs of parsley inside it, season with salt and pepper and lift the ends of the paper, bring them together and fold them over to seal and make a loose package. Put the package on a baking sheet, slide it into the oven, and bake for 20 minutes for every 1 pound of fish. Remove and leave to rest for a couple of minutes before opening and serving.

To cook the fish on the grill, preheat the grill pan over medium heat until it smokes gently. Brush the fish with olive oil and season it with salt and pepper. Place it on the hot grill pan and leave it there until it's time to do the other side. The rule of thumb is that a 1-pound fish takes 8 minutes on each side on the grill pan, so a ½-pound fish will take 4 minutes on each side, and a 1½-pound fish, 10 minutes. Don't move the fish until it's time to turn it, and then do so carefully so as not to tear the flesh, or do so as little as possible, at least. If I doubt my own timing I check the fish by making a small nick with a knife near the spine and checking whether the flesh is white, not clear, and firm but still moist. I also taste it.

Cozze in tegame
A pot of mussels

On Friday night there is nothing I like more than a sleeping child, a glass or three of chilled Sauvignon Blanc, a couple pounds of mussels cooked with garlic, parsley, and wine, and a pile of toast to mop up the broth. Mussels are cheap, sustainable, and readily available, and my fishmonger always has a net bag of pearly, jet-black, barnacle-covered, beard-sprouting *cozze* sitting on the icy counter. They are laborious to clean (I once cleaned 22 pounds and was hallucinating barnacles and beards for the rest of the day), but it's a task made considerably easier by a glass of wine, which you have to open anyway in order to cook them.

Once cleaned, mussels are a cinch to make: oil and garlic, mussels in, wine too, lid, shake, peek to see if they're open. You could divide the mussels and broth between two bowls or simply bring the pan to the table, with bread or toast for the broth and another bottle of wine.

serves 2
2¼ pounds mussels
1 shallot or small white onion
2 garlic cloves
4 tablespoons olive oil
1 bay leaf
⅔ cup white wine
flat-leaf parsley, to serve
toasted sourdough, to serve

Soak the mussels in cold water, discard any open or cracked ones, and then scrub the rest clean, scraping off any barnacles and pulling away the beards. Rinse, then cover them with clean cold water for 30 minutes. Drain.

Finely chop the onion and garlic. In a large pan with a lid, heat the olive oil, add the onion, garlic, and bay leaf, and cook gently until soft. Add the mussels and stir, then add the white wine and cover the pan with the lid. Cook for 4–6 minutes (shake the pan from time to time), or until the mussels have opened. Discard any that haven't. Meanwhile, finely chop some parsley and add it to the pan. Divide the mussels and broth between 2 warm bowls and serve with lots of sourdough toast.

Roman Jewish cooking

In the past, the Tevere river, which curves and cuts through the city, was prone to devastating floods that invaded low-lying parts of the city. When Rome became capital of Italy it underwent a makeover that included enclosing the Tevere within heavy embankments. Protect the city they may, but these stout walls also isolate the river, making it seem solitary and dislocated. This is why the newly minted cycle lanes that run along the river banks and are shaded by the embankments are so welcome—not just as a safe place to pedal and find a satisfying echo with a two-year-old, but as a means of proximity to the river, which for hundreds of years played a fundamental role in city life and was home to boats, mills, fishermen, and 90 varieties of fish. We pedal a few miles along the path at least once a week, more often than not on our way to a part of Rome the river used to devastate periodically: the ghetto.

From the sixteenth to the nineteenth centuries, a struggle between the papacy and the empire resulted in Rome's Jewish community being forced to live in a walled ghetto between the Portico di Ottavia and the river, which was locked at sundown and reopened at dawn. It was, my neighbor Emilia once told me before sharing her family recipe for *carciofi alla giudea*, a dark, claustrophobic place, exposed to floods and disease, but also one of fierce, self-sufficient community-mindedness and, even at the worst of times, good food.

The walls were knocked down in the mid-nineteenth century, allowing the light in and those who wished to, to leave. Today the ghetto, which is still home to a tight-knit Jewish community, is one of the most atmospheric and beautiful parts of the city, a rabbit warren of tiny cobbled streets and alleys, some of which conjure up images of Rome that have become clichés: the damp washing strung across the street, the group of men sitting in a circle of mismatched chairs, the teenager mending his motorbike, the woman prepping artichokes. Picturesque, yes, but never cloyingly so, even in the most touristic trattorias (of which there are many), which has much to do with the history that permeates every cobble. The faded *palazzi* that rise up may indeed be beautiful, but it doesn't take much of a leap to imagine how isolated and insalubrious they must have been, how damp and starved of light. Evocative, too, is the knowledge that it was in the dark, ill-equipped kitchens of ordinary families that Roman Jewish cuisine developed, a true *cucina povera*, poor food in the sense that it used ingredients available to the poor or those spurned by the wealthy, such as squash blossoms, offal,

small fish, or bitter greens, which were transformed into richly flavored dishes.

Since true Jewish food is kosher, and therefore prepared according to principles laid down in the Bible, Roman Jewish food is perhaps the vein of Roman cooking that has remained truest to its gastronomic origins. "This food," Emilia tells me, "is only found in people's homes." However, places like Nonna Betta and C'è Pasta e Pasta in Trastevere still serve traditional and largely kosher dishes that are still made the way they always have been. They are some of my favorites: deep-fried artichokes and squash blossoms; battered salt cod; baked anchovies with *indivia* (bitter greens); salt cod with tomato, raisins, and pine nuts; a very particular take on a cherry and ricotta tart; and soft almond cookies.

Baccalà in guazzetto
Salt cod with tomatoes, raisins, and pine nuts

Cod, heavily salted to preserve it, was widely imported into Catholic Europe as a cheap way of providing fish for the masses on Fridays and fast days, when meat was avoided. As a consequence, people sought out the tastiest ways to cook it. Times have changed and salt cod is no longer cheap, but the traditions live on, notably in Rome, where salt cod is called *baccalà* and is sold ready-soaked by weight on Fridays. My local *norcineria* is proud of the way their salt cod is soaked, and there is often a scrabble for the last fat fillet.

It is very likely that this Roman Jewish preparation of salt cod, tomatoes, raisins, and pine nuts migrated north from Sicily. In fact, I first ate this dish when it was cooked by Carmela, Vincenzo's mum, who migrated from Sicily to Rome with his dad, Bartolomeo, 25 years ago. The combination of the firm and fleshy cod, simmered until tender and falling in deep flakes into a tomato sauce enriched with onion, nuts, and the sweetness of the plump raisins, is a wonderful one.

You are most likely to find salt cod in Italian, Spanish, Portuguese, Greek, West Indian, or Asian food shops. Look out for fillets that are thick and white; if they are yellow and thin, they are most likely old and therefore stringy and tough. You will need to soak the fish for at least 36 hours, changing the water at least 6 times. This probably sounds like a right palaver, which it is, but worth it if you like the distinctive texture and flavor of salt cod.

If you can't find salt cod, ordinary cod works well too; it just requires less, and more attentive, cooking. Like so many braised dishes, this one benefits from a rest, and from being served just warm rather than hot. Make sure you have plenty of light red or rosé chilling to drink alongside.

serves 4

1¾ pounds salt cold, soaked
1 large onion
1 (14.5-ounce) can plum tomatoes
4 tablespoons extra-virgin olive oil
⅓ cup raisins or golden raisins
⅓ cup pine nuts
salt and freshly ground black pepper

Rinse and pat the salt cod dry with paper towels. Cut it into pieces roughly 2½ inches long and ¾ inch wide. Thinly slice the onion and either pass the tomatoes through a food mill or chop them.

Heat the olive oil in a deep sauté pan or casserole dish over medium-low heat, add the onion, and cook gently until softened. Add the salt cod and gently fry it until lightly golden, using a spatula and a wooden spoon to turn the pieces. Add the raisins and pine nuts and then the tomatoes. Half cover the pan and leave it bubbling gently for 30 minutes, turning the salt cod halfway through the cooking time. If the sauce seems to be getting too thick, add a little water. Taste and season cautiously—the salt cod will do most of the seasoning.

I also make a variation of this dish with fresh cod fillet, which is considerably less robust than salt cod. I make the sauce as above, but instead of adding the cod after the onion, I fry it briefly in another pan until the outside is opaque, then I add it to the sauce for the last 10 minutes of the cooking time.

L'orata con le patate di Miriam
Miriam's sea bream baked with potatoes

Our favorite place to eat Roman Jewish food isn't in the ghetto, but in the other direction down the river, where classical Rome makes way for industrial Rome, just over the Ponte Testaccio in via Ettore Roli. It's called C'è Pasta e Pasta ("There Is Pasta and Pasta").

One of the owners, Miriam, is a beautiful woman for whom Vincenzo can't hide his admiration. She is formidable too, which he also admires. For months, while he grinned over the glass counter, I bristled while looking at the lasagne, pretending to be nonplussed.

One day last year, when my enthusiasm for her food and curiosity about the setup in this small *tavola calda* (canteen-style café) got the better of me, I asked her to give me her recipe for this book.

In short, what I learned was that a wishful conversation between Jewish friends about making and selling fresh egg pasta had become a reality a few years back when they took a long lease on a property on the corner of via Ettore Roli. As well as the pasta, they also decided to serve a small selection of hot dishes from the counter, the sort of simple, traditional, genuine kosher home cooking that they felt was missing from Rome. Almost immediately the hot food was a success, both in the Jewish community and among the locals, who queued up for the freshly fried *fritti*, daily *minestre*, and lasagne. C'è Pasta e Pasta is one of the few places in Rome that serves *indivia*, a type of bitter greens, baked with anchovies, and salt cod with tomato, pine nuts, and raisins. They also make a dish I have adopted at home: baked fish with a potato crust.

By covering fillets of fish with a layer of finely sliced potatoes, the fish both steams and bakes and therefore remains tender. The potatoes in turn are soft and forgiving underneath and crispy and slightly chewy on the top. Even if you do some elaborate, fish-scale-like arranging of the potato, it's an extremely simple dish to make, good with a green salad and a glass of something fragrant.

serves 4
olive oil, for greasing and baking
1½ pounds fish fillets, ideally bream, with or without skin
salt and freshly ground black pepper
1¾ pounds Yukon Gold potatoes

Preheat the oven to 400°F and grease a square ovenproof dish or baking sheet with olive oil.

Arrange the fish fillets, skin-side down if they have skin, in a single layer and season them with salt and pepper. Slice the potatoes very thinly (a mandoline is helpful here) and arrange them—neatly or not so neatly—over the fish so that the fillets are completely covered. Zig-zag the potatoes with olive oil and season them with a little more salt.

Bake for 20–25 minutes, or until the potatoes are tender underneath, golden on top and crisp at the edges.

4
VEGETABLES

Roots and Routine

In Rome, as in the rest of Italy, the structure of a meal is important, and vegetables are mostly treated as a separate course. They often follow a first course of pasta or soup instead of meat or fish, or serve as a starter before a heavier main course. Either way, they are usually called *contorni*, which is generally translated as "side dishes." That said, served in larger portions and with appropriate additions, such as bread, eggs, or cheese, all the dishes in this section can be meals by themselves.

Can be, and *are* meals by themselves in this house, mostly at supper time. They include some of our favorites: a red pepper and tomato stew called *peperonata,* topped with a lacy-edged fried egg; *vignarola* (spring vegetable stew) piled on toast; greens cooked in garlic-scented olive oil, served with several slices of halloumi grilled until almost the wrong side of golden; a dish of lentils finished with a poached egg. They can mostly be made in advance, and keep well (some would say beautifully and beneficially, as a wait improves the flavor). This makes them useful dishes for the mother of a toddler who turns from delightful to hungry and fractious in the blink of a dinosaur eye any time between five and seven o'clock, and needs a spoonful of whatever with an egg on top right now—his mother too.

The market

First, a small proviso: in a chapter about vegetables I am, of course, going to talk about the market, which was—and still is—one of the reasons I live so happily in Testaccio. It still surprises me every day with its produce and ordinary charm. What if you don't live near a charming market in Italy, though, where cranberry beans in their pods and zucchini showing off their golden flowers roll into your arms? The answer, of course, is that it doesn't matter: you want the very best you can find, and what you can find will do. These recipes bring out the best in vegetables, and will fit around you and what you have. Now, to market.

Every quarter of Rome has a market, some large and some small, most of them open six mornings a week. Testaccio is home to one of Rome's most famous, or infamous—I'm not quite sure which. During my first seven years here, it inhabited Testaccio's central piazza, right next to my old building in via Mastro Giorgio. It was built in the 1960s, a covered home for the historic market that had previously simply gathered in the piazza. From a distance, the big square building, roofed but open, was unprepossessing, ugly even, especially in the afternoons when its metal grilles and gates were padlocked down, making it look like a vast fortified bus shelter. Inside, the first thing to strike you was the not-quite-half-light; the grimy glass roof held by iron uprights kept things muted even on the sunniest day. After the light came the smell of flesh, the nature of which depended on whether you had entered next to the meat or fish stalls. Either way, it gave way to the thick, vegetal, and sweet smell of freshly picked produce piled high on the dozen or so central stalls, the low light emphasizing the almost unnaturally brilliant colors.

The image of the old market most etched in my memory is that of late spring, when it was still awash with leafy greens and tangled wild ones, lettuces, pods of peas and broad beans like gnarled fingers, and stalks of asparagus. Green, but splattered with color like a Cy Twombly canvas: the gaudy gold flowers at the tip of every fluted zucchini, the violet tips of the artichoke flowers and pink-tinged spinach stalks, the marbled elegance of the white-and-pink cranberry bean pods, the flush of early peaches and apricots, and the stain of cherries and Sicilian tomatoes. Beside several of the stalls was a chair at which someone sat doggedly shelling peas, peeling tiny onions, trimming artichokes, or divesting leafy greens of their tough stalks with impressive speed and skill. All this was accompanied by the market hum of (mostly) good-natured shouting and banter. Beyond the food stalls were those selling shoes, more shoes, cheap clothes, bags, and household goods, each stall's wares spilling into the already narrow walkways that were patchworked with pieces of cardboard for balancing on while you tried on shoes. It was an extraordinary place, both makeshift and functional, adhering to none of the EU guidelines for health and safety and making you feel as if you were in another time.

There was so much talk and so many delays (building sites in Rome inevitably become archaeological digs) that it seemed as if market vendors would never move. Then, one day two years ago, they did, to a newly constructed brick and glass structure a few hundred yards across Testaccio, in front of the old slaughterhouse. A few weeks later the men and bulldozers arrived, and before an audience of *testaccini*, including my old neighbor Marcella shaking her head and muttering *dio mio*, glass panes shattered and iron uprights twisted as the old market was pulled to the ground.

I was with another neighbor the first time I visited the new market, and the experience was a little like an Alan Bennett play in Italian, Sofia giving a running commentary of *ohhs* and *oh nos*, *isn't this lovely and clean* and *oh dear, I don't like that*. Whereas in

the old market you had to adjust your eyes to the almost half-light, in the new market you have to make allowances for the brightness. We walked and watched the residents of Testaccio exploring the new space as if it were some queer new planet, peering at the stallholders they had known all their lives in a completely new light.

It took me ages to find Gianluca and Giancarlo, each aisle seeming rather like the next. Then there they were at stand 32, Frutta & Verdura, il Velletrano, Gianluca with a cigarette in his hand (an EU rule still reassuringly broken). "*Eccoci*," ("Here we are") he said, as if he had been waiting for us, and there was his produce, much of it grown on the family's land southeast of Rome: the reds and greens, the wild and the tame, the bulbs, roots, and leaves, the same glorious stuff, just in a different frame. "What do you think about the new market?" I asked. "Boh," he said. "We had to move and now we have to get used to it." Then he passed me a paper bag to help myself, with a gesture that seemed to say "just get on with it." As I took the bag, another customer, a much older *signora*, elbowed me strategically in order to maneuver herself to the front, at which point I used my height advantage to reach up and over, at which point she used her lack of height to grab the fruit from below. Not that we needed to fight over fruit—there was more than enough to go around. I was glad for the tussle, though, because it felt familiar. Gianluca replenished the depleted sections with an avalanche of tomatoes and bunches of basil, the smells of which filled the air. People jostled, voices were raised, free parsley was stuffed in the tops of bags. Everything had changed, yet nothing had changed. My fruit and vegetables in my bag, I went to visit my butcher, Sartor, now occupying a spot as prime as their steak, right in front of an opening at the heart of the market that allows you to look down on the archeological remains of an ancient Roman road. It was clear from Daniele's eyes that he was pleased with the move and position. "*Bello*, eh?" he said as he handed me my parcel. Then I went over to see how my fishmonger was settling in. He complained about the higher rents, but then gestured to the running water that meant he no longer needed to ferry buckets of water from the communal pumps, before trying to overcharge me for a couple pounds of clams. Again, nothing had changed. Before leaving, we sat on one of the concrete benches in the wide central opening, which gives you a clear view through Testaccio one way and across to the old slaughterhouse in the other, a pleasing view of a part of the city to which I am so attached.

I would be lying if I said I don't miss the old market with its roguish charm and sweet, stale breath. That said, I know it had to go and I am now, after two years of daily visits, extremely fond of the new market, which, although still rather too bright, is starting to feel lived in, its Roman market spirit kicking a little against the imposed order. Alongside the stalls I've been visiting for years, there are also new ones that breathe even more life into the place: Sergio with his superb sandwiches filled with classic Roman dishes, Artenio with his Lariano bread, Emanuela with her kitchenware, Gabriele Torrefazione (coffee roasters), Costanza and Roberto bringing Sicilian traditions to Rome, much to Vincenzo's delight.

As I write, the site of the old market is still cordoned off, and work on reopening the piazza is, it appears, as fraught with bureaucratic delays as closing a piazza. We have petitioned the mayor and it appears someone has finally listened. By the time you read this, the fountain of amphorae on the edge of Testaccio will have been brought back to its original home at the center of the old market piazza at the heart of Testaccio, and will be surrounded by majestic trees.

Eating my greens

"Eat your greens" is something I've never needed to be told, cajoled, or forced to do. As a child I happily plowed my way through large servings of cabbage, Brussels sprouts, spinach, spring greens, chard, and broccoli. If they were glistening with butter, better still. I was one of the few who ate the ambiguous heap of greens whose odor lingered, like us, in corners and corridors around the school and appeared on every lunch plate. "What a good little eater," relatives and cafeteria ladies would say. This confused me, since surely they meant a good *big* eater?

Eating my greens in Rome has been even more of a pleasure. Rome's climate, which can hover above freezing for a few weeks each year but rarely goes under it, produces excellent greens throughout the winter, both domesticated and wild, such as emerald spinach, curly endive, chard, hairy borage, and various types of broccoli. Sweet, mild, and full of flavor, they are mostly served simply. Anything small and tender enough is eaten in salads, and the rest are customarily boiled or steamed and dressed at the table with salt, best olive oil, and a squeeze of lemon. Spinach and green beans are particularly nice served like this. The quality of the ingredients is important: the spinach should have a bouncing, bright appearance, and crunch and squeak as you stuff it in the bag. The beans, too, should be bright and crack decisively if you break them.

As for cooking them, spinach is best cooked in a large pan with nothing more than the water clinging to its just-washed leaves. I am always amazed at how unruly spinach wilts so obediently into such a small pile. Beans are best cooked hard and briefly in plenty of well-salted, fast-boiling water; the time needed depends on the age and size of the beans, but they should be cooked long enough to develop a rounded, nutty flavor, and they should not squeak. In Roman trattorias or people's homes, you are encouraged to dress the beans or spinach yourself with a little salt, some olive oil, and a spritz of lemon—after all, you know best.

Verdura strascinata o ripassata
Greens with garlic and chile

Another classic way of serving greens is *strascinata,* which is Roman for "dragged," a word that can also be used to describe the way you get a small boy to leave a playground. *Strascinata* refers to the habit of dragging or sautéing boiled or steamed vegetables in olive oil scented with garlic and possibly chile. It's also known as *ripassata* or "re-passed." It's an extremely simple technique that works well with most leafy green vegetables, the garlic working like a strong outline, giving the vegetables sharper definition.

After choosing fresh, vigorous vegetables, the key is frying the garlic gently in plenty of olive oil until it is golden and fragrant. The best way to prepare the garlic is to crush the clove gently with the back of a knife so it breaks apart but is still more or less holding together and the skin almost comes away of its own accord. The garlic should never burn, or it will leave a horrid bitter taste. Once the garlic has imparted its soft but volatile perfume, you remove it before adding the greens and turning them in the fragrant oil until glistening.

In Rome the most popular vegetable to be dragged is *cicoria* (chicory), which grows in exuberant heads with lots of saw-toothed leaves in the Roman countryside. It is distinctly bitter and slightly metallic tasting, but deliciously so. If you can't find chicory, or curly endive, or it isn't to your taste, any leafy greens work well. I particularly like *broccoletti* (sprouting broccoli) cooked in this way, then piled on toast and topped with a poached egg or a slice of goat's cheese.

serves 4–6 as a side dish, or 2 as a main course
about 1 pound greens, such as curly endive, chard, or broccoli
2 garlic cloves
1 small dried red chile or a pinch of red pepper flakes
4 tablespoons extra-virgin olive oil
salt

Carefully pick over the greens, discarding any that are discolored or particularly tough. Wash them well in cold water and drain.

Bring a large pot of well-salted water to a fast boil, add the greens, and cook until they are tender, which can take anywhere from 4–8 minutes, depending on the type and age of the greens. Use a slotted spoon to lift them into a colander to drain.

Peel and gently crush the garlic cloves with the back of a knife and finely chop the chile. In a large frying or sauté pan, warm the olive oil, garlic, and chile over medium-low heat until the garlic is just turning gold and fragrant and the chile sizzles. You can remove the garlic at this point if you wish. Add the greens, and a pinch of salt and sauté for 3–4 minutes, or until they glisten with oil.

Spinaci in padella con pinoli e uva sultana <u>Spinach with pine nuts and raisins</u>

You need only take a few steps up leafy via Pallone to put the chaos of Testaccio behind you and enter the quiet, residential gentility of the Aventine, one of Rome's seven hills, with its shady, tree-lined streets, small parks, and some of Rome's loveliest early churches.

I walk up to the Aventine hill a few times a week, inevitably ending up in Parco Savello, a gravel-and-grass park shaded by orange trees and pines. I used to sit and read, or nod off with my mouth open like my grandpa. These days I am more likely to be arbitrating between my son and the poor dog he is throwing gravel at. The garden is often busy, but never overwhelmingly so, with locals, tourists, lovers, and nuns, most of whom take a moment or

five to look at the view across Rome from the terrace at the end of the garden, over the sepia and terra-cotta city, domes gleaming with bronze or dull and leaden. From this particular point the city seems disconcertingly small to bear the weight of so much history. The view when you turn back is lovely, too, of the small, walled garden lined with pots, scented with orange blossom, and framed by umbrella pines. These are extraordinary trees, with long, gangly trunks that bend like disjointed limbs, capped with a toupée of branches fringed with pines that fan out like their namesake.

It is umbrella or stone pines that produce the pine nuts known as *pinoli*, slender, resinous things that are incomparable in pesto. I hadn't made the connection until one day I saw three small boys smashing open the tiny nuts they had collected with a stone and then either eating or flicking them into their companions' faces. Unless you are tenacious and patient enough to do what the three little boys did, it is nearly as hard to find Italian pine nuts in Rome as it is in London. But when you do, a handful of them work beautifully along with raisins soaked in warm water until plump, then mixed into wilted spinach glistening with olive oil. The combination of green leaves with the sweet grapeyness of the raisins and the resinous nuts is an excellent one. I like this dish served next to or after a grilled lamb chop or some grilled cheese, such as scamorza or halloumi. It is not at all Roman to mix butter with oil, but I am not Roman and I love a little butter with my spinach: it soothes its metallic edges, especially if the richness is tempered by some lively extra-virgin olive oil. You can, of course, use all butter or all olive oil.

serves 4–6 as a side dish, or 2 as a main course
¼ cup raisins or golden raisins
about 1 pound leaf spinach
2 garlic cloves
2 tablespoons extra-virgin olive oil
1½ tablespoons butter
¼ cup pine nuts
salt

Soak the raisins in warm water for 10 minutes. Rinse the spinach well in 2 changes of cold water, discard any wilted or bruised leaves, and trim away any thick, woody stalks. Put the spinach in a large pan with nothing but the water that clings to the leaves, cover the pan, and cook over low heat until the spinach has collapsed and is tender. This should take 4–6 minutes, depending on the freshness and age of the spinach.

Remove and drain the spinach in a colander. Once it is cool enough, squeeze it to eliminate any excess liquid. Peel and gently crush the garlic cloves with the back of a knife. In a large frying or sauté pan, cook the garlic gently in the olive oil over medium-low heat until it is fragrant and lightly golden, then remove it. Add the butter, let it foam slightly, then add the pine nuts and turn them in the oil before adding the spinach and a pinch of salt. Cook for 2 minutes, or until the leaves glisten. Drain the raisins and add them to the pan, turn ingredients a couple more times, and serve.

Zucchine al tegame
Zucchini cooked in olive oil

Zucchini can be bland. Even the gorgeous, fluted Romanesco variety, which are at once dense and sweet and look a bit like a Las Vegas showgirl with their gaudy flower headdress, can be timid. The key, I think, is cooking rounds of zucchini in far more garlic-scented olive oil than most recipes would dare to suggest, over low heat until they are just tinged with gold, then adding a little hot water and cooking until it has been absorbed and the zucchini are soft and extremely tender. It's the combination of oil and water that gives the zucchini a creamy consistency. In the last moments of cooking you can add the ripped-up flowers and some torn basil, then inhale before serving them with a slice of milky mozzarella and some bread, or stirred into some al dente pasta.

serves 4 as a side dish, or 2 as a main course
6–8 zucchini (approximately 1¼ pounds), ideally the pale, creamy green or ribbed variety, with flowers still attached, but otherwise the zucchini you have
6–9 tablespoons extra-virgin olive oil
2 large or 3 small garlic cloves
salt
basil leaves

Remove and reserve the zucchini blossoms, if you have any, then slice the zucchini into thick coins.

Pour a generous amount of olive oil into a heavy-bottomed sauté pan. Peel and add the whole garlic cloves to the pan. Warm the oil over medium heat, allowing the garlic to sizzle gently and turning the cloves every now and then. Cook for about 3 minutes, or until it is soft,

golden, and fragrant. Do not let it burn. Remove and discard the garlic.

Add the zucchini to the pan along with a generous pinch of salt. Turn the zucchini in the oil until each coin is glistening. Allow them to sizzle gently, turning them occasionally, over very low heat for about 15 minutes, or until they are just golden. Add about 7 tablespoons hot water, then continue cooking until the water is absorbed and the zucchini are very soft and creamy, which can take anywhere from 15–45 minutes. Add a little more water if the pan seems dry.

Tear the basil and zucchini blossoms into small pieces and add them to the pan. Remove the pan from the heat and stir, allowing the flowers and basil to wilt in the residual heat. Serve immediately.

Peperonata
Bell pepper and tomato stew

Peperonata consists of red bell peppers, onion, and tomatoes stewed in olive oil and butter until they soften, collapse, and thicken into a rich, vivid stew. It is one of the simplest and most delicious vegetable dishes I know, and I make it constantly.

There is a moment of stovetop alchemy when you make *peperonata*. It's when, having softened the sliced onion in butter and oil, you add the sliced red peppers and cover the pan; in just

a matter of minutes the crisp, taut slices of pepper surrender their juices, then simmer and soften in their own cardinal-red liquid.

Thick, rich, silken, and tasting of somewhere warm and brilliant, *peperonata* is delicious served warm with chicken, veal, or fish. It makes a good bed for an egg: fried, poached, or soft-boiled, the yolk spilling into the red stew and making your plate look like a desert sunrise. I like it as part of an *antipasti*-style lunch next to soft, sharp cheese, lean, pink *lonzino* (air-cured pork loin), and a few salty black olives. It's also fantastic stirred into pasta. It keeps well, so make plenty, then spoon some into a clean jar and float enough olive oil over the surface to seal the contents. Once opened, keep it in the refrigerator.

serves 8

1 large white onion
4 tablespoons olive oil
a knob of butter
4 large or 6 medium red peppers (approximately 1¼–1½ pounds)
about 1¼ pounds good, ripe tomatoes or canned peeled plum tomatoes
salt and freshly ground black pepper
1–2 teaspoons red or white wine vinegar (optional)

Slice the onion. Heat the olive oil and butter in a pan and cook the onion gently until soft and lightly golden. Meanwhile, cut the peppers into strips, discarding the stems, seeds, and pith. Add the sliced peppers to the pan, stir, then cover the pan and cook over medium heat for 15 minutes. Peel the tomatoes by plunging them into boiling water for 60 seconds, then transferring them to cold water, by which point the skins should split and slip off easily, then roughly chop them. If you are using canned plum tomatoes, chop them roughly directly in the can using scissors.

After about 15 minutes, add the tomatoes, which will also relinquish their juices. Let the peperonata cook, uncovered, at a lively simmer for 30–40 minutes, reducing until almost all the liquid has evaporated and you are left with a thick, vivid stew that is slightly jammy. Season with salt, pepper, and a dash of vinegar to sharpen things up, if you like.

Fagiolini corallo in umido
Flat green beans with tomatoes and onions

This is a full-flavored, slow-cooked stew of flat green beans, onion, tomato, and basil. Ideally, the green beans should be flat and so fresh that they crack decisively when you break them. The tomatoes should be red, ripe but firm, and with a lick of real sweetness (if they're on the acidic side, a pinch of sugar should do the trick).

The key is to cook the onions gently until very soft in plenty of olive oil, then add the beans and stir until each piece glistens. Then you add the tomatoes and cover the pan. The steamy heat trapped under the pan lid helps the tomatoes relinquish their juices, at which point you remove the lid and leave the beans to cook in the rich, red stock until it reduces into a dense sauce.

It's a straightforward dish, but one that requires attentive stirring and tasting, particularly toward the end of cooking, when the beans are reaching that perfect point of tenderness and the sauce is thickening and clinging. Watch that the stew doesn't catch on the bottom of the pan. If the sauce reduces too much before the beans are cooked, a spoonful or two of water should loosen things up. It's best to make it a few hours, or better still a day, before you want to eat it, so that the flavors can settle and the sauce thickens and takes hold of the beans.

The stew can be served warm with rice or meat, or topped with a frilly-edged fried egg. Served at room temperature with a wedge of ricotta or mozzarella or a slice of cold roast beef, it makes a lovely summer lunch.

serves 8 (it keeps beautifully for up to 3 days in the fridge)
1 large or 2 medium white onions
5 tablespoons olive oil
salt
about 1 pound flat green beans
about 1¼ pounds ripe tomatoes or canned plum tomatoes
a small handful of torn basil leaves

Thinly slice the onion. Warm the oil in a heavy-bottomed pan with a lid over medium-low heat, then add the onion and cook gently with a pinch of salt until soft and translucent.

Cut or break the beans into 2-inch lengths. Add the beans to the pan and stir well until each piece is glistening with oil. Continue cooking and stirring for a few minutes. Peel the tomatoes, if you like (by plunging them into boiling water for 60 seconds, then transferring to cold water, by which point the skins should split and slip off easily), then coarsely chop them and add to the pan with another pinch of salt. Stir, then cover the pan. After a couple of minutes, uncover the pan and stir; the tomatoes should be relinquishing their juices. Cover and cook for another 5 minutes or so.

Once the tomatoes have given up their juices, uncover the pan and allow it to simmer, uncovered, stirring every now and then, for 40–50 minutes, or until the beans are tender and the tomatoes have reduced to a thick, rich sauce. During the last 10 minutes of cooking, add the ripped basil leaves. Taste and season with salt if necessary. Allow the dish to sit for a couple of hours before serving. It's even better made a day in advance, kept in the fridge overnight, and then brought to room temperature before serving.

Pomodori al riso
Tomatoes stuffed with rice

I've eaten some dreary stuffed tomatoes in my time. I've also—thanks to a respectable number of holidays in Greece and now nine years in Italy—eaten some very good ones, particularly here in Rome, where they're called *pomodori al riso*. Romans adore their *pomodori al riso*. They make them at home, but are just as likely to buy them from a canteen-like *tavola calda* or the local *forno* (bakery), where vast trays of stuffed tomatoes surrounded by a sea of diced potatoes are baked in the bread ovens until their red flesh is tantalizingly wrinkled and intensely flavored, the rice plump, and the potatoes golden on top but soft and sticky underneath, a consequence of wallowing in the oily, tomatoey juices that collect in the tray.

Pomodori al riso, like much of Rome's traditional cooking, are without frills, simple and delicious. Good tomatoes are hollowed out and the jumble of pulp, flesh, and seeds is mixed with rice, garlic, basil, olive oil, and salt to make a stuffing. After a good rest, the stuffing is spooned back into the tomato shells, which are then nestled among diced potatoes on a shallow baking pan before being baked. Then—and this is important—the baked tomatoes are left to rest for half an hour or so, during which time the flavors settle, the rice swells, and the oily juices from the pan soak back into the tomatoes and potatoes. Good stuffed tomatoes do indeed come to those who wait. When you serve them, make sure everyone has their fair share of both crispy and soggy potatoes. To drink, try a soft, unobtrusive but generous red like Cerasuolo di Vittoria.

serves 4

8 firm, fruity, fleshy, and flavorsome tomatoes
salt
2 garlic cloves
8 basil leaves
10 tablespoons risotto rice (I use Arborio)
7 tablespoons extra-virgin olive oil, plus extra for the potatoes
freshly ground black pepper
2¼ pounds potatoes (ideally roasting potatoes, but whatever type you have will do)

Cut the tops off the tomatoes and set them aside. One by one, hold the tomatoes over a bowl and, using a teaspoon, scoop out their insides—flesh, seeds, and juice—and let it all fall into the bowl. Sprinkle a little salt in the cavity of each tomato, then place them cut-side down on a clean tea towel so that any excess liquid can drain away.

Pass the tomato flesh, seeds, and juice through a food mill or process briefly with an immersion blender. Peel and chop the garlic very finely and add it to the tomato. Rip the basil into small pieces and add it to the tomato. Add the rice and olive oil. Season the mixture very generously with salt and pepper. Stir, then leave to sit for at least 45 minutes.

Cut the potatoes into ⅜-inch-thick, 1-inch-long matchsticks. Put the potatoes in a bowl, pour over a little olive oil, sprinkle lightly with salt, and using your hands, toss the potatoes until they are well coated with oil.

Preheat the oven to 360°F. Sit your hollowed-out tomatoes in a lightly greased ovenproof dish. Spoon the rice mixture into the shells until they are three-quarters full, then put the tops back on the tomatoes. Scatter the potatoes around the tomatoes. Slide the tray into the oven and bake for 1–1¼ hours, or until the tomatoes are soft and just starting to shrivel, the rice is plump and tender, and the potatoes are soft and golden. Allow them to sit for half an hour before eating.

Uova con la salsa
Eggs in sauce

This dish tastes like the childhood I never had, somewhere warm
and dusty with a vegetable garden that produced more tomatoes
than we could manage, chickens that laid fresh eggs, and suppers
of eggs coddled in thick tomato sauce. It's the childhood Vincenzo
actually had, for four months of the year at least, when he spent
long summers on his grandparents' farm in southern Sicily, and
where there were tomatoes—fields of them—and a man who
brought a chicken every Thursday (which his *nonna* [grandmother]
then strangled in the garage), along with two dozen eggs and some
breakfast egg biscuits. Vincenzo also likes to remind me that there
was a petroleum plant that cast an ugly shadow over the bay of Gela,
and coarse threads of menace and corruption woven into the fabric
of daily life. Better to talk about tomato sauce (*la salsa*), which was
ubiquitous, mostly on pasta but also on meatballs, and occasionally
as a red bed for coddled eggs. In other parts of Italy this dish is
known as *uova con la purgatorio* (eggs in purgatory), but the D'Aleo
family called it *uova con la salsa* (eggs with the sauce), so we do too.

This is my version of eggs in sauce, an absolute favorite in this
house for Sunday breakfast or a weekday tea. A little finely chopped
parsley over the top is nice, and good bread is essential.

serves 4
1 small white onion
1 celery stalk
5 tablespoons olive oil
salt
about 1 pound fresh or canned plum tomatoes, chopped
a pinch of sugar (optional)
4 large eggs
finely chopped flat-leaf parsley, to sprinkle (optional)
good bread, to serve

Very finely dice the onion and celery. Warm the oil in a heavy-
bottomed pan over medium-low heat, add the onion, and cook gently
until soft and translucent, then add the celery and a pinch of salt.
Stir well so that all the vegetables are well coated with oil. Reduce the
heat and cook, stirring every now and then, until the vegetables are
soft and lightly golden. This should take about 5 minutes.

If using fresh tomatoes, peel them by plunging them into boiling
water for 60 seconds, then transfer them to cold water, by which

point the skins should split and slip off easily. Cut the tomatoes into quarters, add them to the pan, and gently mash them with the back of a wooden spoon. Increase the heat so the sauce comes to a gentle boil, then reduce the heat and simmer very gently, uncovered, for 20 minutes, or until it is dense but still saucy, and dark red. Taste and season with salt or sugar if your tomatoes are sharp.

Now you have two options. The first is to keep the pan over low heat, make four wells in the sauce as best you can, and break the eggs into the wells. Cover the pan and allow the eggs to cook gently for 9 minutes. Once cooked, serve them directly from the pan with a spatula and spoon. Alternatively, divide the sauce among 4 warmed individual ovenproof dishes, make a well in the sauce, break an egg into each one, then bake in a preheated oven at 350°F for 4–6 minutes, or until the eggs have set. If you like, sprinkle with parsley to serve.

The *Vegetable Book*

My earliest cookbook memory is of my mum's much-loved copy of Jane Grigson's *Vegetable Book*; I remember looking intently at the cat curled up on a chair next to a basket of cabbages on the front cover, amazed and appalled that it was the only picture in the whole dog-eared book. Years later, when I was at drama school training not to be an actor, I bought my own copy from the Waterstones on Camden High Street. If the notes in the margin are to be believed, the first thing I made was ratatouille, a recipe I had already absorbed as if by kitchen osmosis from my mum. She in turn had learned it from Jane Grigson, so having my copy open on the counter felt fitting. Over the next ten years I would make a lot of ratatouille, smoke a lot of cigarettes, and drink a lot of oaky Chardonnay—often while making ratatouille. It was also during this time that I bought cookbooks earnestly, falling particularly for Simon Hopkinson's *Roast Chicken and Other Stories*, Elizabeth David's essays, Nigel Slater's *Kitchen Diaries*, Nigella Lawson's *How to Eat*, and Claudia Roden's *A Book of Middle Eastern Food,* and the way they wove together words, wit, stories, and recipes gave me complete escapism and quiet domesticity, and made me want to cook. I read and used all five books attentively, but the *Vegetable Book* remained my favorite, the one I read like a novel and turned to for advice or reassurance when I made roast potatoes, roast peppers, tomato sauce, cauliflower cheese, chili con carne, and hummus (I made nearly as much bloody hummus as I did ratatouille). More marginal notes remind me that on my thirty-first birthday I made Grigson's fennel baked with Parmesan cheese and tomato tart, neither of which were appreciated by my then boyfriend, since we were busy arguing our way to the end of the relationship. Not long after my thirty-second birthday, the *Vegetable Book* was packed, along with the rest of my cookbooks, books, and belongings, in boxes and stored in my parents' garage when I left England for Italy.

I arrived with nothing but the clothes I stood up in and a shoulder bag large enough for my purse, diary, phone, a guidebook, and a floral toiletry bag for my specs, lens case, and travel toothbrush. So liberating was this fact that I managed to buy little else for the month and a half I traveled: some underwear, another T-shirt, a hairbrush, and a tube of face cream that split when I fell over on my way up Mount Etna. Even when I decided to stay in Rome for a while, I resisted buying anything that wouldn't fit in a smallish rucksack. This continued when I rented a studio flat in Testaccio, which was very modestly furnished. It never felt like a liberating, minimalist exercise, it was just rather nice not to be surrounded by stuff. This was particularly nice in the kitchen corner, and suited my cooking life at the time—that of relearning. I bought the bare

all are Rome. Though my original minutes of claustrophobia never repeated themselves, or threatened to, I set about looking for the gates.

I shrink from the feeling of being foreign—who does not? Mine may be a generation with an extra wish to acclimatize, to identify. Anywhere, at any time, with anyone, one may be seized by the suspicion of being alien—ease is therefore to be found in a place which nominally *is* foreign: this shifts the weight. Rome is the ideal environment for a born stranger; one does not, it is true, belong, but one can imitate—here is much to imitate. The injunction to do when in Rome as the Romans do was superfluous: what else is there to do? I copied the Romans

27

minimum of equipment: a pasta pan, a frying pan, and a decent knife. At times I've told myself (and others) that the meals made in those first two years were some of the best I've ever cooked. They weren't. They were good, though, and an important part of making sense of where I was, thoughts about which I'd write down, a bit too earnestly, in notebooks, wondering if one day I might write a book.

It was when I really began writing about food that I realized I missed something I'd left behind: other people's writing about food. Although inspiration came from where I was living, the inspiration about how to write about food came from the books I had read and used years before, the distinctive voices I'd so enjoyed reading and cooking with. This coincided with a trip back to the UK, during which I opened the damp boxes in my parents' garage and pulled out my favorites. It took me a while to find the most important one, the *Vegetable Book*, which still fell open at the words "Ratatouille, properly made without wateriness, is an adaptable and excellent dish."

I managed to saunter past the eagle-eyed check-in agent with an extremely overweight bag, only to be caught out by a helpful hostess who came to my assistance as I tried to heave a bag containing nine books into the overhead locker. She gave me a knowing look and heaved the bag up with me. I got back to Rome and lined up the books from England on a shelf in Rome, which felt like two halves of the same thing coming together. The shelf sagged in the middle. That night I went to bed with Simon Hopkinson, and the night after that with Jane Grigson. I remember the first time I made ratatouille in Rome; it caught on the bottom of the pan.

New books have joined my pile of favorites, notably Oretta Zanini de Vita's books about Roman food and pasta, a heavyweight volume called *The Regional Recipes of Italy*, Fergus Henderson's *Nose to Tail*, everything by the marvelous Laurie Colwin, and David Tanis's *A Platter of Figs*. However, the favorite books, the ones I brought with me from London, are still the ones I find myself turning to again and again for inspiration and information, and none more so than the brilliant *Vegetable Book*, in which history, wit, advice, recipes, good sense, and good taste are woven together into a fat volume with no pictures.

Asparagi in tre modi
Asparagus in three ways

By the time I arrived in Rome in 2005, the Campo de' Fiori market was already limping, and these days the few stalls merely hint at the vigorous market it used to be. That said, it is still unquestionably worth a visit, the earlier the better, when the light is still limpid and the market is coming to life, since its location is simply extraordinary: it's in the middle of some of Rome's most appealing streets, which turn doglegs around small piazzas and Renaissance palazzos that fade and flake around hidden courtyards.

I cycle up there once every couple of weeks, first to buy *pizza bianca* from Antico Forno, then to visit the flower stall, a neat reminder that Campo de' Fiori means "field of flowers," a pretty name for a place that was once the site of executions. In fact, I've been known to eat my pizza on the steps of the dark, cowled statue of Giordano Bruno (executed for holding the heterodox belief that the planets moved around the sun) in the middle of the piazza. Then, before the sun is too high, I visit one of the (expensive) stalls that continues the spirit of the market as it once was: that of Claudio Zampa, to buy quince and porcini mushrooms in autumn and asparagus in spring.

I am nearly as fond of asparagus as I am of fresh peas, and I have absolutely no problem with its pertinent aftereffects. I also like the fact that English and Italian asparagus can both be exquisite, a celebration of good ingredients in common rather than a battle of better. This much I know: asparagus must be very fresh, so look for stalks that are firm, bright, unblemished, and with tightly closed tips that appear to be pointing rather than nodding off. Intriguingly, asparagus continues to grow once it is picked, fulfilling its natural inclination to go to seed. As it continues to grow, the sweetness turns to woodiness and the tips open up in nature's warning not to buy it.

I have never owned a special asparagus pan, although I used to improvise one with a wire basket and a tea-towel turban on top of the pan until I steamed-burned myself. These days I simply lay the asparagus flat in well-salted water and boil it gently until it is tender but not floppy. I like asparagus served three ways: with olive oil and flakes of Parmesan, with melted butter, and, as Jane Grigson suggests, with boiled new potatoes. Asparagus is opinionated and needs wine to match. Aromatic whites from northern Italy, such as Müller-Thurgau, work particularly well.

serves 2

about 1 pound fresh green asparagus
salt
either 5 tablespoons olive oil, a spritz of lemon juice,
    and 1 ounce Parmesan
or 5½ tablespoons butter
or about 1 pound new potatoes, 2 eggs, a little melted butter,
    and good bread

Examine the asparagus stalks to see where the skin is inedibly thick. Break off the thick ends of the spears and discard them. Alternatively, pare the thick ends away with a vegetable peeler. If the stalks are very thick I pare away the skin of the whole spear, but this is controversial among asparagus aficionados.

Fill a large pan that will accommodate the asparagus lying down with water, bring it to a boil, and salt it generously. When you are ready to eat, put the spears in the boiling water and let them simmer briskly for 3–7 minutes, depending on their thickness. Lift them out when they are tender but al dente and still bright green, and let them drain on paper towels for a minute. They will continue cooking while you choose your serving method.

One: serve the asparagus with the olive oil and lemon juice and shavings of Parmesan, which has a harmoniously sulfurous nature.

Two: melt the butter until it foams gently at the edges, pour it into a small bowl, and serve it alongside the asparagus spears, encouraging everyone to dip the spears in the melted butter.

Three: boil a few small new potatoes with the asparagus and serve with *mollet* boiled eggs (which means that the whites are solid enough to peel but the yolk is soft enough to yield), melted butter, and fresh bread.

Piselli al prosciutto
Sautéed peas with prosciutto

"Pea" was Luca's fourth word ("mamma," "pasta," and "up-up" being the first three), and he seems to have inherited my love of these tiny pouches of sweet and savory, both in fresh and frozen form. As I write, we are still very much in frozen pea mode. We had them last night with fresh egg pasta in broth, and a few nights back beside mashed potatoes and a fried egg, but spring is in the air and soon the emerald-green pods will appear at the market.

Like asparagus and new potatoes, peas are an ingredient that both England and Italy can be proud of, and since my feet are firmly in both food worlds, this shared pride makes me happy. We eat them English-style with butter, in fat frittata-type omelets, with rice and pasta, and pureed into a coarse paste reminiscent of grass in both color and taste, to be smeared on toast. A relatively new favorite is a delicious Roman habit of sautéing peas with a little prosciutto until tender and deeply flavored, then finishing them off with a shower of finely chopped parsley. I particularly like peas cooked in this way with roast chicken.

serves 4–6
2 pounds unshelled fresh peas, or 10½ ounces frozen ones
2 garlic cloves
3 tablespoons extra-virgin olive oil
2 ounces pancetta, prosciutto, or bacon, chopped
2 tablespoons finely chopped flat-leaf parsley
salt and freshly ground black pepper

If you are using fresh peas, shell them, and if you have the time (or inclination) pull the stringy thread and thin membrane away from half a dozen of the pods. If you are using frozen peas, thaw them.

Peel and gently smash the garlic with the back of a knife. In a large frying or sauté pan, warm the olive oil over medium-low heat and add the garlic and pancetta. Cook until the garlic is fragrant and just colored and the pancetta has rendered its fat. Remove the garlic before adding the peas (and pods if you have them) and turn them so that each pea is glistening with oil. Add the parsley, a grind of pepper, and 4 tablespoons water if you are using fresh peas. Cover the pan, turn the heat down, and cook for 5 minutes if you are using frozen peas, or 10–15 minutes if you are using fresh ones. If the water seems insufficient, add another tablespoon, but cautiously: there should be no liquid by the time the peas are tender, just a green-tinted oily sheen. Taste and add the chopped parsley, a grind of black pepper, and salt if necessary, stir again, then serve.

Artichokes

I have a friend from London who arranges his annual business trip to Rome in April so that he can eat *carciofi* (artichokes). The exact nature of his business is ambiguous, but the ambiguity may be more intriguing than the reality. Anyway, over three days, in between business appointments, he eats *carciofi alla romana* (whole, trimmed artichokes braised stem-end up with wild mint and garlic); *carciofi alla giudea* (whole artichokes deep-fried until they look like a bronze flower); *vignarola* (a spring vegetable stew of artichokes cooked with peas and fava beans); on pizza and in pasta. If he has time—what with all the business—he will take a train out to Velletri for the festival of *carciofi,* where he eats more of the above while drinking plenty of local wine. In between business and artichokes he also finds time to go to Gammarelli, the pope's tailor, to buy socks. He then goes home with cardinal-red and bishop-purple socks and a dozen artichokes in his suitcase.

The beauty and sheer quantity of artichokes in Roman markets in late winter and spring is extraordinary, from bulbous *romano* or *mammola* artichokes as big as cricket balls with violet-stained leaves, coarse ribbed stems, and silvery glaucous green leaves; slim *spinosi* artichokes that look like beautiful weapons; to baby artichokes, purple-tinged and the size of a walnut. Extraordinary too—at least to me, who was used to only the occasional beauty to be admired and eaten leaf by leaf—is the nonchalance with which Romans treat them. Rather like going past the Colosseum every day on the way to work, it just *is*: buy them by the dozen and trim them. The first time I saw a woman trimming artichokes was at Testaccio market. She was sitting on a chair beside the stall, ankle deep in leaves and whittling something with such speed that I couldn't tell what it was. When I finally realized that it was an artichoke I was shocked, in the same way you might be on first seeing a friend whose beautiful mop has been crew cut. Once you understand, it isn't shocking at all, but makes absolute sense. Romans have found a cunning way to whittle away in a circular motion everything that is inedible, so that what you are left with is a pale, tulip-like heart that cooks beautifully.

One of the very best ways to eat artichokes is *alla giudea*, which is traditional in the Jewish community in Rome: trimmed artichokes fried until the leaves are burnished bronze, shattering, and crisp and the heart is as yielding and tender as it is possible to be (see page 55). Beyond frying, there are countless ways to prepare artichokes. I have chosen two ways that I think work well in kitchens anywhere you can find them: braised with mint and garlic, and in a spring vegetable stew. On a practical note, trimming artichokes, although it is pesky and initially makes you feel like Edward Scissorhands, is not particularly difficult once you've got the knack (see the recipes below).

Wine and artichokes are a tricky combination, as the chemical compounds in artichokes make everything you taste afterward seem oddly sweet or metallic. My wine-knowledgeable friend Hande suggests that if you are eating artichokes on their own, you should drink only water, resuming wine afterward. If, however, the artichokes are combined with something else, wines can be carefully matched. I often follow the "what goes together grows together" rule and eat artichokes from Lazio with a Malvasia from Lazio.

I will finish by mentioning an Italian drink called Cynar, a pale green, bitter aperitif based on artichokes, which comes in a green bottle with artichokes on it. You may well have seen one at the back of your parents' well-traveled friends' liquor cabinet in about 1979. It is weirdly delicious stuff, tasting medicinal, oddly sweet, and tinged with delicious bitterness. I love it served over ice as an *aperitivo* with salted almonds.

Carciofi alla romana
Roman-style artichokes

Artichokes are like Tilda Swinton as the White Witch in Narnia: beautiful, formidable, and with an insincere sweetness, which comes from the cyanin. Their flavor is intriguing and subjective (I say it's a combination of cooked asparagus, hazelnuts, and truffle). It's the thick, velvety, and yielding texture, though, of the gray-green saucer of a heart that's so special. I think one of the best ways to appreciate this is in *carciofi alla romana*, a quintessentially Roman dish of trimmed artichokes stuffed with wild mint and garlic, then cooked slowly in a little water and olive oil, stems to the sky, until all the liquid has been absorbed and they are meltingly soft and tender. In the spring, on entering a trattoria or restaurant in Rome, you will often see a platter of artichokes cooked this way, like fat, gray-green tulips, stems upward. If you do, that is what you should order. They are also surprisingly simple to make at home.

5 large globe artichokes
1 lemon, halved
2 garlic cloves
2 tablespoons very finely chopped flat-leaf parsley (optional)
2 tablespoons very finely chopped mint, ideally *mentuccia*
   (lesser calamint)
salt and freshly ground black pepper
8 tablespoons extra-virgin olive oil
½ cup white wine

You will need a large, heavy-bottomed pan with a tight-fitting lid, tall enough to accommodate the artichokes, which are to go in standing up.

Prepare the artichokes by pulling the dark, tough outer leaves downward and snapping them off just before the base. Then, using a sharp knife, pare away the tough green flesh from the base of the artichokes and stem. As you work, rub the cut edges of the artichoke with a cut lemon or sit them in a bowl of water with lemon juice.

Chop the garlic very finely. In a bowl, mix together the chopped herbs and garlic, and add a generous pinch of salt and a few grindings of black pepper. Using your thumbs, open up the artichoke flower and use a teaspoon to scrape out the hairy choke (if they are not a chokeless variety). Next, press one-fifth of the herb-and-garlic mixture into the hollow cavity. Sit the artichokes, stems upward, in the pan. Add the olive oil, wine, and enough water to come a third of the way up the leaves. Cover the pot with a damp tea towel or a piece of doubled-over paper towel and put the lid on over the towel. Bring the edges of the towel back over the top of the pan. Place the pan over medium-low heat and cook for 40 minutes. The liquid in the pan should bubble and steam purposefully but not aggressively. The artichokes are ready when a fork easily pierces the thickest part of the stem near the heart.

Once cooked, use a slotted spoon to move the artichokes onto a serving plate, stems upward. Allow them to cool to room temperature. Reserve the cooking juices and pour these over the artichokes just before serving.

Vignarola
Spring vegetable stew

Rome through the eyes of a two-year-old is simple. The Colosseum is the house of the giants; the Roman Forum is the dinosaur house; San Pietro is a big *chiesa*; and the fountains are taps, except the fountain in piazza Navona, which is a tap with a fish (the fish being the dolphin that Neptune is wrestling with). Each landmark, however familiar, is greeted with a comedy gasp, announced as though for the first time, then repeated until I have a headache: "House of the giants! House of the giants! House of the giants!", possibly trailing off into a whisper, *"house of the giants."* The market is similarly straightforward. Yesterday, Luca marched three feet ahead, pointing and announcing the stalls like a town crier: fish, meat, flowers, *pane*, dog (a pet stall), fruit, and then, at our stall— having eaten the first of this year's fresh ones yesterday—yelled *peas, peas, peas!* Gianluca immediately obliged and handed Luca a pod, which he grabbed while I made a futile attempt at "What do you say when you are given something?" But Luca was too busy opening the pod—crack!—and then, at discovering six tiny green balls suspended in the bright green case, said, "babies!"

They were babies: tiny pouches of sweet and savory that pop in your mouth, the sort of peas that elude me most of the time. We bought 3 pounds. Then, rather than listening to myself and getting us out of the market as quickly as possible by offering and revoking the usual bribes, I listened to Luca, who was shouting and pointing at a bench. So we sat in the sun and ate 1 pound, straight from their pods.

With the remaining peas I made something I look forward to each year: a spring vegetable stew, a *vignarola* of sorts, a dish of scallions, artichokes, fava beans, and peas braised in olive oil and water or white wine until tender. The key is adding the ingredients according to their cooking requirements, ending with the peas, which just need a caress of heat and the warm company of the other ingredients to release their sweetness and tease out their color. Important, too, is to add just enough liquid to moisten the vegetables and encourage them to release their own juices, the effect being an intense but gentle, graduated braise in which flavors remain distinct but harmonious. Precise timings are impossible to give, so tasting it regularly is imperative.

Tender wedges of velvety artichoke, sweet peas, buttery but slightly bitter fava beans, all bound by a weave of smothered scallion, make a dish that celebrates and captures the fleeting

brilliance of spring vegetables, and one of the best lunches I know. It's especially good with a piece of quivering-but-tensile *mozzarella di bufala* that erupts beneath your knife, and a toddler standing on a chair singing "*Voglio* peas and cheese!" before falling off and taking the glass water bottle with him.

serves 4
3 large artichokes
1 lemon
2¼ pounds fava beans in their pods
2¼ pounds peas in their pods
2 large or 6 small scallions
6 tablespoons olive oil
½ cup white wine or water
salt

Prepare the artichokes by pulling the dark, tough outer leaves downward and snapping them off just before the base. Then, using a sharp knife, pare away the tough green flesh from the base of the artichokes and stem. Detach the trimmed stems and slice them into 4 lengthwise. Cut the trimmed artichoke globes into 8 wedges. Drop the wedges and stems of artichoke into a bowl of cold water acidulated with lemon juice.

Shell the fava beans and peas. If the fava beans are large and have tough outer coats, remove them by plunging the shelled beans in hot water for 1–2 minutes, then into cold water, then squeezing and pinching off the opaque coats. Thinly slice the scallions.

Warm the olive oil in a heavy-bottomed sauté pan or enamelled cast-iron pan over medium heat. Add the scallions and cook until soft and translucent. Add the artichoke wedges and stems, stirring well so that each piece is glistening with oil. Add the wine and a pinch of salt, then stir again and cover the pan. Cook for 15 minutes, stirring and jiggling the pan from time to time.

Add the peas and fava beans, stir, cover the pan, and cook for another few minutes. Taste, season with salt, and taste again. The vignarola is ready when the vegetables are tender and the stew has come together into a soft, moist, tumbling whole. Let it settle for a few minutes, then serve just warm. It's also good at room temperature.

Patate e fagiolini conditi
Potatoes and green beans

This is an assembly more than a recipe, but it's a good one that we eat all the time in the summer: waxy boiled potatoes, tender green beans, mint, olive oil, salt, and a dash of vinegar.

There are five things to remember. Scrub, but don't peel, the potatoes, then cook them whole. Cook the beans in well-salted, fast-boiling water until they are tender with just the slightest bite, but absolutely no squeak. Tear the mint into tiny pieces with your fingers. Dress the vegetables while they are still warm with a generous pinch of salt, launched from high above so that it disperses evenly, and enough extra-virgin olive oil to make a dietician bristle and each chunk and bean glisten. Let your dressed vegetables sit in a cool place, but not the fridge, for a while before serving.

Patate e fagiolini conditi are delicious served with grilled lamb. Romans call briefly cooked young lamb cutlets, burnished outside but still pale pink and tender within, *costolette di abbacchio alla scottadito,* or simply *abbacchio a scottadito.* Literally translated, this means "lamb cutlets to burn your fingers," reminding you that they should be eaten as quickly as possible from the grill or coals—so blisteringly hot—with your fingers.

serves 4
4 large Yukon Gold potatoes, or 8 smaller ones
about 1 pound fine green beans
salt
a few small fresh mint leaves
extra-virgin olive oil, for the dressing
red wine vinegar (optional)

Scrub the potatoes and top and tail the beans. Put the potatoes whole in a large pan, cover them with cold water, add salt, and bring to a boil. Reduce the heat to a lively simmer and cook until the potatoes are tender to the point of a knife.

Bring another large pan half filled with salted water to a rolling boil, add the beans, and boil them hard, uncovered, for 8 minutes, or until they're tender but still have the slightest bite. Drain the beans.

When the beans and potatoes are cool enough to handle but still warm, put the beans in a large bowl. Using a sharp knife, pare away the potato skins, then roughly chop and break the potatoes over the beans. Tear the mint leaves into the bowl. Season generously with salt, then pour over some olive oil and the vinegar, if you are using it. Use your hands to gently turn and mix the ingredients. Taste and add more salt and olive oil if necessary. Leave to stand for at least 30 minutes before serving. Turn again before serving.

Pressed potatoes

The English cookbook most at home in a Roman kitchen is Fergus Henderson's *Nose to Tail Eating*, a favorite book from a favorite London restaurant, St John. That's mostly due to the meat and offal (*Nose to Tail*, as its name suggests, is about eating the whole animal, something offal-loving Romans know all about); to the recipes involving salt cod (about which the Romans are fanatical); but also to the vegetable and salad recipes, which are punctuated by brilliant Roman ingredients like capers, curly endive, anchovies, lemons, olive oil, mint, and parsley. The recipes have much in common with Roman food philosophy (if I can call it that): simple, good, unfussy. This is adapted from one of them.

Pressed potatoes is a brilliantly simple dish that consists of layers of sliced potatoes alternating with scant layers of tiny capers, which grow just a few yards from my flat here in Rome—not that I pick those. Having built up your layers in a loaf pan lined with plastic wrap, you put a heavy weight on top, which presses the ingredients into a sliceable loaf. The slices are both beautiful and delicious, especially with a spoonful of *salsa verde* (green sauce) and some smoked fish, ham, or hard-boiled eggs draped with anchovies.

You really do need a heavy weight, as the potatoes need to compress fully to form the sliceable loaf that's so appealing. I use an old iron that usually acts as a doorstop, which works a treat, as does a slim book with a large can of tomatoes on top. If the loaf does fall apart, don't panic: simply reinvent it by crumbling it into a potato and caper salad.

serves 4–6
4½ pounds waxy potatoes (such as Yukon Gold or the like), peeled
a healthy handful of capers (extra fine, if possible, roughly chopped if not)
salt and freshly ground black pepper
salsa verde (page 268), to serve

Put the potatoes in a large pan of salted water, bring it to a boil, and cook until tender but not falling apart—check with a sharp knife in order to catch them at the right moment, then drain well.

Line a loaf pan or terrine mold (I use a 9 × 5 × 3-inch loaf pan) with plastic wrap, leaving it to overhang the sides. As soon as the potatoes are cool enough to handle but still warm, slice them into ⅜-inch-thick rounds. Place a layer of sliced potatoes in the bottom of the loaf pan—don't be afraid to patchwork this, breaking pieces into bits if needed—sprinkle cautiously with some of the capers, and season with salt and pepper. Cover with another layer of potatoes, more capers, and salt and pepper, and repeat until the pan is full. Cover with plastic wrap and place a heavy weight on top. Place in the fridge overnight. The next day, tip the pressed potatoes out of the mold and slice with a thin, sharp knife.

Salsa verde
Green sauce

At times, I have found myself paralyzed by kitchen advice, strong opinions, and *come si fa* (how to do something); or rather, *non si fa*, (how not to). I brought it upon myself, of course, by being eager to learn, eager to be authentic—whatever that means—and eager to please. This was very much the case with green sauce, or *salsa verde*, until a good friend and even better cook reminded me that once you've listened to all the advice and tried and tested something, you must make the recipe your own.

So I did. This is my version of *salsa verde*, which owes something to every spoonful I've tasted, from Milan to Sicily, and every recipe I've read. It doesn't contain chopped egg or bread crumbs, and I don't usually include vinegar, just masses of green herbs—parsley, basil, mint, and I'd fling some dill in there if I had any—along with anchovies, the best I can find in oil, and capers, ideally those packed in salt, otherwise slightly fewer of the vinegar-packed ones, chopped and loosened with extra-virgin olive oil into a gorgeous green goddess of a sauce that precipitates a number of adjectives you could be fined for overusing: grassy, peppery, warm, musty, briny, fishy, oily, brilliant.

It's wonderful and companionable beside or over pressed potatoes, boiled meats, grilled fish, hard-boiled eggs, in sandwiches, on your face. These are merely guidelines, since in reality for a sauce like this there are no rules or strict measures. It's important you keep tasting, as the exact quantities will depend on the strength of the ingredients. In short, make the recipe your own.

When it comes to hand versus machine, it's not that one is better than the other, only different. I personally prefer it chopped by hand, as it has more substance and a more distinct, coarser texture, which is obliterated into a more consistent, pleasing smoothness by a food processor. You really do have to try both ways to decide which you like best.

makes enough to fill half a standard jam jar
a large bunch of flat-leaf parsley
a large bunch of basil
a handful of mint
a small tin of anchovy fillets in oil, drained
a handful of capers, rinsed if salted
2 garlic cloves
1 teaspoon red wine vinegar
extra-virgin olive oil
black pepper

To make the sauce by hand, chop the herbs very finely with a knife or, better still, a *mezzaluna* (a two-handled crescent-shaped chopper). Roughly chop the anchovies and capers and mix them with the herbs in a large bowl. Peel and smash the garlic with the back of a knife, then chop it very finely and add it to the bowl. Add the vinegar, if using, then stir in the olive oil a little at a time until you have a dense, spoonable sauce. Taste and season it with pepper. The anchovies and capers mean you probably won't need extra salt.

To make it in a food processor or blender, pulse-chop the herbs, anchovies, capers, and garlic until roughly blended. Transfer to a large bowl, add the vinegar, if using, then add the olive oil, stirring continuously until you have a dense, spoonable sauce.

Patate al forno con rosmarino, aglio e limone
Roast potatoes with rosemary, garlic, and lemon

I was an extremely diligent and irritatingly helpful little girl who thrived on being given jobs. One of these was being sent out into the garden with the big kitchen scissors to cut a sprig of rosemary from the bush by the garage wall. I took this job very seriously. My brother, Ben, however, took sabotaging it almost as seriously and we inevitably ending up scrabbling in the bush, the strident pine and eucalyptus scent rushing up our noses and the woody branches scratching our calves. The final blow would be Ben, faster and keener, stealing my job by grabbing the branch and taking it into the kitchen to Mum.

Despite the childhood bush incident, I like rosemary very much. Romans do too, and pair it beautifully and boldly with lamb, pork, and rabbit. They also put it with potatoes for a quintessential Roman *contorno* that you find in every trattoria every day of the year: *patate al forno* (roast potatoes). It also features on one of the best pizzas ever, the unlikely sounding *pizza con le patate* (potato pizza). In both cases the sap-green and pine-fresh flavor of the rosemary needles jolt the sturdy, yielding potatoes.

I have come to the conclusion that the more primitive my oven, the better my roast potatoes. I have never made such good ones as in the comedy gas oven I'm using now. I'm also vaguely cabbalistic about my baking pan, never washing it with detergent and turning it three times before I put it away. That said, I have also asked my

entire family to test this recipe in various ovens and various pans. It's hardly a recipe, just lots of yellow potatoes, peeled and cut into half wedges, tossed with extra-virgin olive oil, good salt, garlic, a sprig of fresh rosemary, and lemon juice, roasted (door opened and pan shaken), roasted (door opened and pan shaken), and served hot.

serves 4

2¼ pounds potatoes (not too floury or too waxy)
3 garlic cloves
a sprig of rosemary
salt
4–8 tablespoons extra-virgin olive oil
juice of ½ lemon

Preheat the oven to 400°F. Cut the potatoes into quarters, and the quarters into eighths if they are large. Smash the garlic with the back of a knife. Tip the potatoes into a baking pan, pull the rosemary leaves off the stem and sprinkle them over the potatoes along with a good pinch of salt, the garlic, lots of olive oil, and the lemon juice. Roast for 50 minutes–1 hour, or longer if they need it, shaking the pan every 10 minutes, until they are crisp and golden.

Fennel

Alice Jones, my mum's mum, was happiest when her name was written above the door of the Gardeners' Arms pub in Oldham, Manchester. I have a photo of us all standing in the pub doorway in 1977, which captures her happiness and pride quite precisely. It also captures her style: practical-with-flair blue trousers and polo neck with a belted tunic, hair set and secured with Elnett lacquer, lips tilting into a smile.

She didn't want to leave the pub and did her best to forget this fact by diligently looking after her grandchildren, my cousins, and gardening, rambling, making wine, and cooking. She was a good cook, possessing both resourcefulness and fastidious good taste. This resourcefulness, along with Grandpa Gerry's cautious stomach, meant she mostly cooked straightforward English food: a stew made with beef skirt, a breast of lamb cooked slowly in the oven while they went to the pub for a drink, a steak-and-kidney pie. Every now and then, though, when we were staying, she would pull her Jane Grigson or Elizabeth David down from the shelf and cook us something different and suggestive of somewhere else. I always had the sense that Alice wished she was somewhere else, however happy she claimed to be.

Rather incongruously, it was in her small kitchen near Dewsbury that I first helped cook fennel, which seemed a most exotic and curvaceous vegetable. She peeled away the outer layers before slicing it thickly, steaming it, and layering it in a well-buttered dish, and scattering over bread crumbs and Parmesan. I still make this dish in Rome, where the sweet, bulb or Florentine fennel known as *finocchio* is one of the prizes of the market in autumn and winter. Resembling a swollen hand, with stems like pointing fingers sprouting feathery fronds, fennel is related to anise but has none of its cousin's aggressive sharpness, but rather a clean, faintly licorice aroma. It's crisp, cool, and sweet, and one of my favorite vegetables. Mostly we eat it shaved very thinly and dressed with salt and oil, or if it is particularly succulent and sweet, more simply still, in fat wedges instead of fruit.

Finocchio alla parmigiana
Fennel baked with Parmesan

This is the Jane Grigson recipe that my granny Alice followed. The combination of soft, tender fennel in melted butter and a golden lattice of baked Parmesan, alongside a large dose of nostalgia, makes it my favorite fennel dish.

serves 4
6 fennel bulbs
butter, for greasing
salt and freshly ground black pepper
4 tablespoons grated Parmesan
2 tablespoons bread crumbs

Preheat the oven to 400°F and generously butter an ovenproof dish. Prepare the fennel by trimming the base of each bulb, cutting away the finger-like fennel tops where they meet the bulb, and pulling away any outer layers that seem particularly tough, damaged, or bruised. Quarter them lengthwise.

Bring a pot of well-salted water to a boil, add the fennel, and cook until tender but not floppy. Drain the fennel and arrange it in the prepared dish. Season with pepper, then sprinkle over the Parmesan and bread crumbs. Bake for about 15 minutes, or until the cheese is golden and the fennel is bubbling in the buttery juices.

Finocchio al tegame
Braised fennel with olive oil

Rather like the recipes for zucchini, potatoes, and artichokes, this one calls for the fennel to be braised very slowly in olive oil and a little wine or water until it is extremely tender and all the cooking juices have been reabsorbed. Cooking vegetables in this way—it works for nearly all of them—produces the most deeply flavored dish of utmost tenderness. I love this with baked fish or alone with nice bread and a lump of cheese.

serves 4 as a side dish, or 2 as a main course
2 large fennel bulbs or 4 smaller ones
6 tablespoons extra-virgin olive oil
salt
⅞ cup white wine or water

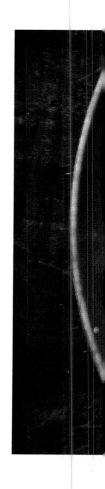

Prepare the fennel by trimming the base of each bulb, cutting away the finger-like fennel tops where they meet the bulb and pulling away any outer layers that seem particularly tough, damaged, or bruised. Cut each bulb in half, then quarters, then eighths.

In a deep sauté or frying pan, warm the olive oil over medium-low heat and arrange the fennel wedges in a single layer. Let them sizzle gently for a moment, then turn them over. Season with salt, pour over the wine or water, and increase the heat until the liquid bubbles for a minute or two, then reduce the heat. Cook the fennel, turning the wedges from time to time, until they are tender, glossy, and caramelized around the edges and the liquid has evaporated, apart from a little of the olive oil. This will take 20–40 minutes, depending on the age of the fennel. If the pan starts to look a little dry, add a couple more tablespoons water. Once cooked, toss the wedges a couple of times in the oil at the bottom of the pan, turn onto a warm serving dish, and serve immediately.

Braised lettuce with scallions

It seems counterintuitive to cook lettuce, or at least it did to me at first. Surely the whole point was that it was raw and vital, especially crisp varieties like romaine or little gem, whose job was to crunch virtuously, offering contrast to my sluggish nature. It was the inclusion of lettuce in the spring vegetable stew *vignarola* that convinced me otherwise. Salad it may be, but lettuce is a green vegetable too, and one that braises surprisingly well. I promptly found several recipes for and including cooked lettuce, which I adapted into this recipe for braised lettuce and scallions. As Simon Hopkinson says, if you have never braised a lettuce you should start now.

The method is similar to several others in this section: the smothering method. That is, having been turned in the melted butter and oil and doused with a little white wine or water, it is covered and left over a low flame so the lettuce—in a sort of pan steam-room—can cook in its own juices. Nothing of its flavor is lost, but simply reabsorbed into the leaves, which collapse into a tender and floppy pile. It's simply delicious. I serve it with roast chicken and fish cakes.

serves 4
6 little gem or 2 large romaine lettuces
a bunch of scallions
1½ tablespoons butter
3 tablespoons olive oil
7 tablespoons white wine
salt and freshly ground black pepper

Remove any dark or damaged outer leaves from the lettuce, then cut the little gem in half, or the larger lettuces in quarters, lengthwise so they remain connected. Trim and slice the scallions into 2-inch pieces.

Melt the butter and olive oil in a deep frying or sauté pan with a lid over medium-low heat, then add the scallions and lettuces and turn them in the oil and butter before adding the wine, a pinch of salt, and a grind of black pepper. Cover the pan.

Turn the heat to its very lowest and cook gently for 20–30 minutes, turning the vegetables every now and then, until they are tender and floppy. If at any point the pan looks dry, add another tablespoon of water or wine, or remove the lid and increase the heat to reduce any excess liquid. Serve immediately or at room temperature.

The traditional Roman salad is *misticanza* ("a mixture of things"): an assortment of leaves, field herbs, and aromatic shoots collected at the first signs of spring from the fields around Rome, then eaten as a salad. Italian food historian Gillian Riley reminds us that this habit of collecting wild plants is a legacy of the days when the poor, unable to afford a doctor, were cared for by country women and their collections of wild medicinal plants. Until fairly recently, women dressed in black would bring the *misticanza* they had collected to the market to sell.

We may not have a field to collect herbs and aromatic shoots from, but it's still possible to assemble a *misticanza* of sorts with an assortment of green leaves and herbs from your garden or the market, such as baby lettuce, arugula, mâche, radicchio, escarole, watercress, sorrel, baby borage, and dandelion. You need a combination of tender green leaves, some small crisp ones, something strong and peppery, and something very soft. The leaves should be washed and dried carefully (wet lettuce is the enemy of dressing, and therefore my enemy) and dressed simply with salt, lemon juice, good red wine or balsamic vinegar, and extra-virgin olive oil. I usually put these in the bottom of a large bowl, put the leaves on top, then toss them at the last minute.

My brother, Ben, and my dad are both big fans of a plain lettuce salad ("nothing fancy," Dad might say): the heart of a soft English lettuce, ripped into manageable pieces, with some of Dad's dressing (5 tablespoons olive oil, 4 of grapeseed, 1 of wine vinegar, 2 teaspoons Dijon mustard, 1 of honey, put in a jam jar, shake like mad until it emulsifies). I like this salad too and think of them both when I eat it. For four people you need three lettuces, as you're only going to use the soft heart, which should be separated into leaves and washed and dried carefully, then tossed with your favorite dressing, and served with or after most things.

Insalata di puntarelle
Puntarelle with anchovy and lemon dressing

The mere mention of *puntarelle* has me shooting off on a sentimental tangent that involves my friend Alice, a trattoria in an irritatingly pretty piazza, a paper tablecloth, Pyrex glasses, a liter of hair-curling wine, a grumpy waitress, braised rabbit, and a bowl of pale-green curls of gently bitter salad leaves with anchovy dressing.

I'd heard about an idiosyncratic salad from a Roman friend in London long before I moved here, of a Catalonian chicory with dandelion-like leaves called *puntarelle*, which, once trimmed, cut, and immersed in cold water, curled in much the same way as Shirley Temple's hair. The pale green curls are dressed with a pungent and loudly delicious dressing of anchovies, garlic, olive oil, and lemon or vinegar. I ate it with Alice during the first spring I was in Rome, and neither the wine nor the waitress could spoil our delight in the *puntarelle* salad that we, in the proprietorial manner of new arrivals in Rome, had so happily "discovered."

Nine years later, less proprietorial and pretty comfortable about still being in Rome, I prepare *puntarelle* a lot during its winter-spring season. I say prepare, but curl, pulse, and assemble is a better description. Some people say that the dressing should be made with a mortar and pestle, but I make mine with my immersion blender—not just for speed, but because I like the more consistent, thicker dressing that a few pulses creates. I also prefer lemon juice to vinegar, as it gives the dressing a citrus-sharp but less aggressive edge. *Puntarelle* is becoming more widely available, but in its absence you can use frisée.

serves 4

1 head puntarelle or frisée
1 garlic clove
4 anchovy fillets packed in oil, drained
1 teaspoon lemon juice or red-wine vinegar
4 tablespoons extra-virgin olive oil

To prepare the puntarelle: holding the whole head, pull away the dark green external leaves. Separate the individual tube-like stalks and pull off any dark green leaves. Cut away the tough lower part of each stalk, then cut the tubes in half lengthwise and then each half into strips about ⅛ inch wide. Rinse the strips under cold water, then immerse them in a bowl of iced water for 30 minutes, or until they curl. Once curled, drain and dry thoroughly.

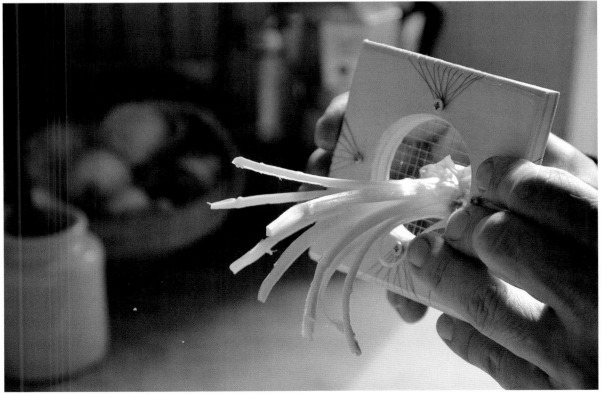

To prepare the frisée: discard the tough outer leaves (or use them for soup), then wash and carefully dry the paler inner leaves. Tear the leaves into bite-size pieces.

Peel the garlic, then cut it in half and remove the green shoot, if there is one. Pound the garlic in a mortar and pestle, then add the anchovy fillets and grind to a rough paste. Stir in the lemon juice or vinegar and then the olive oil. If you're using an immersion blender or small food processor, blend all the ingredients until they form a textured dressing. If not, just blend the ingredients in the mortar and pestle.

Tip the leaves into a bowl or serving dish, pour over the dressing, toss to coat evenly, and serve immediately.

Cauliflower with hard-boiled egg, black olives, and anchovy-lemon dressing

I follow Jane Grigson's advice when I buy a cauliflower: "If the cauliflower looks back at you with a vigorous air, buy it; if it looks in need of a good night's sleep, leave it where it is." Although we could debate what vigorous looks like, it's a good rule of thumb when choosing most fruit and vegetables. Except avocados, that is,

which taste better when they appear to have been out on the razzle two nights in a row. It's a rule of thumb that can also be applied to people, which in my case—sadly no razzle, just a wakeful toddler—means leaving me exactly where you found me.

Rather confusingly, Italians sometimes call winter cauliflower *broccolo*. Not my *fruttivendolo* Gianluca, though; he calls it *cavolo*, which usually means "cabbage," but is also an abbreviation of *cavolfiore*, which literally means "cabbage flower." To which we could reply "*che cavolo?*," which, beyond meaning "what cabbage?", is a standard response to anything flummoxing or vexing, including cauliflower etymology. Rather than looking like flowers, I've always thought good cauliflowers with unblemished, creamy-white whorls look like cumulus clouds, the ones that cluster in an otherwise blue sky.

This dish was a happy consequence of having made too much *puntarelle* dressing and a handsome cauliflower with which I was going to make cauliflower cheese until I remembered we didn't have any milk or cheese. *Che cavolo!* The anchovy and lemon dressing, bold and uncompromising, brings out the tender sweetness of the cauliflower, the olives contribute a fruit-sweet, pleasingly leathery bite, and the hard-boiled eggs round it off into a pleasing and satisfying lunch.

serves 4
1 cauliflower
4 eggs
2 garlic cloves
6 anchovy fillets packed in oil
8 tablespoons extra-virgin olive oil
2 teaspoons freshly squeezed lemon juice
2 tablespoons flavorful black olives, ideally Taggiasca olives in extra-virgin olive oil
black pepper

Pull away the tough outer leaves, cut away the hard central stem, then break the cauliflower into florets. Bring a large pot of well-salted water to a boil, add the cauliflower, and cook until tender to the point of a knife. Drain and set aside.

Hard-boil the eggs. Once they are cooked, plunge them into cold water until they are cool enough to handle, then tap the shells, peel them, and slice each one in two.

Meanwhile, make the dressing. You can either use a mortar and pestle, in which case first pound the garlic, then add the anchovy fillets and pound them to a rough paste before stirring in the olive oil and lemon; or an immersion blender or small food processor, in which case add all the ingredients and pulse rather than blast to make a consistent but slightly textured dressing.

Arrange the florets in a shallow serving dish, cutting any large ones in two, scatter over the olives, arrange the hard-boiled egg halves on top, and season with black pepper before spooning over the dressing. Serve while the cauliflower and eggs are still warm.

Pinzimonio di ceci
Chickpeas with greens

My copy of *The River Café Cook Book* sat on my mum's kitchen bookshelf during the first six years I was in Italy. Then, one Christmas, much to her dismay I reclaimed it. It was a long-lost favorite, and in my opinion ranks alongside Elizabeth David's *Italian Food* as the English cookbook that best captures the spirit and soul of Italian ingredients and cooking. It still looks as sharp and uncompromisingly good as it did when I bought it 17 years ago, and I still want to make everything in it.

It falls open at page 172, at a recipe for something Rose and Ruth call *pinzimonio di ceci,* or chickpeas with Swiss chard. As much as I like a nice food picture, it's not usually that which inspires me to cook. Quite the opposite, in fact. Pictures, especially if too pretty, styled, or framed with incongruous bits of this and that, leave me cool. This picture, however, unstyled and unframed, makes me eager to cook and eat. A woman in a white apron is holding a platter on which there is a pile of glistening chickpeas and chard flecked with tiny nubs of carrot, red onion, parsley, and chile, sitting in a generous, golden puddle of extra-virgin olive oil.

After *pasta e ceci* and hummus, this is probably my preferred way to eat chickpeas. The combination of the soft greens (which offer, as Fergus Henderson would say, "structural weave"), sweet and tender nubs of carrot and onion, heat from the chile, and depth from the wine and tomato is a full and delicious one. Wholesome but generous. It is very much a meal in itself, but I like a spoonful of ricotta beside it or an egg on top.

serves 6

about 1¼ pounds greens, preferably Swiss chard, but collard greens work well

1 red onion

2 carrots

5 tablespoons extra-virgin olive oil, plus extra to serve

salt and freshly ground black pepper

1 dried chile, crumbled

1 cup white wine

2 tablespoons tomato passata, or 1 tablespoon tomato paste

2½ cups cooked chickpeas

a generous handful of chopped flat-leaf parsley

juice of ½ lemon

Bring a large pot of well-salted water to a fast boil, add the greens, and blanch them briefly. The timing will depend on the greens; collard greens take 3–5 minutes. Taste them to check. Drain them well, and once they are cool enough to handle, chop them coarsely and set aside.

Chop the onion and carrots. Warm the oil in a heavy-bottomed sauté pan, add the onion, carrots, and a pinch of salt, and cook them

slowly for 15 minutes, or until tender. Season with a little more salt and pepper and add the crumbled chile. Add the wine to the pan and allow it to bubble away until it has almost completely reduced. Add the tomato passata or paste, greens, and chickpeas, stir, and cook, stirring every couple of minutes, for 10 minutes.

Add three-quarters of the chopped parsley and the lemon juice, stir, remove from the heat, and allow to sit for 10 minutes. Transfer to a large platter or serving plate, sprinkle with the remaining parsley and a little more extra-virgin olive oil, and serve.

Una ricetta per lenticchie
A recipe for lentils

The last recipe in this section is one of my most tried-and-trusted, if rather unimaginatively named, favorites. Perhaps it should be called "one way with lentils," as there are various. This, however, is the way I cook lentils as a side dish to serve under sausages, slices of rudely pink *cotechino*, a small wheel of baked goat's cheese, or a fried egg. It really is worth seeking out good lentils, such as Castelluccio; they become soft and gently floury, which means they will absorb all the other flavors but retain their lentil identity.

You do have to keep an eye on the lentils as they cook, as you want them to absorb all the water, but not dry out. If the pan looks dry, you can add a little more water. The final panful shouldn't be soupy, but it should ripple a little like risotto, and the lentils will of course thicken a little as they sit. Working on the principle that these lentils are delicious and almost better the next day (keep them in the fridge, pull them out an hour before you need them, and reheat them gently with a little more water), this is a double quantity for 4.

serves 8
1 onion
1 carrot
1 celery stalk
1 leek
2 garlic cloves
4–6 tablespoons extra-virgin olive oil
2½ cups small brown lentils
salt and freshly ground black pepper
a handful of finely chopped flat-leaf parsley

Finely chop the onion, carrot, celery, leek, and garlic. Coat a large, heavy-bottomed frying or sauté pan with olive oil and heat over medium-low heat. Add the chopped vegetables and cook very gently until they are soft, but not colored.

Pick over the lentils to check for tiny stones, then rinse them and add them to the pan, stirring for a minute or two so that each lentil glistens with oil. Cover them with water (the water should come about 1 inch above the lentils), bring to a boil, and reduce the heat to a simmer. Cook the lentils, stirring occasionally, keeping a beady eye out and tasting often, until they are tender but not squishy. They should still have lentil integrity and the water should have been absorbed. If the pan seems dry, add a little more water. This will take 25–40 minutes, depending on the lentils.

Season them generously with salt and pepper, and stir in the chopped parsley and another tablespoon or 2 of olive oil for shine.

5
DOLCI

A Sweet Finish

Spiced quinces in syrup

Poached apricots in spiced syrup

Baked peaches with butter and almonds

Baked pears with Marsala and cinnamon

Caramel oranges

Panna cotta

Tiramisù

Gelato drowned in coffee

Melon granita

Coffee granita

Kitty's vanilla ice cream scented with citrus

Pine nut, rosemary, and sea salt caramel brittle

Ricotta and lemon bundt cake

Cherry jam

Cherry jam tart

Rather-like-ricotta curd cheese

Ring cookies with wine and fennel seeds

Almond, pine nut, and fennel seed biscotti

Soft almond cookies

Chocolate salami

Angel wings

Sweet yeasted buns

Candied orange peel

Spiced fruit cake with saffron

I like the Roman attitude to sweet things. I like it that after a meal, especially a long one, sweetness is often provided by fruit or the spoonful of sugar you stir into your espresso, plus the knowledge that you'll walk out for a gelato later. I love the way that, should a dessert be called for, it's perfectly acceptable—encouraged even—to ask one of your guests to call in at one of Rome's countless *pasticcerie* (pastry shops) to buy something that's luscious and brassy in equal measure. It makes me smile that if you do make pudding, it may well wobble.

I like that in Rome, gelato is considered beyond the bounds of mealtimes and can be eaten whenever the heck you want, ideally while walking down the street. (The same could be said about cream cakes. I've never seen so many men eating cream cakes as I have since moving to Rome.) I adore the fact that sweets and festive food mark the year better than any calendar, and that cakes, tarts, and cookies are eaten for breakfast. Cookies, I should note, are also dipped in wine, a good thing in my book. It seems fitting that for the Romans, a spiced fruit cake for Christmas means as much as it does to the English.

The recipes in this section reflect this Roman attitude: fruit, some wobbly puddings, a breakfast cake that's at home anywhere, cookies for dipping, a chocolate salami, and a spiced fruit cake painted yellow. As with the rest of the book, the recipes are inspired by, and I hope loyal to, Roman food traditions, but are also influenced by my English roots, by Vincenzo's Sicilian ones and—perhaps most importantly—by how we like to eat.

The time for fruit

My friend Ezio knows how to choose a good watermelon: the color, the bowling ball weight, the full B-flat when given a proper thud. He also knows how to cut one, which might sound like the most obvious thing in the world, but isn't. After inserting the point of the knife he uses his significant body weight to lever it down, cracking as much as cutting, until the fruit splits and exposes two bright rounds of almost rudely red flesh. The same movement is used to cut one of the halves in two, then swifter cuts and cracks divide the fruit into craggy wedges that are passed around the table. Some people approach their wedge with a knife and fork, but most forgo any cutlery intervention and meet the crystalline flesh head on, spilling ruby-tinted juice and black seeds, leaving lips cold, chins glistening,

and wrists a temptation for the wasps that hover nearby. Vincenzo is the only one at the table who squeezes lemon juice on the red flesh, because he is Sicilian and squeezes lemon over whatever he can.

There is, I think, no better place to observe the place and importance of fruit in an Italian meal than at the table with Ezio, Ruth, and their four kids. However long or short the meal, and whether there's another dessert to come or not, fruit is always served. Sometimes it's from their garden, sometimes not. Either way, it's always served generously and with a sense of easy ceremony. In winter there's what I used to consider the boring but reliable fruit: apples, pears, oranges, or clementines with bright green leaves. Ezio peels the fruit and passes the slices or segments around the table to those who can't peel as niftily as him. The arrival of spring is marked by strawberries, and then, a little later with the heat of June, the first figs, pale green with white cracks, and if you're lucky a teardrop of nectar at the tip of the stalk. Melons next: fragrant cantaloupe, or better still an almost-white galia melon to

be carved into new moons, and soon after the stone fruit, as flushed as self-conscious teenagers: apricots, peaches, *nespole*, and plums. As summer progresses, the cherries darken from cerise to purple and arrive at the table in the biggest colander, to be grabbed by the handful, bitten into, and have their stones spat out from mouths to hollow fists. Ezio, the king of cherry eating, is the fastest. By late July the watermelons are humming like Pavarotti and provide abundant, careless refreshment, both sweet and thirst quenching. Autumn is marked by the arrival of grapes in huge bunches with vine handles, and soon after orange persimmons forewarn the return of winter, telling us that the fruit cycle at the Ferraro-Duffy table is about to begin again.

Choosing a partner to serve with the fruit is really no different from ordinary matchmaking in that you consider a suitable partner, introduce them at the table and then leave things be, or rather leave your guests to get on with it. A bowl of sugar and wedges of lemon for the strawberries, a lump of deep yellow Cheddar for a rough-skinned Russet apple, a piece of blue-veined cheese for the figs, a round of goat's cheese for the grapes or cherries. There's an Italian saying that goes something like "Don't let the farmer know how good cheese is with pears." I suppose this is because if we do tell him—although I suspect he already knows—he might not share his pears, or his cheese, depending on what sort of farmer he is. Anyway, in case you don't know—which I think you probably do—pears pair extremely well with cheese. I particularly like a ripe Comice or Bosc, peeled, sliced, and eaten with craggy pieces of pecorino or Parmesan, the sweet, vinous flavor of the pear contrasting with the salty, granular cheese. What I like even more is pear, cheese, and a slice of what Vincenzo's Sicilian family call *cotognata*, or quince paste.

We had a quince tree in the garden of the house I grew up in. The fruits that hung from its branches were small and hard, their flesh astringent; we'd dare each other to take a bite and then, our mouths puckering, hurl the rest in fruit warfare. "Benjamin, do not throw fruit at your sisters," Mum might shout from the kitchen door, when the real culprit and fast bowler was my younger sister Rosie. Occasionally, Mum had a bowl of quinces from the tree on the kitchen table, which I thought looked nearly as odd as the ornamental pumpkins she also liked. Odd, but I did recognize that they smelled beautiful. Now, years later, in my Roman kitchen at the right time of year, I sometimes have a bowl of quinces on the table, and Luca, as if to take me down a peg or two, tries to take a bite, says *blurgh*, and hurls the fruit across the kitchen.

The quince is an ancient fruit, part of the rose family and cousin to the apple and pear, which accounts for its unmistakable scent: apple, pear, rose, musky honey, and a dash of something exotic. It is odd-looking, bulbous, and could be the love child, conceived during a night of passion at the back of a fruit crate, of a knobby yellow pear and an underripe cooking apple. Quinces are covered in a downy brown coat, and their hard, astringent raw flesh gives little clue as to the delights in store when they are cooked with sugar or honey.

Quinces were beloved by the ancient Romans, and were also used in English medieval and Italian Renaissance cooking. The food historian Gillian Riley notes some wonderful-sounding dishes in her companion to Italian food, such as roasted duck with quince cooked in sweet wine; a sauce of quince with spices and bitter orange for serving with meat; a *minestra* of quince cooked in broth, thickened with cheese and egg. Jane Grigson, too, has a whole section on quinces in her book about traditional English food. These days, quinces have become rather rare and unfamiliar, particularly in England. They're less so in Italy, where they are still used to make compotes, jams, clear jellies, and a firm jelly called *cotognata*. They're not the easiest fruit; they require a bit of attention and a keen hand to deal with the hard flesh. Like me on a Monday morning, quinces need sweetening up; a patient simmer, a slow bake or poach, to bring out the best in them and transform them into something delicious.

Cotogne in composta
Spiced quinces in syrup

Quinces poach beautifully, becoming tender and succulent while resolutely holding their shape and pleasing grainy texture. They taste like buttery poached apples, fragrant pears, sweet honeyed wine, and something sharp and tropical all at the same time. Poaching also changes their color from honey yellow to anything from peach to—if you're lucky—an extraordinary deep red. The addition of lemon, cloves, and pepper lends a soft, spicy warmth. Poached quinces are delicious with thick cream or Italian mascarpone; and they make a good breakfast with yogurt and muesli. They also have an affinity with cheese, particularly Parmesan, and cold meat such as boiled bacon, chicken, or turkey, acting rather like a spiced fruit chutney.

serves 6
2¼ pounds quinces
zest of 1 organic lemon
1¼ cups granulated sugar
6 cloves
6 black peppercorns
⅞ cup white wine

Wash, peel, core, and cut the quinces into eighths. Using a peeler, pare away the lemon zest. Put the quince pieces, along with the cores and lemon zest, in a large, heavy-bottomed pan along with all the other ingredients and 2 cups (500 ml) cold water.

Bring to a gentle boil, then reduce the heat to a simmer and cook for about an hour, or until the quinces are tender. Lift the quince pieces into a serving dish with a slotted spoon, then continue simmering to reduce the syrup until it is thick enough to coat the back of a spoon. Strain it through a sieve and pour it over the quince pieces. Serve warm.

Cooking fruit

If the quince tree provided ammunition, the large Bramley apple tree, with its branches spread wide, provided a place from which to fire it at the unsuspecting enemy emerging from the house. There were also a pair of smaller apple trees, a huge old crabapple, and rhubarb in the vegetable patch in the garden of the house I grew up in. It may have been a piddling orchard but it provided plenty of fruit, most of which needing cooking into submission. Consequently we ate a lot of poached, stewed, and baked fruit. My brother and sister protested, but I rarely did. My absolute favorites were apples stuffed with butter and raisins and baked until they burst into a juicy fluff, or rhubarb poached with just enough sugar to soften the sharpness but not enough to completely mask it, served warm with cold cream. There were pies and crumbles too, of course, which nobody complained about, but fruit cooked until tender and served with custard or cream was what I liked best. It still is.

Bramley apples and rhubarb may be hard to come by in Rome, which I don't mind (they're good things to be missed and looked forward to when I go back to England), but there's plenty of other fruit to be baked and poached, most notably in our kitchen apricots in spiced syrup, peaches baked with butter and almond, and pears with Marsala and cinnamon.

Poached apricots in spiced syrup

Some years ago my best friend threw a spoonful of crème fraîche in my face. Although not planned, it was inevitable. Romla tells the story well: the restaurant near Villefranche-sur-Mer, the chicken roasted in a wood oven, the jars of poached apricots in syrup, the pail of crème fraîche, the ex-boyfriend, the throw. So here we were, coming to the end of a long meal that had involved plenty of wine, and there they were, the clip-topped jars of poached fruit, and beside them the pail of white and a large spoon. Our eyes locked, in much the same way they had locked just before Romla had had to slap my face repeatedly during an earnest scene of overacting at drama school. Her eyes narrowed. The blob landed just short of my left eye and sent a little snowstorm across my head. Everyone at the table looked shocked, and we laughed for the next two days.

The apricots may have been overshadowed by the slapstick, but they were a good enough food memory to be filed away. The memory was nudged years later by a recipe that caught my eye and a pile of pale orange apricots blushed with pink at the market. After quinces, apricots are my favorite fruit for poaching in syrup because their texture changes, becoming somehow tighter and plumper but always tender. The scrolls of cinnamon bark lend warm spice, the pepper heat, the lemon a sharp edge, and the cloves some spicy intrigue. Although good right away, poached apricots are infinitely better after a few days spent wallowing in their spicy syrup. I like them for dessert with crème fraîche (throwing is optional). I also like them for breakfast with Greek yogurt or ricotta and some toasted hazelnuts that have been broken into bits. This is not real preserving, so the jar should be kept in the fridge, but will do so happily for a couple of weeks.

makes 1 quart
20 ripe-but-firm apricots
1 vanilla pod
1 cup plus 2 tablespoons superfine sugar
7 thick strips organic lemon zest
   (you'll need 2 or 3 lemons)
2 cinnamon sticks
4 cloves
6 black peppercorns

Rinse and cut the apricots in half and remove the stones. Split the vanilla pod in half lengthwise and scrape out the seeds from the pod with the tip of a sharp knife. Put them in a large, heavy-bottomed saucepan with the empty pod, 1 quart filtered water, the sugar, lemon zest, cinnamon, cloves, and peppercorns. Gently bring to a boil and cook, stirring, until the sugar has dissolved.

Now you are going to cook the apricots in two or three batches, depending on the size of your pan. Add the first batch and simmer, stirring once or twice, for 2–6 minutes, or until tender. The length of time will depend on the ripeness of the fruit. Using a slotted spoon, lift the apricots out of the syrup and into some very clean canning jars. Put the next batch in the syrup, poach in the same way, and lift into the jars. Repeat, if necessary, with a final batch.

Next, scoop out the lemon, peppercorns, cloves, and cinnamon and divide them between the jars. Bring the syrup to a fast-rolling boil and leave it boiling energetically until it has reduced by about one-third. Divide the syrup between the jars.

Seal and store the jars for a few days in the fridge before serving the apricots cold or at room temperature with a dollop of crème fraîche, mascarpone, or thick Greek yogurt.

Peaches, apricots, plums, and fresh purp... ...
cut up into rather small squares. Make it in the morning for the
evening, add a little sugar and lemon juice, which will dissolve to
a syrup, and serve it very cold.

ZABAIONE

For each person allow the yolks of 2 eggs, 2 teaspoonfuls of sugar and 1 small sherry
glassful of Marsala.

Beat the yolks and the sugar together until they are white and
frothy. Stir in the Marsala, and put the whole mixture into a

Pesche ripiene
Baked peaches with butter and almonds

Peaches, like apricots, have a kernel inside their stone that
is reminiscent of bitter almonds. In fact, apricot kernels are
sometimes used instead of bitter almonds to make tiny, domed
amaretti biscuits. That's why there's such a pleasing symmetry
to this dish, in which peaches are stuffed with butter and crushed
amaretti, the removed stone having left a perfect hollow. In the
absence of amaretti, ground almonds work just as well.

Good things happen when peaches are baked with butter and
almonds: the fruit shrivels and its flavor is intensified, the butter
and juices create a sticky, rose-tinted syrup, and the amaretti or
almonds give a crumbing texture. By the time they're ready, the
peach halves should be slumped as deeply in the dish as my family
are in armchairs after Sunday lunch. I think these peaches are best
about 45 minutes after coming out of the oven, so they are still just

a little warm and the sticky juices are thick but still spoonable. Having said that, I made a tray for a supper last week and they sat for about 5 hours before we finally ate them with a spoonful of mascarpone. If you do keep them overnight, keep them in the fridge, but remember to pull them out about half an hour before eating. I also like two halves for breakfast with Greek yogurt.

serves 4

4 tablespoons soft unsalted butter, plus extra for greasing
4 ripe peaches
6 amaretti biscuits, or scant ½ cup almond flour
¼ cup brown sugar
1 egg yolk
grated zest of 1 organic lemon
mascarpone, to serve

Preheat the oven to 360°F and butter an ovenproof dish.

Rinse the peaches and rub them dry. Cut them in half, remove the stone, and use a teaspoon to scoop away any hard flesh or fragments of stone that might be left in the hollow. Arrange the peach halves cut-side up in the oven dish.

Wrap the amaretti in paper or put them in a small plastic bag, then crush them using a rolling pin. In a small bowl, mash together the butter, sugar, crushed amaretti, egg yolk, and lemon zest. Spoon a walnut-size blob of this mixture into the hollow of each peach half.

Bake for 40 minutes, basting a couple of times, or until the fruit is tender, golden, and a little wrinkled at the edges. Allow the peaches to sit for at least 30 minutes before serving with mascarpone.

Pere al forno con marsala e cannella
Baked pears with Marsala and cinnamon

I ate pears baked with Marsala and scrolls of cinnamon at the River Café restaurant in west London several years before I came to Italy. I think it was the same meal at which I first ate linguine with crab and baked sea bass. It was certainly when I tasted their infamous Chocolate Nemesis, a spectacular pudding made with chocolate, eggs, and sugar that I later tried and failed (and wasted 12 eggs) to make at home in my flat on Haverstock Hill.

Years later in Rome, having been given a bottle of Sicilian Marsala and having rescued my *River Café Blue Book,* which had been curling at the edges in a damp box in my parents' garage ever since I moved to Italy, I made these pears for the first time. It's a simple and clever idea: pears are rubbed with butter (which is one of my favorite recipe instructions), placed in a shallow dish, doused with Marsala, sprinkled with sugar and bits of broken cinnamon stick, and then baked, first under an aluminum foil tent, then uncovered, until they're tender and sit in a pool of sticky Marsala sauce. The key then is to roll them around in the sauce, letting them soak up as much as possible, and serve them just warm with a blob of mascarpone. Of course, the last pear eaten for breakfast the next day is the best one of all.

serves 6
6 Comice pears
3 tablespoons soft unsalted butter
1 cup dry Marsala
1 cup sugar
2 cinnamon sticks
mascarpone, to serve

Preheat the oven to 360°F. Slice the bottom off each pear so that they sit flat. Using a sharp knife, cut out the central core as best you can. Rub some butter over the skin of each pear and sit them, stalk upward, in an ovenproof dish. Pour over the Marsala, sprinkle on the sugar, and break the cinnamon sticks roughly over the pears. Cover the dish loosely with foil.

Bake for 25 minutes, then remove the foil and reduce the oven temperature to 325°F. Continue baking for another 25 minutes, or until the pears are very tender and slightly shriveled. Serve warm or at room temperature, with some of the sticky juices and a spoonful of mascarpone.

Arance caramellate
Caramel oranges

One of my favorite pieces of food writing is from Elizabeth David's *Italian Food,* in which she describes the kitchen of the Taverna Fenice in Venice. The colors of the kitchen, she notes, are reminiscent of a Venetian painting: saffron-colored polenta bubbling in a copper pan, an orange and umber sauce of tomatoes, rose-colored scampi and vermilion crabs contrasting with the marble table, coils of gold fettuccine drying in braided baskets, Sicilian oranges luminous with their sugary coating sitting in the larder. It is clearly writing from another time—1954, to be precise—but it's incredibly evocative and I come back to it again and again, not least because it's the introduction to one of my favorite fruit desserts with that luminous fruit in the pantry: caramel oranges.

Just three ingredients—oranges, sugar, and water—are interplayed cleverly. Oranges are peeled and then dipped in a simple sugar syrup. The peel is thinly sliced and caramelized in the same syrup before being piled on top of the now-glistening oranges. The sugar syrup, by now scented with orange essential oil, is reduced further and poured over the fruit. Once chilled, the oranges look like big jewels with a Philip Treacy headpiece sitting in a simmering puddle. They feel more like 1979 than 1954 because they remind me of the helix-print curtains with orange and copper swirls in my school friend's living room.

serves 4
4 large organic oranges
¾ cup (150 g) superfine sugar

Using a vegetable peeler, carefully pare away the zest, taking as little pith as possible, from 2 oranges. Cut this zest into matchstick-size lengths and cover it with cold water in a small pan. Bring to a boil and cook for 7 minutes to remove the bitterness, then drain and set aside.

Now, working with a sharp knife, pare off the white pith from the zested oranges, and remove the peel and pith from the other ones. Set the oranges aside.

Make a syrup by dissolving the sugar in about ⅔ cup water over low heat, then increasing the heat and boiling until it reduces and forms a syrup that coats the back of a spoon. Roll the oranges in the syrup, letting them sit for about 5 minutes, turning and rolling from time to time so as to soak up as much syrup as possible. Arrange the syrup-soaked oranges on a serving plate.

Put the blanched zest matchsticks in the syrup over medium heat, bring to a boil, and cook until they are transparent but still floppy. Arrange a little pile of caramelized zest on top of each orange, pour the syrup over each one, then chill before serving just so.

Panna cotta

Panna cotta, which literally means "cooked cream," is not in fact cooked. Cream, perhaps with a little added milk, is gently warmed with sugar and often a vanilla pod, mixed with softened gelatin, then molded and chilled. The resulting custard is a delicate set cream turned out on a plate, and looks like a smooth, milky-white sandcastle, which—and apparently this is the key—quivers and wobbles like a woman's breast.

That wobble means that the panna cotta is softly set. It should tremble as you bring it to the table, and your spoon should sink easily into the milky-white mound. The texture should be soft, smooth, silky, and untroubled. The taste should be simple and clean, delicate and dairy, of cream sweetened with sugar and flavored with real vanilla.

For such a simple dessert, there's a lot of panna cotta advice around, and as with almost all Italian culinary wisdom, even the simplest of recipes comes with the obligatory suggestion: practice. So it was with the advice a friend gave me while we leaned against the bar in Barberini one gray Wednesday afternoon. When an Italian shares a recipe with you it's likely to be dotted with variables and gestures that suggest "some" or "to taste" or, bewilderingly, "enough." This is because they know and understand that ingredients, whether tomatoes, potatoes, butter, flour, cream, or vanilla, vary from kitchen to kitchen, from place to place, from season to season; that what may seem sweet to one person is not to another; that gelatin can be unpredictable; that wobbles are personal.

With the spirit of Italian culinary wisdom in mind, and working on the principle that panna cotta, once made, is something you'll probably want to make again and again, I suggest you treat the recipe below as a template. I use *panna fresca,* which is technically single cream but seems a little richer, but you will likely use heavy cream or half-and-half or a mixture of both. My friend was vague about sugar, making a tipping gesture when it came to telling me the quantity, which was charming but not very specific. A bit of trial and error ensued. I err on the not-so-sweet side and find that 6 tablespoons is about right. Vanilla? I like it, you might not; if I didn't have the real thing I wouldn't bother with vanilla essence, though. Gelatin is pesky stuff. You need enough to set your cream to the requisite quiver, but not so much as to seize it into the consistency of a car tire. I do hope you can find gelatin leaves; the powder is a pest and agar agar is just odd. You need 3 leaves in my book.

Even though panna cotta looks very pretty served in a glass with a layer of fruit sauce or syrup poured on top, I like mine turned out on a plate in all its milky-white, wobbly glory. I am happy to eat it just so, but I really like panna cotta with some fruit, or even better, a spoonful of fruit sauce. The idea of caramel or chocolate sauce might seem appealing, but I think it all ends up being too much. Panna cotta pairs well with sharp, edgy, acidic fruit, such as sour cherries, blackberries, cranberries, black currants, or red currants, all of which, cooked briefly or simply mashed with a tiny bit of sugar, offset and accentuate the creaminess and look wonderfully dramatic, like red lips and pale skin, next to your innocent white pudding.

serves 4 (6 at a stretch, but who wants to stretch?)
vegetable oil, for greasing, if needed
1⅓ cups heavy cream
⅔ cup half-and-half
1 vanilla pod
3 gelatin leaves
6 tablespoons to ½ cup superfine or confectioners' sugar

You'll need 4 metal panna cotta molds or ramekins (which need to be lightly greased with vegetable oil). If you don't want to turn them out, use 4 glasses.

Pour the cream into a pan. Use a small sharp knife to split the vanilla pod lengthwise, then scrape the seeds out. Add the seeds and split bean to the pan. Warm the cream gently over low heat, but do not allow it to boil. Remove from the heat and set aside for 10 minutes so that the vanilla infuses into the milk.

Soak the gelatin leaves in a bowl of cold water for 5 minutes, or until they are very soft and floppy.

Remove the vanilla pod from the pan. Return the pan to low heat, add the sugar, and stir until it has dissolved. Squeeze the water out from the gelatin leaves and add them to the pan. Stir until the gelatin has dissolved. Remove the pan from the heat.

Divide the mixture between your molds or glasses and chill in the fridge for at least 3 hours. To turn them out, dip the base of the molds briefly in boiling water, then invert onto serving plates. Serve just so, or with a spoonful of sharp fruit sauce or coulis.

Caffè

Before arriving in Italy I hadn't drunk coffee for several years, for several reasons, none of which are particularly interesting. I returned to coffee-drinking with a *ristretto* in a noisy bar near Napoli airport about an hour after I first landed. As the intense half-inch of dark liquid invaded every crevice of my palate and seeped into my system, I enjoyed a moment of caffeine ecstasy that I'm not sure will ever be repeated. Tiredness banished, I then ignored advice and decided to find my bed-and-breakfast on foot. After an hour spent dodging cars and mopeds ridden by helmetless youths and walking down alleys strung out with damp washing, their walls encasing shrines to the Madonna framed with pink plastic flowers, and the air thick with Neapolitan dialect, I found myself back where I'd started. I had another espresso and caught a taxi.

In standard Italian, *caffè* means coffee, while *bar* means café, as in coffee shop or coffee bar. Romans love their *caffè* and the city is punctuated by bars in which the real business of life is conducted over small cups. In Testaccio alone there are 16 bars, all of which I have visited, but only one with any real loyalty: Barberini on via Marmorata.

In the early days I lived on the other side of the quarter, but now I live just around the corner from Barberini. These days I also have a companion, my little boy, Luca, who walks with me each morning, past the pet shop, the *tabacchi*, the bank, and then through the pale wood door up to the cashier of the bar I have visited most days for the last nine years. Despite the familiarity I will always be a *straniera* (foreigner), a term I don't mind anymore; after all, I am. Luca, however, is not: he has grown up here, this is his bar. He pummels his fists on the front of the glass counter for a *maritozzo*, a sticky, yeasted bun, then pummels on my leg so that I will lift him up onto the lip that runs around the sickle-shaped bar. I have barely touched the 10 *centesimi* coin and the receipt on the counter before Paolo puts a cappuccino in front of me, its thick *schiuma* (frothed milk) resting in promising folds. Luca is given an espresso cup of the same creamy folds, which he eats with a teaspoon. Here it is, one of the best moments of the day and one of the things I love most about living in Italy: standing at the bar in a bar with a coffee before me. I drink in the moment and the contents of the cup quickly. People ebb and flow throughout the morning at Barberini. The bar might be surrounded by a three-deep throng, or just dotted: the woman from the launderette, a fireman from the station opposite, the girl from the *canestro*, and Laura from the spice shop, all engaged in breakfast contemplation, together but alone.

Later in the day I will return for an espresso. If it's after three o'clock, the other Paolo is usually working and the bar is quiet, the machine shining accordingly, and the top stacked with warm cups. Watching a good barista make an espresso is something I never tire of, the series of movements and sounds that conclude in a small, white cupful: the dark roasted grounds deposited into the basket and pressed firmly, then twisted into place; the hiss of steam pressure within that forces the correct measure of water through the compressed coffee, resulting in a dribble of essence finished with *crema*, the thin layer of foam on top. I'm told the pour time is 20 seconds, but it depends on the machine. Vincenzo is habitual about having a glass of water before an espresso—in Sicily you are given one as a matter of course—and I have picked up the habit, since the flavor is heightened in a cold, clean mouth. The cup is placed on the saucer. Here it is again: that moment, which I drink in quickly, although not quickly enough to catch Luca, who is running round the bar as if he's had several espressos and may well be trying to turn off the switch of the cake fridge. We say good-bye and leave.

At home I make coffee in the *moka*, or metal stovetop coffee maker, of which I have three different sizes that stand like unpacked Russian dolls next to the stove. Although it's a simple device— a top and bottom screw together to enclose ground coffee in a compartment between them—a moka takes a little getting used to, to perfect the amount of coffee and water and recognize the

delicious gurgle of the coffee erupting into the top section, at which point you turn the heat down. Made well, with the correct coffee grind, moka coffee has an enormous, full flavor and intensity—perfect in fact for the following two desserts, and the coffee granita.

Tiramisù

Well made, a tiramisù is a bloody good dessert, a sort of extra-boozy, fruitless, caffeinated trifle dredged with cocoa. It's prepared—constructed, really—by alternating layers of savoiardi (ladyfingers) soaked in espresso and dark rum with a cream made from mascarpone cheese, eggs, sugar, and more booze, then finished with a liberal dusting of unsweetened cocoa powder. Literally translated, *tiramisù* means "pull-me-up" or "pick-me-up." It's a pick-me-up of considerable force, but one that shouldn't impose or sit heavily. Rather, it should delight and leave you wanting more.

After gelato, which is more a way of life than a dessert, tiramisù is probably Italy's most popular and ubiquitous *dolce*. You'd be hard pressed to find a restaurant or trattoria that doesn't have a vast cocoa-dredged tray of it somewhere, to be served in much the same way as lasagne, or a cluster of individual tiramisùs in the fridge. It is, however, a relatively recent invention. Apparently—and who am I to doubt it?—the original was created in the 1970s at the restaurant Le Beccherie in Treviso. The idea caught on, and today there are as many recipes, tips, and tiramisù secrets as there are tiramisù cooks.

I'm not sure why, but I think it tastes better when eaten from a glass, ideally a tumbler. The modest depth and sloping sides provide a perfect vessel for the six graduating layers. Actually, nine layers if you include the cocoa, which can be sprinkled on top of each of the three layers of cream. A glass tumbler is also the perfect way to both display your imperfect layers and contain the inevitable chaos as you plunge your teaspoon down to the bottom of the glass in order to get a perfect spoonful: a soft clot of coffee-and-rum-soaked sponge, a nice blob of pale, quivering cream, a good dusting of cocoa, and just a little of the coffee and rum pond at the bottom of the glass.

makes 6 (ideally in ⅔-cup glass tumblers)

⅔ cup strong espresso coffee, still warm
2 tablespoons dark rum or brandy
½ cup plus 1 tablespoon superfine sugar
3 eggs
⅓ cup Marsala
8¾ ounces mascarpone
12 ladyfinger cookies
good-quality unsweetened cocoa powder, for dusting

Mix the espresso with the rum and 2½ tablespoons of the sugar and stir until the sugar has dissolved.

Separate the eggs, putting the yolks in one bowl and the whites in another. Add the Marsala and remaining sugar to the egg yolks and whisk until the mixture is light and fluffy before adding the mascarpone and stirring it in carefully. Whisk the egg whites until they form stiff peaks. Gently but firmly, fold the egg whites into the egg yolk mixture with a metal spoon.

For each tumbler you will need 2 ladyfingers. Submerge a ladyfinger into the coffee mixture until it is sodden but not collapsing. Gently break it in half and tuck half in the base of the glass. Spoon over a tablespoon of the mascarpone cream before placing the other half of the biscuit on top and covering it with another spoonful of cream. Using a fine-mesh sieve, dust the surface with cocoa powder. Take another biscuit, soak it as before, break it in half, and place both halves side by side on top of the cocoa-dusted mascarpone cream. Cover the surface with more cream.

Repeat this process with the other 5 tumblers. Keep them in the fridge for at least 8 hours before eating, so that they are absolutely set. Before serving, dust the surface of each one very liberally with more cocoa powder. Eat.

Affogato al caffè
Gelato drowned in coffee

Affogato means "drowned," so *affogato al caffè* means "drowned in coffee," a state I am very familiar with. It's simple: a single scoop of gelato drowned in a single espresso. The effect of pale and dark, hot meeting cold, sweet and lactic meeting a full, tannic espresso is delicious, and one of my favorite ways to end a meal. Time is of the essence: you need to plunge your spoon in quickly so as to appreciate the contrast between hot and cold and the still-distinct flavors before the cream melts into the dark liquid and you are left with a toffee-colored inch to be drunk from the glass. With its fleeting nature in mind, the best way to serve this is to keep the gelato and coffee separate and let people do the drowning themselves.

serves 4
4 scoops good vanilla gelato, or *crema* or *fior di latte* gelato
4 shots freshly brewed espresso

Give everyone a glass containing a scoop of gelato, a cup of espresso, and a spoon. On your marks, get set, pour the espresso over ice cream, then eat.

Granita is a coarse-textured water ice, a slightly slushy, grainy mass of sweetened flavored water that is frozen and crushed to produce something between a drink and sorbet. It is the simplest and easiest of frozen treats. Vincenzo likes to remind me that granita originates, like him, from Sicily. It can be made from nut milk—almond is particularly good—and most fruits and vegetables. Melon and Campari, lemon and mint, blood orange, and of course coffee are all favorites. There are two ways to make granita. The first involves no intervention and a food processor. The second, for those of us without a processor, is more of an affair, but rewards you with lovely, distinct crystals.

One: pour the sweetened liquid into ice cube trays. Once frozen, blend into fine, soft crystals in a food processor.

Two: pour the sweetened liquid into a bowl or plastic container and put it in the freezer. After a couple of hours, move, stir, and—for want of a better word—agitate the granita as it starts to freeze. Do it again an hour later, disturbing the surface of the granita before sliding it back into the freezer. Repeat this process every hour or so (probably not more than 4 times in total), making sure you scrape down the sides, until you have an icy slush like the snow by midday, ready to spoon into glasses. In my freezer, in a medium-size metal bowl, this generally takes 4 hours and 4 agitations, which makes it sound like a lot of bother, which it isn't, or a 1980s dance.

Granita di melone
Melon granita

It needs to be hot for me to have any real enthusiasm for granita. There was one day last week, for example, while coming home on the 280 bus, the temperature flirting around 86 degrees, my son kicking my calf, when I could think of nothing but diving into water and icy shards of pink. There was no hope of diving, but at least I could make granita. I blasted the chunks of melon with such force that I sent an arc of splatters almost as high as the mark the moka coffee pot made the day it exploded. Luca and I had two glasses each, though, and might have had a third, were it not for a kamikaze wasp.

I make melon granita with both fragrant cantaloupe and watermelon. In both cases, I blast the seedless cubes with my

immersion blender. I then add the juice of a lemon to the melon pulp and taste. If the melon is as sweet as it should be, I don't add sugar; if not I add 1 or 2 heaped tablespoons of superfine sugar. I sometimes add a tablespoon of orange flower water to the cantaloupe pulp too. I then prepare the granita in one of the two ways described above and serve it in glasses. Melon granita is especially good if you pour a little Campari over the top.

serves 6
1 large or 2 small melons, ideally cantaloupe or watermelon (you need about 1¾ pounds melon flesh)
1–2 heaped tablespoons superfine sugar (as needed)
juice of 1 large lemon
1–2 tablespoons orange flower water (optional)

Quarter the melon, scoop out the seeds, and cut away the flesh from the rind. Cut the flesh into large chunks and blend it into a pulp using a food mill, immersion blender, or ordinary blender. Transfer the pulp to a bowl. Add the sugar, lemon juice, and orange flower water, if using, and stir well. Tip the sweetened pulp into a freezerproof container or ice cube tray and prepare according to one of the methods above (page 321).

Granita di caffè
Coffee granita

This is what I want at about four o'clock on a hot afternoon, when the caffeine lifts my weary spirits and the iced shards cool me from the inside.

serves 4
scant 1¾ cups very strong espresso
2 tablespoons superfine sugar
1⅓ cups very cold heavy cream

Make the espresso, and while it is still hot, stir in the sugar until it has completely dissolved. Once the coffee is cool, prepare the granita using one of the two methods above (page 321). While it freezes, whip the cream. Serve the granita in glasses, topped with whipped cream.

Grattachecca

It seemed only right that before writing this, on a hot Saturday afternoon in late June, I should walk about 300 yards through streets that echo with afternoon naps to a small kiosk on the corner of via Branca and via Beniamino Franklin. For a moment I thought it was closed, the black metal grilles pulled and padlocked, until I heard an unmistakable sound from the side of the kiosk: the distinct grating swipes, like a coarse spade shoveling tenacious snow, of a metal tool against a block of ice.

In the hot summer months, *grattachecca* is a Roman institution, served from historic bottle-lined kiosks dotted throughout the city. The name comes from *grattare*, "to grate," and *checca,* an old word for a solid block of ice, and that's precisely what *grattachecca* is: ice, shaved or scratched coarsely from a solid block with a metal grater surrounded by a box, then tipped into a plastic cup, embellished with chopped fruit, and covered with fruit syrup. It is the simplest of icy treats, reminiscent of the very first ices made hundreds of years ago from snow. Each *grattachecca* comes with a spoon and a special straw that has one end flattened into a tiny shovel, making it ideal for prodding, scooping, and sucking. Once you have disciplined the grated ice and the summer heat has reduced everything to a slushy mess, you switch to the spoon, only to return to the straw once the ice has given up completely and you're left with an inch of sweetened water.

We live in between two kiosks, each of them good, so I try to show loyalty to both and alternate visits as best I can. Maurizio, on the corner opposite the fire station, wears a bandana and both grates and decorates. I generally have lemon and coconut or sour cherry *grattachecca* decorated with burnt-red bottled *amarena* (cherries). At the other, Roberto and Rosaria, who have run the black kiosk on via Branca for 25 years, work together in brusque harmony, Roberto grating quickly but precisely and Rosaria doing the rest, cutting the moons of pith and flesh from huge, almost sweet lemons to decorate, then impaling defiantly with the spoon and straw.

Both *grattachecca* kiosks are well positioned, allowing space for cars to double and triple park, or for *motorini,* driven with arrogant ease by young Romans with helmets balanced like top hats, to swerve in. On really hot days the queue can stretch for yards and the crowd spills like a dropped *grattachecca* across the pavement, some leaning on nearby cars, others against walls, the lucky ones having commandeered the sole pair of plastic chairs. At night the kiosks are like beacons, their lights shining almost as luminously as the fruit

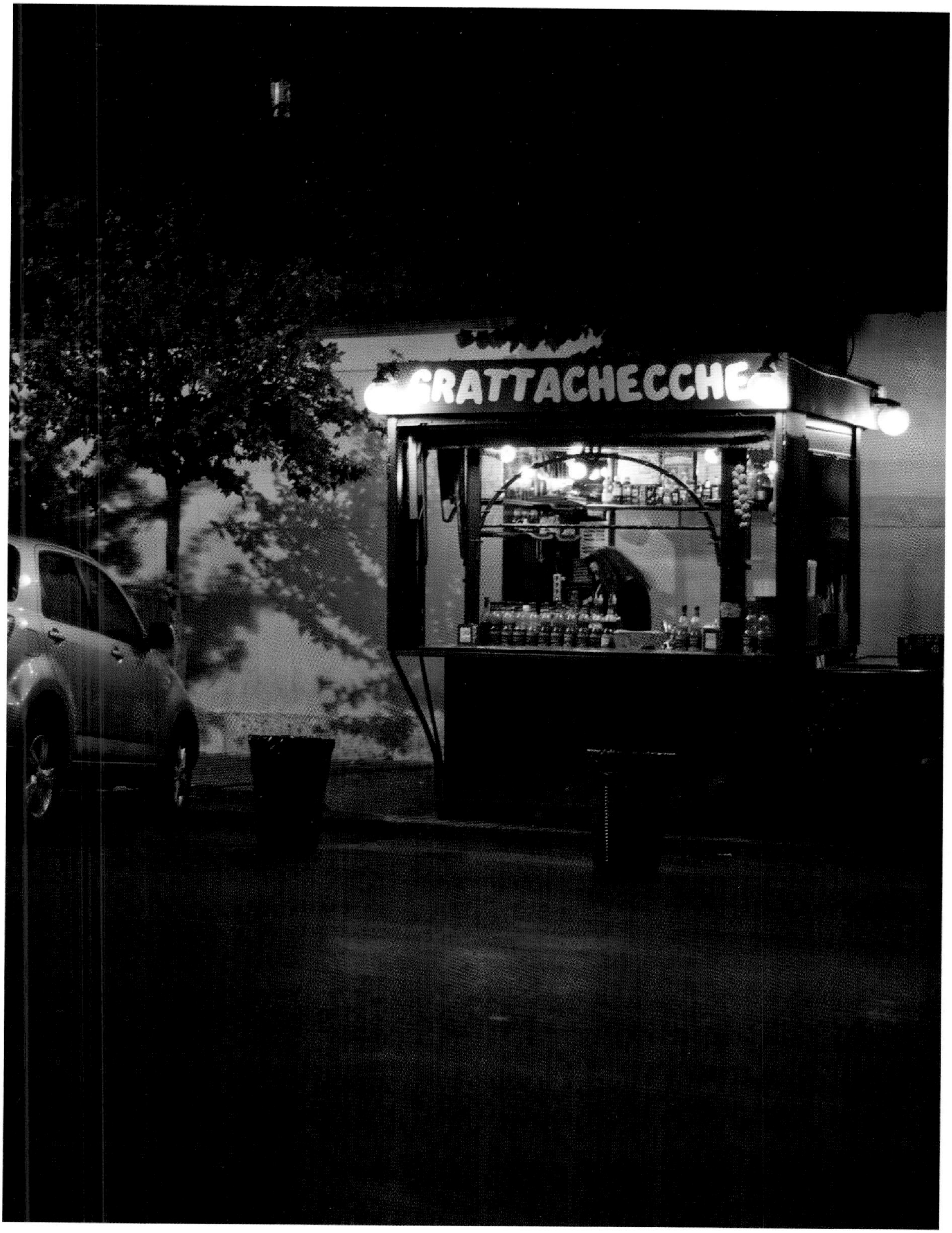
GRATTACHECCHE

syrups, the atmosphere warm, slightly sticky and quintessentially Roman.

"*Ahò, Nonna, Nonna, che vuoi?*" ("Oi, Grandma, Grandma, what do you want?") a young boy who has reached the front of the queue shouts across the street. "*Amarena,*" an older woman yells back in flint-hard Roman: "*Sempre amarena!*" ("always cherry"), before dipping her head back through the window. By the time Luca and I have our icy drinks, the boy has joined his *nonna* and both are leaning out of the window, their *grattachecca* balanced on the windowsill, a perfectly framed snapshot of Rome on a hot day.

Gelato

Like the local bar scene, the gelato scene is one of the all-inclusive glories of Italian life. Most towns have at least one good *gelateria,* which, regardless of the season but especially in summer, is a gathering place for young and old, families, colleagues, and friends in noisy groups, who throng onto the pavement with their cups of gelato*, sorbetto*, or granita.

Rome is a big city, dense with Romans, tourists, pilgrims, and passersby, most of whom have time for a gelato, which means that this glorious gelato scene can be tricky: there are plenty of scoundrels out to make easy money by bending the ambiguous rules about what "artisan" means (not a lot) and tempting with their enormous, flabby conefuls scooped from dubious mounds whipped up from powdered mixes. When I arrived in Rome, the scoundrels seemed to have had the upper hand, and I was naïve to say the least. However, as I write ten years later, there have never been so many good *gelaterias* that are reclaiming and redefining what good gelato really involves: small-scale production, natural, carefully sourced ingredients, and heaps of creativity and passion to boot.

My hands-down favorite gelato in Rome is made by Mirella at Settimo Gelo, and I put anyone who cares enough about it on the 280 bus and tell them to get off at via Oslavia to visit her. I'm not the best person to ask about creative flavor combinations since I rarely deviate from my trusted five with their ten possible pairings: vanilla, coffee, chocolate, pistachio, and hazelnut, all of which are exceptional; Mirella's coffee gelato is the best you will ever eat. If I had to choose, it would be coffee with hazelnut. The man who taught Mirella to make gelato was Claudio Torcé, who is the master behind my second favorite *gelateria*, which is outside Testaccio but still only a couple hundred yards from our front door, Il Gelato on viale Aventino.

I like Il Gelato best at about half-past nine on a summer night, when the heat has subsided and the light is just slipping away. Aventino is a well-heeled part of town, so suede loafers, jeweled sandals, and photogenic *bambini* in shoes with buckles are to be expected. As are courting couples, which always impresses me, a woman who is almost incapable of any sort of courting without the assistance of wine or beer, or both. Having considered a new flavor I default to hazelnut and coffee, while Luca shouts for chocolate. Gelato paid for, we take our cones over to the bench in front of the shop.

While Luca refuses any sort of assistance with his cone and holds it uncomfortably close to the suede loafers, two police bikes lurch from nowhere onto the pavement before us. All eyes turn to watch the bikes park and two leather-bound officers dismount. Kids stand open-mouthed while adult eyes dart around trying to ascertain the reason for the visit, but then roll when it becomes clear: the two officers stroll up to the counter, order two *coppette* with extra cream, then walk back to the bikes and lean. "*I poliziotti mangiano gelato?*" ("Policemen eat ice cream?"), a boy whispers to his father, who has thankfully unsullied suede shoes. "*Certo, tutti mangiano gelato, piccolo. Tutti.*" ("Of course, everybody eats gelato, sweetheart. Everybody.")

Kitty's vanilla ice cream scented with citrus

Like several other significant people in my Roman life, I met Kitty Travers in a pub in Trastevere called Big Star. These days it has a sign, but back then it didn't, just a faded star above the door if you looked very closely. Kitty was standing on the steps wearing a tartan mini skirt, drinking a beer and smoking a Marlboro red, and although clearly English she fitted in nicely with the crowd of *trasteverini*.

I liked her immediately, and liked her even more after having established, through a fog of guilty pleasure, that we were both from London (where we had friends in common) and that she, a pastry chef, was working with a friend of mine in Rome. We also talked about gelato, a shared preoccupation, which she was still learning to make. Several years, many visits, and a few kids later, we are still good friends and she is back in London making the most brilliant ice cream at La Grotta Ices in Spa Terminus in south London, and serving it out of her converted three-wheeled Ape van.

I don't make ice cream in my Roman kitchen because I don't have
a machine, or the space for one. However, when I go back to England
I churn happily in my mum's machine, and it's often one of Kitty's
recipes. That's why it seemed fitting to include one here, a classic,
delicious, and essential one: proper vanilla that can be drowned with
coffee, placed next to poached or baked fruit, or eaten in a cone just so.

The mere mention of the word custard used to make my heart
sink. This recipe and my desire to make proper vanilla gelato with
a custard base changed that. The secrets are a gentle heat and
constant stirring. Overnight resting is also key. The addition of
lemon peel and coffee beans is inspired, the citrus cutting through
the richness of the cream and eggs, and the beans (which you then
remove) adding a just perceptible touch of pleasing bitterness.

makes 1 quart
1 vanilla pod
1½ cups organic whole milk
1 cup heavy cream
a pinch of sea salt
½ cup sugar
3 large egg yolks
1 organic lemon
**5 fresh coffee beans (a nice addition but not essential,
    so use only if you have them)**

Split the vanilla pod in half lengthwise with a sharp knife and scrape
out the seeds. Heat the milk, cream, salt, and vanilla pod and seeds
together in a heavy-bottomed pan (stainless steel is ideal) until it is
barely simmering.

Whisk the sugar and egg yolks together until combined. Pour
the hot milk over the yolks in a steady stream, whisking constantly,
then return everything to the pan. Cook over low heat, stirring
constantly with a heatproof spatula, until the temperature reaches
180°F. Peel the outer zest (leaving the white part behind) from the
lemon with a sharp vegetable peeler and add it to the hot custard
along with the coffee beans, if you have them. Cover the pan tightly
with plastic wrap and let it sit in a sinkful of iced water until cool.
Make sure the water comes up to the level of the custard inside the
pan, otherwise it will take far too long to cool.

Refrigerate the mixture for at least 8 hours, preferably overnight,
then strain it to remove the vanilla pod, coffee beans, and citrus zest
and blend with an immersion blender for 30 seconds to emulsify it.
Churn it in an ice cream machine according to the manufacturer's

instructions, or until it has increased in volume by about 20 percent and looks dry. Scrape the ice cream out into a clean, freezerproof container, cover with wax paper and a lid, then label it and place it in the freezer to harden until ready to serve.

Pine nut, rosemary, and sea salt caramel brittle

When I asked Kitty for her vanilla ice cream recipe she also sent me a recipe for pine nut and rosemary brittle. Not only was it delicious, she wrote, but also seemed fitting for a Roman cookbook of sorts, what with the pine nuts and the rosemary. My heart sank when I saw the word "caramel," but then my curiosity got the better of me because it sounded good, and what's more, reminded me of the salted nut brittle that Leonardo at trattoria Cesare serves with coffee, which I have been meaning to make ever since it nearly took my crown out. I decided I would try it.

I have adapted Kitty's rather precise and technical recipe into something that works in my thermometer-less kitchen: an informal caramel. Once you've added the nuts to the caramel, work fast and don't worry if it looks like a mess—it should. The combination of almonds, resinous pine nuts, the cool sap-green flavor of the rosemary, and the salt and sugar is dangerously nice. Bring the craggy whole to the table, then impress or terrify your guests by smashing it into manageable pieces with the nearest heavy object to serve with ice cream or coffee.

makes about 12 small pieces
½ cup sugar
a sprig of fresh summer rosemary
½ cup chopped almonds
a large pinch of sea salt
⅓ cup pine nuts
¼ teaspoon baking powder
1½ tablespoons unsalted butter

Heat a heavy-bottomed pan (stainless steel is ideal) over medium-low heat for 1 minute, then add the sugar and leave it, not touching it at all but keeping an eye on it. Shake the pan occasionally once the sugar starts to turn liquid.

While the sugar is melting, pick the rosemary leaves and chop them roughly. Put them in a bowl with the chopped almonds, salt,

pine nuts, and baking powder and stir well to combine, making sure there are no lumps of baking powder. As soon as the sugar has turned a dark caramel color, add the butter carefully, stirring with a whisk or heatproof spatula, then add the almond mixture and mix to combine. Turn off the heat. Turn the hot brittle mixture quickly and evenly onto a nonstick silicone baking mat or large piece of oiled parchment paper placed on a heatproof surface, and use a spoon dipped in hot water (I use my hands dipped in cold water) to spread it out if needed as it starts to cool. Leave to cool completely.

Once cooled, break it into large pieces and store between layers of wax paper in an airtight container.

Lemons

Even a tiny wedge of lemon garnishing a drink was enough to make my grandpa shudder and suck his breath through his teeth. Vincenzo's grandfather, on the other hand, ate a lemon a day, skin, pith, flesh, and all. To be fair, there was a continent of difference between the leather-skinned, shockingly sharp ones my grandpa would have encountered in a northern English pub in 1980, and the muted, fragrant, almost sweet lemons Vincenzo's grandfather grew on his farm in Sicily. That said, I still like the unjust comparison between the two: John Roddy grimacing at the sight of a small yellow triangle in a pub near Sheffield and Orazio D'Aleo eating the whole fruit in a field in southern Sicily. Apart from the citrus and language differences, we think our Lancastrian and Sicilian grandfathers would have got on well, in an awkward, silent way.

Lemons are important in our flat. Vincenzo doesn't quite eat them whole, but almost. He squeezes them in and on the obvious—fish, salad, vegetables, tea—and the less obvious: strawberries, watermelon, bread, potatoes, espresso. He also washes the dishes with the squeezed-out halves. Although less exuberant with my squeezing, and still trying to get in the washing-up habit, I am devoted to Italian lemons, their pale, unwaxed skins and oily spritz, gentle pith that's as thick as a thumb, and flesh that tastes clean and citric.

Perennial, beautiful, and essential, I pretty much always have a bowl of lemons on the table to lift, cut, sharpen, encourage, and brighten. They are squeezed with blood oranges to make juice the color of a desert sunrise, spritzed on greens or fat-fringed pork chops, and into my eyes when I'm doing things too quickly, twisted into dressings for salads and vegetables, and then, once a week, grated into a cake batter.

Ciambellone di ricotta e limone
Ricotta and lemon bundt cake

This is the only cake I make with any sort of regularity, usually once a week, more often than not on Sunday night so that the impact of Monday morning is softened by cake. It's based on the yogurt-pot cake my friend Ruth taught me, for which you use a carton of plain yogurt, then use the carton to measure out the rest of the ingredients. But I decided to double quantities, substitute ricotta for yogurt, and add lemon zest, which meant the proportions of oil and sugar changed; in short, a set of scales seemed wise. It's still a cake for the baking-inhibited, though, the kind you can rustle up quickly with minimal mess. The ricotta gives it a creamy depth and means it stays moist, the olive oil provides the necessary fat, and the lemon zest gives it a little warm whiplash and a dose of mood-lifting citrus. It's simple and extremely good—as Vincenzo says, an everyday cake—and accommodating too, as comfortable on a breakfast table as it is wrapped in a paper napkin and stuffed into a pocket for a morning snack; as good beside a cup of tea at four o'clock as it is with a glass of sweet wine after dinner, or a shot of brandy at nine o'clock.

makes 12–16 slices
1 cup (200 ml) extra-virgin olive oil, plus extra for greasing
2 cups (250 g) all-purpose flour, plus extra for dusting
2 teaspoons baking powder (I use a packet of *lievito*,
    an Italian raising agent of seemingly magical powers)
a pinch of salt
¾ cup (150 g) sugar
1 cup (250 g) ricotta
4 large eggs
grated zest of 2 organic lemons

Preheat the oven to 350°F and grease and flour a ring or bundt pan approximately 9 inches in diameter, or a standard 9 × 5 × 3-inch loaf pan.

In a large bowl, mix together the flour, baking powder, salt, and sugar. In another bowl, whisk together the ricotta and olive oil, then add the eggs one by one, beating between each addition, until smooth. Add the ricotta mixture to the flour mixture and whisk until

you have a thick batter. Add the lemon zest, stir again, then pour the batter into the prepared pan, making sure it does not come more than two-thirds of the way up the sides.

Bake for 30–40 minutes if you are using a bundt pan (40–50 for a loaf pan), or until the cake is golden and fully set. I check it with a strand of spaghetti, but you can use a knife or skewer: insert it into the middle of the cake and it should come out clean. Allow the cake to cool before turning it out of the tin and onto a plate.

Confettura di ciliegie
Cherry jam

This is a satisfyingly simple jam, which I always make in small quantities. The purple-tinged froth that rises as the cherries simmer reminds me of my auntie May's purple rinse, and the addition of lemon zest gives the jam a sharp lemon edge reminiscent of sour cherries. I love this, but you may not, in which case omit the lemon zest and be frugal with the lemon juice.

makes 3–4 (8-ounce) jars
3¼ pounds cherries, washed, with stems and stones removed
1 organic lemon
4 cups superfine sugar

Put the washed, stoned, and stemmed cherries in a large, heavy-bottomed pan suitable for making jam. Pare away 5 thick strips of lemon zest with as little pith as possible attached. Add them to the pan, cover the fruit with the sugar, stir, and leave to sit in a cool place for 3 hours.

Squeeze the juice from the lemon over the cherries. Stir, place the pan over medium heat, and bring to a boil, stirring occasionally and skimming away any purple froth. Reduce the heat to a gentle simmer and leave the deep purple jam to bubble and burp quietly for just over an hour. The jam is ready when it is thick, clings to the back of the spoon, and is of an even consistency and decidedly sticky. I also do the saucer test to see if the jam has set. That is: put a saucer in the freezer for a few minutes, then put a spoonful of jam on the cold saucer, wait a minute, then run your finger through the jam. If it wrinkles, remains divided in two parts, and doesn't run back into a single puddle, it's ready.

Ladle the jam into warm sterilized jars while still hot. Screw on the lids immediately, then leave the jars to cool upside down, which creates a seal. The jam will keep in a cool, dark place for up to a year, but as I make such small quantities I tend to keep it in the fridge.

Crostata di visciole o ciliegie
Cherry jam tart

This is another recipe in which my two food worlds collide: the simple, not-too-sweet pie crust jam tarts of my English childhood and the crisscrossed sour cherry *crostate* so beloved of the Romans.

When I was eight years old, drinking a Snowball in a Champagne saucer topped with a cocktail cherry was the height of sophistication. My granny ran a pub on Dunham Street in Oldham called the Gardeners' Arms, a traditional free house serving Robinson's ale, bitter, and stout. I knew full well that my cocktail had barely a whiff of alcohol—just enough Advocaat to tinge the lemonade pale egg-yolk yellow—and that I'd be whisked off to bed as soon as the pub got busy. But that didn't bridle my joy at sitting up at the bar, Snowball in one hand and cheese-and-onion crisp in the other, listening to jukebox tunes I didn't quite understand.

Although I'm still partial to a cocktail cherry or three, these days I prefer my cherries still warm from the tree at my friends' house, straight from the brown paper bag on the way home from the market, or chilled until they're so cold and taut they burst between your teeth. Once I've had my fill of cherries hand to mouth, I poach a few, soak a few in alcohol, and make some jam, which is even better if I have a few *visciole* too. *Visciole* are sour cherries and Romans adore them, whether preserved in deep red syrup, steeped in red wine for an inky liqueur, or most commonly simmered into a jam which is then baked into biscuits or *crostata*. You can make this tart with any jam, but cherry is particularly nice, and sour cherry jam nicer still. One especially Roman variation includes a thick layer of ricotta, which bakes into a soft, baked-cheesecake-like lid. It's my favorite tart.

serves 8–12
2⅓ cups (300 g) all-purpose flour
11 tablespoons (150 g) cold unsalted butter, plus extra for greasing
½ cup (100 g) superfine sugar
a pinch of salt
grated zest of 1 small organic lemon
3 eggs
2 cups (500 g) cherry or sour cherry jam

for a cherry and ricotta tart:
2 cups (500 g) fresh ricotta (you may not need all of it)
5 tablespoons (60 g) sugar

1 egg plus 1 egg yolk
1¼ cups (350 g) cherry or sour cherry jam

1½ cups whipped cream

Sift the flour into a large bowl. Cut the butter into small dice and add it to the bowl. Working quickly with cold hands, rub the butter into the flour until it resembles fine bread crumbs. Add the sugar, salt, and lemon zest and toss everything together. In a small bowl, lightly beat 2 eggs with a fork, then add them to the other ingredients. Use your hands to bring everything together to a smooth, consistent dough. Wrap the dough in plastic wrap and leave it in the fridge to rest for 1 hour.

Preheat the oven to 350°F and grease a 9½-inch tart pan. On a lightly floured work surface, roll two-thirds of the pastry dough into a round a little larger than the pan. Lift the pastry into the pan using the rolling pin and press it gently into the corners. Trim off any excess around the edge. Prick the pastry base with a fork. Spread out the jam on top of the pastry. Roll out the remaining pastry and cut it into strips, then use these to crisscross the tart. Beat the remaining egg in a small bowl, then brush the crisscrossed strips with the egg. Place the tart pan on a baking sheet and bake for 45–50 minutes.

Serve warm or at room temperature, alone or with a spoonful of whipped cream.

To make the cherry and ricotta tart, make the pastry and line the tart pan as described above. Mix together the ricotta, sugar, and eggs until smooth. Spread the cherry jam onto the pastry, then cover with the ricotta mixture. Cover with the crisscrossed strips of pastry as above. Place the tart pan on a baking sheet and bake for 45–50 minutes.

Ricotta

I've mentioned ricotta in each of the first four parts of the book, which means that along with extra-virgin olive oil, salt, and flour, it's one of the most significant and sociable ingredients in the book. This seems fitting, since it's one of my favorite things, a quintessential Roman ingredient that's at home in most kitchens, and last but not least a standard-bearer for my imagined fifth quarter: ingredients made out of things that would be otherwise discarded, in this case the leftover whey from cheese making.

Before we move on to ricotta's sweeter role, it seems important to reiterate a couple of things here rather than referring to a distant appendix of ingredients. Ricotta can be made from sheep's or cow's milk. It can also be made from goat or buffalo milk. In all four cases, the technique is the same: the leftover whey from whichever cheese was being made is reheated, or re-cooked (*ri-cotta*) with more whole milk, rennet is added, and then the curds are packed into conical baskets so that the excess liquid can seep away. The most beloved ricotta in Rome is *ricotta di pecora* (sheep's-milk ricotta), which is protected by a DOP status. Authentic *ricotta di pecora* is wonderful stuff, porcelain white and bearing the imprints of the basket. It has a clean, fresh flavor, a sheepish nature, and creamy texture. It is these qualities that make it an indispensable part of many antipasti, pasta, savory, and sweet dishes. Good cow's-milk ricotta, although without the distinctive sheepyness, is every bit as delicious and useful as *ricotta di pecora*. What isn't as good is the tubs of long-life, fine-textured soft cheese that masquerade as ricotta in Italy and elsewhere, which is often the only thing you can find. If this is the case you might like to consider making your own curd cheese, which, although not ricotta, is remarkably similar: sweet, gently curdy, and perfect for four of the recipes here.

Rather-like-ricotta curd cheese

This was my first foray into cheese making (although it isn't strictly
cheese, so this is actually rather-like-ricotta curd cheese made by
rather-like-cheesemaking means). Making curd cheese also meant
that at long last I had a reason to turn the kitchen stool upside down
on the table and drain something into a bowl, as I'd seen my mum
do years ago. Obviously, the better the milk, the better the final
product, and if you can find unpasteurized milk, better still. You can
buy rennet from the health food store, although if you wish to do

this in Italy, I suggest you look up the word in Italian first, since trying to explain and/or mime the word "rennet" is no easy task.

343

makes about 1 pound
2 quarts fresh whole milk (unpasteurized if you can find it)
a pinch of salt
4 teaspoons rennet

Bring a large saucepan of water to a boil to sterilize the pan. Throw away the water (or use it to do the washing up), then put the milk in the pan and add the salt. Over medium-low heat, bring the milk to blood temperature, using a thermometer if that reassures you, then remove the pan from the heat.

Add the rennet to the milk, stir well, then leave to sit for 15 minutes, or until the milk separates into curds at the top and whey at the bottom.

Use a slotted spoon to lift the curds from the pan into a colander lined with a double layer of cheesecloth. Tie up the corners of the cheesecloth and hang it over a bowl or the sink to drip for 2 hours. Once drained, unwrap the cheese, put it in a bowl, and keep it in the fridge until you are ready to use it. It will keep in the fridge, covered, for 2 days.

A story about cookies

I was too confused and cross to appreciate anything. It was six o'clock on Monday and I was late and lost, fooled again by the exaggerated curves of the Tevere River, staggering with an oversized child in an undersized sling down yet another cobbled street. The man at the bus stop shook his head and made a gesture which confirmed that I was, as suspected, a long way from where I wanted to be. No directions were forthcoming. Mad-dog Englishwoman tourist, his eyes seemed to snigger. "I've lived here for nearly nine years!" I wanted to tell him, but every word of Italian eluded me.

Relief at finding myself on via del Corso was short lived. In front of me was the bus stop from which I'd caught the first of two ill-advised buses an hour earlier. The sun beat down and Luca pounded his hot little hands on my chest. We walked some more, wading against a tide of shoppers and tourists. "You want the 116," said a kind woman at another bus stop. "I know, I've lived here for

nine years, I take buses every day," I wanted to say, but "*Grazie*" was all I could manage.

The 116, a dwarf bus, bumped along via del Babuino. Women with expensive shoes and immaculate toenails teetered on, so I tucked my shabby ones under the seat. We stopped just after the piazza di Spagna and there it was, Europe's broadest staircase and another mass of bodies, shopping bags, and blinking cameras. "Get off here," said the kind woman, "but walk up the other staircase just behind." This we did, and at last I appreciated something: in these cool, quiet, stone steps we had our own private staircase, just yards away from the busiest one in Europe. Not as marvelous, of course— but at that moment, nearly.

Almost nine years ago, on a similar evening, the view from the Pincio at the top had made my heart swell and skin flush. It had also made me cry. That happened again now, partly from relief that we were no longer lost and I was no longer furious. But mostly it was down to the sublime view across Rome: a hazy patchwork of terra-cotta, brown, and gold, gleaming *cupolas*, uneven tiles, fading *palazzi*, hidden roof gardens, and the distant plateau of Janiculum with its shadowed umbrella pines. "Mamma, mummy, mamma, look, look!" Luca insisted, tugging at my shirt, his eyes full of wonder. "Look mamma, dog!" A large dog, leg cocked, was relieving itself against the curb. At this we turned and walked briskly, our Tupperware box of *ciambelline al vino* keeping time, across Villa Borghese to the picnic party we had started out for so many hours ago. Fortunately, *ciambelline* are hardy cookies that will happily withstand hours of hot sun, inept traveling, and a brisk jolt across the park. They are also rather particular, as only a cookie made with olive oil and fennel seeds can be, and delicious, as only a cookie intended to be dipped in wine can be.

Ciambelline al vino
Ring cookies with wine and fennel seeds

Ciambelline al vino are quintessentially Roman, and a good recipe in which to mention *q.b.*, or *quantobasta*, which literally means "how much is enough?"—or, as Vincenzo puts it, "whatever you think is the right quantity." You find q.b. dotted liberally throughout Italian recipes, and the older your book or more southward-leaning your travels, the more you encounter it. It isn't a question, but an assumption that you know how much salt, pepper, flour, oil, wine, sugar, fennel seeds, and so on, is enough for the recipe in question, according to your preference. It's an assumption that you have good taste, good instincts, and/or that the recipe is good enough for you to make it again and again until q.b. has become second nature.

Unlike some recipes I've bookmarked, in which every ingredient is followed by q.b., this one has measurements of sorts. That is: a glass of wine (red, white, or fortified), a glass of extra-virgin olive oil, and a glass of sugar. The size of the glass, of course, is whatever you think is right. I use my trusty 3-ounce Duralex glass tumbler. To your pool of sugar, wine, and oil you add salt and fennel seeds. A pinch and a teaspoon seem the right quantity to me. Then you add the flour q.b, little by little, working it in with your hands until the dough has come together into a compliant mass that comes cleanly away from the sides of the bowl. You will know.

I am not going to try and convince you; if you don't like the distinctive taste of fennel seeds you won't like these. Of course, you can leave the fennel out. But without the sweet, grassy, anise whiplash they are, in my opinion, as lost as I was that hot Monday. I've heard you can substitute the wine with milk, but why would you want to do that? "Somewhere between utterly sweet and charming and functional hard work, *ciambelline al vino* are ring biscuits made with wine to dip in wine," says my friend Anna. I think that just about sums it up. Unsurprisingly, I adore them. They keep brilliantly in an airtight tin or box.

makes about 20
1 glass sugar
1 glass wine (white, red, or fortified wine such as Madeira)
1 glass extra-virgin olive oil
salt q.b.
fennel seeds q.b.
plain flour q.b., plus extra for dusting
sugar q.b., for finishing

In a bowl, mix together the sugar, wine, and olive oil. Add as much salt and fennel seeds as you think right, then the flour, a little at a time, mixing with your hands until you have a soft but manageable dough that comes away cleanly from the sides of the bowl. Move the dough onto a board dusted lightly with flour and work it until smooth. Cover the dough and leave it to rest for 1 hour.

Preheat the oven to 350°F and line a baking sheet with parchment paper. Pinch walnut-size pieces from the dough and with floured hands, roll them into slim logs, roughly 3–4 inches long. Curl each

log into a round shape and pinch the ends to form a ring. Invert
it and dip the top of each ring into a dish of sugar until it is well
coated. Arrange the rings on the prepared baking sheet and bake
for 25–30 minutes, or until they are golden and crisp. Allow to cool
completely, then store in an airtight container.

Biscotti di mandorle e pinoli
Almond, pine nut, and fennel seed biscotti

Bis means "again," and it is what Italians shout insistently to singers
instead of *encore*. It's what you say as you hand your emptied plate
back to the person with the serving spoons while eyeing up the
last slice of lasagne, and it prefixes *cotti* to make *biscotti*, meaning
"cooked again" or "cooked twice."

As with the English word "biscuit," biscotti is now the generic
Italian word for cookies, not all of which are re-baked. These
biscotti, though, most certainly are. The first bake is of long, flat
logs of dough until they are almost cooked but still soft enough to
cut. Once you have cut the logs into long, tongue-like slices and laid
them side by side, you bake them again until hard and crisp.

Almond, pine nuts, and fennel seeds make a distinctive,
opinionated combination that tends to divide people. At one
lunch, a friend who bakes seriously said they were one of the most
delicious biscotti she had ever eaten while her husband slid the
rest of his under a napkin and drank a glass of water. You could, of
course, leave the fennel seeds out or replace them with a little finely
chopped rosemary. The almonds can be replaced with hazelnuts.

Biscotti are best with a drink: usually coffee (either milky or
black), dessert wine, or another thing that divides people: a short
glass of herbal, slightly medicinal Amaro. They keep brilliantly in
an airtight tin.

makes about 25
2 cups (250 g) all-purpose flour
1¼ cups (250 g) superfine sugar
½ teaspoon baking powder
⅔ cup (100 g) blanched almonds, chopped very coarsely
½ cup (75 g) Italian pine nuts
1 teaspoon fennel seeds (optional)
1 teaspoon grated organic lemon zest
2 large eggs, beaten

Preheat the oven to 400°F and line a baking sheet with parchment paper.

Sift the flour into a large bowl and add the rest of the ingredients except the eggs. Mix well. Add the beaten eggs and use your hands to bring the ingredients together into a ball of firm dough, making sure the nuts are well distributed. Cut the ball in half. Shape both halves into sausages about 1½ inches in diameter and place them on the baking sheet. Bake for about 20 minutes, by which time the dough will have spread out and should still be soft in the middle, but firm enough to cut into slim slices.

Take the rolls out of the oven and reduce the temperature to 350°F. Let them cool a little, then carefully lift or slide them onto a cutting board. Using a sharp, serrated knife, cut them, on a slight diagonal if necessary, into slices roughly 3 inches long and ¼ inch wide. Put the slices back on the baking sheet, lined up like soldiers, and return to the oven for 15 minutes. Turn them over and cook for a further 15 minutes, or until dry, firm, and crisp. Cool on a wire rack, then store them in an airtight tin.

Pasticcini di mandorle
Soft almond cookies

In Sicily I became preoccupied with, among other edible things, the soft almond cookies called *pasticcini di mandorle* that you find in almost every *forno* (bakery) or *pasticceria*. For about a month, as the shops began to roll back their shutters and unlock their doors at five o'clock after the long lunch break and the hottest hours of the day, I would hunt down and purchase my daily dose of almond. Then, holding a small paper bag, I'd go and buy myself a granita before finding the nearest wall to sit on and eat alternating bites of almond and lemon ice.

The shape and texture of the *pasticcini di mandorle* varied from place to place and from oven to oven. Some were stout and sticky, others more of a cookie. But the best I ate were large, slightly crisp, and cracked on the outside, giving way to a soft, dense marzipan heart. These were the soft almond rounds I wanted to make—and after excessive experimenting, now do. The key to making balls from the sticky mixture is to dust your hands and the dough with lots of confectioners' sugar. The mixture will spread from walnut-size balls into 2-inch cookies, so space them out accordingly and remember that, regardless of how precise you are, they will be different every time.

makes about 20–30
3 cups (350 g) ground almonds
2 cups (200 g) confectioners' sugar, plus extra for dusting
grated zest of 1 large organic lemon
2 eggs, gently beaten with a fork

Preheat the oven to 350°F and line a baking sheet with parchment paper. Mix the ground almonds, confectioners' sugar, and lemon zest in a large bowl. Add the beaten eggs and, using a fork

or your fingers, bring the mixture together to form a soft, sticky dough.

Dust your hands with confectioners' sugar and scoop out a walnut-size lump of dough, then gently shape and roll it between your palms into a ball. Dust the ball with more sugar and put it on the baking sheet. Continue until you have used up all the mixture. Make an indentation in the center of each ball with your finger so that they cook evenly.

Bake for about 14–18 minutes, or until golden brown underneath and cracked, crisp, and very pale gold on top. Transfer to a wire rack and allow to cool. They will keep in an airtight tin for up to a month.

Salame di cioccolato
Chocolate salami

This excellent treat has its origins somewhere between the box of
Calabrian figs stuffed with hazelnuts and coated with dark chocolate
I was given a few years ago for Christmas, and the butter, cookie,
and cocoa powder fridge cake I made when I was thirteen in Mrs.
Carrington's home economics class.

I never fail to be delighted when I make chocolate salami: the
easy squash of it all, how the butter, cookie, egg, sugar, cocoa, nut,

and fig log, once chilled and cut with a sharp knife, does indeed look like slices of salami with particularly dark flesh and cookie-like fat. You can use any nut or dried fruit and most plain types of cookie, but ladyfingers, toasted hazelnuts, and semi-dried figs are particularly good.

Brought to the table still wrapped in its wax paper, then unwrapped and sliced thickly to serve with coffee, it makes a great end to a meal, whether ordinary or not so ordinary. I have never made this for dinner and not been asked for the recipe. It keeps well for 3 days in the fridge—just make sure you wrap it tightly with wax paper.

makes 12 slices
2 egg yolks
½ cup (80 g) sugar
6 tablespoons (80 g) unsalted butter, soft
¾ cup (50 g) unsweetened cocoa powder
½ teaspoon salt
1 cup (100 g) toasted hazelnuts or almonds
¾ cup (100 g) dried figs
12–15 (100 g) ladyfingers

In a large bowl, beat together the egg yolks and sugar with a whisk until pale and fluffy, then add the butter and beat again. Add the cocoa and salt and beat again until you have a creamy paste.

Break the nuts into rough chunks, chop the figs into small pieces (I use scissors for this) and crumble the ladyfingers roughly. Mix the nuts, fruit, and cookies into the creamy paste with a spoon and then with your hands until you have a soft, sticky mass.

Turn out the mass onto a large piece of wax paper and roll it into a log roughly 2 inches wide. Wrap the wax paper tightly around the log and twist the ends like a huge toffee, then put it in the fridge overnight.

To serve, wrap the log in a clean piece of wax paper or dust it with icing sugar and put it on a plate. Either way, use a sharp knife to cut slices and serve it with espresso.

Depending on which part of Italy you live in, the six days of *carnevale*, in which you finish all the rich foods and indulge in festivities before the pious period of Lent, might involve masked balls, fires, feasts, fried things, lasagne, or drunken abandon. I am happy to participate in all of the above, although becoming a mother has meant I have tempered my abandon because I have to supervise someone else's: that of Luca, who gets to dress up as a crocodile (green tights, box on head) and run around the piazza with princesses and pirates, flinging paper confetti and watching bigger kids ambush each other with spray cans of luminous foam string. He is only persuaded to stop by a deep-fried *frappe* dusted with confectioners' sugar that makes him look like a crocodile caught in a snowstorm before he flies off again into another blizzard of fluttering paper.

In Rome, two traditional treats line the counters of every *pasticceria* and *forno* around the time of *carnevale*: *frappe* and *castagnole* (little chestnuts). My favorite are the *frappe*, known in other regions of Italy as *cenci* ("rags"), *bugie* ("lies"), and *chiacchiere* ("chit-chat"): strips of enriched, sweetened dough with crimped edges that are deep-fried until golden and dusted with confectioners' sugar. Good *frappe* will shatter, flake, and then melt in your mouth. Roman women seem to be able to eat them without the snowstorm; I, like my son, can't. Our bakery, Passi, is right next to the confetti-throwing piazza and has a special glass box on top of the curved glass counter full of freshly fried *frappe* to be bought by weight and eaten straight from the bag.

Frappe
Angel wings

This recipe, like several others in this section, is not one passed down through several generations of Romans, but given to me by my friend Dan. I met Dan and his wife, Fran, on the street here in Testaccio. Thinking they were hapless English tourists at the mercy of a card-gobbling bank machine that had eaten mine the day before, I intervened. They turned out be neither tourists nor hapless, and much better than me at spotting a dodgy bank machine. After apologizing in the way that only three English people can, we went for *caffè* at Barberini and there began a friendship conducted over lunch, between my kitchen in Testaccio and theirs up the hill in Monteverde.

While he was in Rome, Dan, who is a keen baker, researched, tested, and documented dozens of traditional Roman recipes, and this is his recipe for *frappe*, which works beautifully, coming the closest to the *frappe* I like so much at Passi. Traditionally, *frappe* were a way of using up animal products and would have been fried in *strutto* (lard), which I can confirm is absolutely delicious. These days, however, they are generally fried in olive or vegetable oil.

makes 12–15
2 cups (250 g) all-purpose flour, plus extra for dusting
½ teaspoon baking powder
3 tablespoons (30 g) superfine sugar
a pinch of salt
grated zest of ½ organic lemon
2 eggs
½ teaspoon vanilla extract
1 tablespoon liqueur, such as grappa, brandy, rum,
  or whatever you like, depending on your inclinations
  and what's in your liquor cabinet
3 tablespoons (25 g) unsalted butter
olive or vegetable oil, for frying
confectioners' sugar, for dusting

Sieve the flour and baking powder into a large bowl, then add the sugar, salt, and lemon zest. In another bowl, beat the eggs, then add the vanilla and liqueur and beat again. Melt the butter in a small pan, then let it cool a little.

Add the eggs and melted butter to the dry ingredients and use a spoon or your hands to bring everything together into a dough. Turn the dough out onto a lightly floured surface and knead for a few minutes until smooth and well integrated, then wrap in plastic wrap and leave to rest for an hour in a cool, draft-free place.

On a lightly floured surface, roll the dough out to about $\frac{1}{16}$th of an inch thick. Alternatively, you can run it through a pasta roller. Using a crimped pasta cutter or knife, cut the dough into rectangles roughly 2 × 4 inches, then cut each rectangle in half lengthwise.

Heat the oil for frying to about 325°F, then deep-fry the dough pieces a few at a time until golden, then lift them out onto paper towels to drain. Dust with confectioners' sugar and serve.

Maritozzi
<u>Sweet yeasted buns</u>

One of the reasons Barberini on via Marmorata became my habitual breakfast bar in Testaccio is that alongside the usual morning pastries sitting behind the curved glass counter—the croissant-like *cornetti* filled with jam or suspiciously yellow custard and the Danish whirls, some of which involved large quantities of Nutella—sit the rather more innocent-looking *maritozzi*.

Maritozzi are not-too-sweet, bread-like buns that are baked until golden and brushed with a light glaze. At breakfast, they are eaten just so, with cappuccino or *caffè*, and later in the day they are split and filled with whipped cream for the Italian equivalent of a cream bun. This is another of Dan's recipes, the research for which involved a trip across Rome with Luca in tow to eat Rome's best *maritozzi con la panna* at the perennially good Regoli. The *maritozzi* are not so much filled as plastered with cream at this historic cake and pastry shop. The bun is split and pulled so far apart it looks as if it is doing the splits before being covered with a mound of whipped cream. Dan was momentarily lost for words; Luca just head-butted the creamy mound.

Maritozzi are much less work than I imagined, although they do require your sporadic attention for a good part of a morning, so I tend to make them on a Saturday or Sunday in time for a late second breakfast. A large coffee with hot milk in the white cup, a warm *maritozzo*, maybe two, a real newspaper and an unreal magazine, and I am all set until lunch.

makes 10
for the sponge:
⅓ cup (40 g) white bread flour
1 cup (250 ml) milk, warmed to blood temperature
2½ teaspoons (7 g) dried fast-action yeast
2 tablespoons (20 g) superfine sugar

for the dough:
2 cups (250 g) white bread flour
½ cup (120 g) all-purpose flour
3 tablespoons (30 g) superfine sugar
½ stick (50 g) unsalted butter, melted
grated zest of 1 organic lemon
1 egg yolk
salt

to serve:
5 tablespoons (50 g) sugar
2 cups (500 ml) heavy cream

First, make the sponge by whisking together the flour, milk, yeast, and sugar until they are the consistency of cream. Leave the sponge, covered, to ferment. You want it nice and bubbly, which will depend on the warmth of your kitchen or chosen location. With all that yeast and sugar, it won't take too long—around 20 minutes.

Once the sponge is active and bubbling, add the dough ingredients and bring it together into a dough, using your hands or

a stand mixer fitted with a dough hook. Knead the dough for a few minutes. Put the dough in a clean bowl, cover it and leave it to prove until it has doubled in size. Again, the amount of time will vary—in my warm kitchen, this took a couple of hours.

Gently deflate the dough with your fingers to regulate the structure. This is called "knocking back" in Britain, but all that business of thumping it with your fist is far too violent—you don't want to lose all the air. Then divide it into 10 pieces, each weighing 3 ounces or thereabouts, and shape each one into a 3-inch-long cylinder, gently tucking the join underneath. Place the buns on a baking sheet lined with parchment paper to prove, covered with a cloth, until doubled in size. Preheat the oven to 400°F.

Bake for 15 minutes, or until golden brown. While they're baking, make a simple sugar syrup with ¼ cup sugar and 3 tablespoons water by putting them in a pan and bringing to a boil. When the rolls are baked and still warm, brush them with the syrup. If you like, whip the cream to soft peaks, then split the buns and fill with cream.

Variation: If you like, you can add ¼ cup of pine nuts, raisins, and chopped peel to the dough before the first rising.

Spices and other good things

When I first moved to Testaccio the shop on via Luca della Robbia was the workshop of a seamstress and button coverer. I never actually went in, only peered through the window and wondered if it really was as small as it seemed, or whether it opened up like a tardis. It closed before I could have anything mended or a button covered, but then reopened as La Bottega delle Spezie. Finally, the one thing missing from my resolutely Roman local shops had arrived: spices, a whole tiny shop full of them, the cumulative scent of which invaded your senses as you opened the door. Not that I had the chance to open the door very often, since the *bottega* was never open, at least not when I passed. I remember once meeting a friend with a bag of spices just outside my old flat. The *bottega,* she told me happily, was open. We caught up for 10 minutes or so in the middle of the road, then grabbed a coffee at Zia Elena before walking back down towards the *bottega*. It was closed.

Then, in August 2008, the 10 × 10-foot shop changed hands once again, this time into the steady and reliable ones of Laura, Fabio, and Arianna, who, seeing the potential of spices and other good things combined with proper hours, opened the Emporio delle Spezie.

They also sell tea, flours, legumes, jams, vinegars, nuts, and dried fruit alongside the hundred or so jars of every imaginable spice, herbs, and seasoning, most of which are sold by weight determined by an old-fashioned set of scales.

Now, I am unabashedly biased about the tiny shop just a few yards from our flat where I can buy a few grams of peppercorns, 8 cloves, and a bag of loose Darjeeling tea, and then sit down for a dose of chinwagging. However, even less biased people agree that the *emporio* is precisely the sort of business that Testaccio, an area reeling from the loss of small shops, changing habits, and a stomping onslaught of supermarkets, needs. A small, independent business where quality and knowledge really matter, where both sides actually seem to care about each other in a nice ordinary way. A shop whose values are as old-fashioned as its scales—but at the same time progressive, since Laura, Fabio, and Arianna are as passionate about the bay leaves and fennel seeds for traditional Roman dishes as they are about the warm, exotic spices of elsewhere.

If all this sounds like a love letter to the Emporio delle Spezie, I'm glad, because it is. All the spices, flour, nuts, and dried fruit for the recipes in the book were bought there and, bar the candied fruit and eggs, every single element of the final recipe, *pangiallo,* were weighed out on the scales in one of the nicest shops in Testaccio.

Candied orange peel

I'd never *even considered* making candied fruit or peel. I imagined it involved complicated and elaborate procedures, that it was fiendishly difficult and bound to end in disaster. Then, a couple of years back, a fellow blogger called Molly with a knack for words made it sound not only delightful but doable, and I began making my own.

I'm bound to make it sound complicated and pernickety, but it isn't. A flurry of activity demanding your full attention is needed to get started, but then it's all about the long, seductive simmer that requires nothing more than a curious prod and satisfied nod every now and then. You slice both ends from each orange (6 is a good number, and make sure they're organic), then score the fruit with a sharp knife so that you can ease away 4 arcs of peel. Now you need to blanch the peel three times: that is, put it in a pan, cover it with cold water, and bring it to a boil, drain it, re-cover it with fresh cold water, bring to a boil again, drain, re-cover, and re-boil.

Having blanched the peel, you need to simmer it in simple syrup (made from equal quantities of water and superfine sugar—I use 2 cups—heated in a pan until the sugar completely dissolves) until the arcs are tender and translucent. Tentative touch and taste are the best gauge; trust yourself, you are right. Mine took 1¾ hours. Once your orange arcs are candied, use a slotted spoon to scoop them out of the amber liquid and onto a wire rack placed on top of a piece of parchment paper. Leave them to dry for a day and a half, by which point they are no longer wet, but still a little bit tacky, and shine like polished leather. Leave them as they are or cut them into whatever shape you like, and store them in a screw-top jar. Don't forget to pour the amber cooking syrup into a bottle and keep it in the fridge. It's good on Greek yogurt or poured over sliced oranges, slivers of dates, and mascarpone.

Of course, you can eat the peel just so. I do. It's heady stuff, the absolute essence of orange: sweet, fragrant, spicy, oily, and acerbic. Not for the citrus faint hearted. It's good with an espresso and a square of Lindt. Or with tea—Darjeeling is particularly nice. You can dip the ends of your fat, fragrant matchsticks in melted dark chocolate to make *scorzette d'arancia candite al cioccolato* (orangettes). Alternatively, you could, and should, make what is possibly my favorite Christmas treat (which is saying something, considering the throng of heavily fruited cakes, suet-laced puddings, *panettone*, profusion of marzipan, and gaggle of spiced delights that clamor for attention during my schizophrenic Anglo-Italian festivities): *pangiallo.*

Pangiallo
Spiced fruit cake with saffron

Pan giallo, or "yellow bread," isn't bread as we know it at all, but a flat, rich, boldly spiced cake that dates back to medieval times. Don't let its looks deceive! A dark, curiously bumpy appearance barely concealed by a saffron-colored glaze, *pangiallo* is a most delicious thing. I've described it as a cake but it's actually more like soft, chewy, heavily spiced nougat with a whisper of cake that's crowded with dried fruit, nuts, candied peel, heavily spiced and then painted with a glaze of egg yolk and saffron.

For a woman like me, with a weakness for toasted nuts, candied peel, heavily spiced confections, and medieval undertones, this is a pretty stupendous slice. Italian food historian Gillian Riley notes that in the 1500s, *pangiallo,* like *panforte* (which literally means "strong bread"), with its strengthening sweetness and stimulating spiciness, was considered an ideal gift for women after childbirth. Now I know it's been a few years, but I'm still in need of strengthening sweetness and stimulating spiciness.

makes 2 small cakes that each cut into 8–10 slices

⅓ cup (100 g) golden raisins

⅓ cup (100 g) dried figs

1 cup (150 g) candied fruit or chopped peel

1½ cups (200 g) mixed nuts, such as almonds, pine nuts, hazelnuts, and walnuts

¾ cup (100 g) all-purpose flour

½ whole nutmeg, grated

a pinch of cinnamon

½ teaspoon black pepper

½ cup (150 g) honey

⅔ cup (80 g) confectioners' sugar

for the glaze:

a few threads of saffron
2 tablespoons warm water
2 egg yolks
1 tablespoon flour
1 tablespoon confectioners' sugar

Soak the raisins in a little hot water for 10 minutes. Chop the figs into eighths and dice the candied fruit if it is in large pieces. Once the raisins are plump, squeeze out any excess water. In a large bowl, mix together the dried fruit and nuts, then add the flour, nutmeg, cinnamon, and pepper and stir again or toss with your hands so that each piece of fruit or nut is well coated.

Preheat the oven to 325°F and line a baking sheet with parchment paper. In a small pan over medium heat, warm the honey with 1 tablespoon water, add the ⅔ cup sugar and stir until it bubbles at the edges. Pour the honey mixture over the fruit and nut mixture, then use a spoon or your hands to mix the ingredients until you have a lumpy and sticky but consistent mass. Divide the mass in half, then shape it into 2 round loaves about 1¼ inches deep and 6 inches wide. Sit them on the prepared baking sheet.

Make the glaze by dissolving the saffron in 2 tablespoons warm water, then add the yolks, flour, and the tablespoon sugar. Beat well until they form a yellow paste, then brush and dab it over the tops of the loaves and bake for 30 minutes, or until it is firm and golden at the edges, and the glaze is bright yellow.

Acknowledgments

This book is dedicated to Vincenzo and Luca with love—
there is no one I would rather share a meal with.

Thank you
to my family; Mum, Dad, Ben, Rosie, Paul, Kate, Beattie, Freya
and Stanley. *Grazie a* Carmela and Bartolomeo.

to Joanna

to Giampiero

to all the readers and supporters of my blog *Racheleats*. Without you
all, this book would never have happened.

to my publishing family; publisher Elizabeth Hallett and Kate Miles at
Saltyard Books, editor Laura Gladwin, designer Myfanwy Vernon-Hunt,
photographer Nick Seaton, Rosie Gailer and everyone at Hodder &
Stoughton and John Murray Press. Also to Honey & Co for being across
the road from the Saltyard office and for feeding us delicious food.

to my agent Jon Elek; also to Mina Holland and Felicity Cloake for
your support.

to my friend and wine mentor Hande Kutlar Leimar—you have
changed the way I think about wine and made my drinking life
so much better.

to my friend and baking mentor Daniel Etherington.

to the hardworking shopkeepers and market traders of Testaccio who
make shopping a local pleasure, especially the Pucci family, Artenio
Fanella, Sergio Esposito, Laura, Fabio, and Arianna at Emporio delle
Spezie, Mauro Pierluigi, the Sartor family, Azienda Agricola Fanelli,
and Azienda Agricola Centrone Pietro.

Thank you too, to those who advised me, cooked with me and for me,
and shared stories, recipes, and tables—particularly the Fioravanti
family, the Ferraro family, Alice Kiandra-Adams and Leonardo Carosi,
Irene Ranaldi, Carla Tomasi, Jo Wennerholm, Kitty Lindy-Travers,
Maureen Bransfield and Marco Gargiulo, Stefania Barzini, Carla
Tomasi, Kat von Tan, Molly Hays, Mona Talbott, Fabrizia Lanza,
Chris Behr, Katie Parla, Elizabeth Janus, Gina Tringali, Enrico Guerra
and Elizabetta la Pera, Carla Costanzi, Stefano Cecchi, Roberto
Liberati, Leonardo Vignoli, Augusto D'Alfonsi, the Caristia and
D'Aleo families, and Paola Lurilli.